the 6 ... Montreal think big

D0731998

Habitat 67

The Biosphere, formerly the American Pavilion

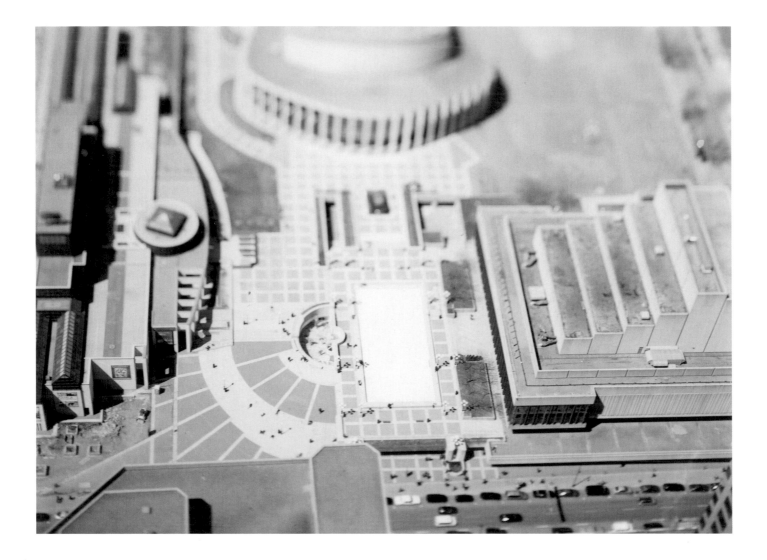

Place des Arts

Complexe Desjardins

Place Ville-Marie

Westmount Square

500 Place d'Armes

Metropolitan Boulevard

site specific_montreal 04
Olivo Barbieri

*You glue the doors into the walls next. You glue the walls
into the foundation. You tweezer together the tiny bits of
each chimney and let the glue dry while you build the roof.
You hang the tiny gutters. Every detail exact. You set the tiny
dormers. Hang the shutters. Frame the porch. Seed the lawn.
Plant the trees.*

– Chuck Palahniuk, *Lullaby: A Novel*

I took my first aerial photo as a child, the first time I flew
in a light plane. For many years after that, however, both
airplanes and photos were infrequent. I took it with
a twin-lens reflex camera, which I had to turn upside
down in order to reach the airplane window. There were
several black-and-white photos, and I still remember the
amazement of the neighbourhood photographer who
developed them when he saw the picture of the town
square. In those days, it was normal to fly over historic
city centres at low altitude, though I believe that taking
pictures was forbidden.

Never has there been so great a concern to talk
about cities as in the past twenty years. We have been
submerged obsessively in a flood of ideas and commentary
from Europe, North America, Japan and, now, almost the
whole of Asia.

Since September 11, however, anything expressed
before that time seems to have lost clarity. A veil of
uncertainty has fallen between our thoughts and the
world. With the *Site Specific* project, I look beyond this veil.

The first constraint of representation is viewpoint;
changing it opens a new drawer full of meanings.
Adopting a fluid position has limited the risk of obligatory
and predictable views.

The world as a temporary site-specific installation,
structures and infrastructures, the foundation of our sense
of belonging and our identity, seen from afar, as a great
scale model: the city as an avatar of itself.

Site Specific is a work in progress that involves several
regions of the planet.

the 6os: montreal thinks big

edited by André Lortie

Olivo Barbieri
Marcel Fournier
André Lortie
Michael Sorkin
Jean-Louis Cohen

Canadian Centre for Architecture, Montréal
Douglas & McIntyre, Vancouver / Toronto

This publication accompanies the exhibition *The 60s: Montreal Thinks Big*, organized by the Canadian Centre for Architecture (CCA), Montréal, and presented at the CCA from 20 October 2004 to 11 September 2005, under the honorary chairmanship of Senator E. Leo Kolber.

The CCA wishes to thank the Ville de Montréal for its generous support of the exhibition.

The CCA also thanks Hydro-Québec, Loto-Québec, RBC Financial Group, BMO Financial Group, and CGI for their support of the exhibition, as well as State Street Global Advisors and Liberty Yogourt for their support of the accompanying public programs.

The CCA gratefully acknowledges the generous support of the Ministère de la Culture et des Communications du Québec, the Canada Council for the Arts, the Department of Canadian Heritage, and the Conseil des arts de Montréal.

Douglas & McIntyre gratefully acknowledges the financial support of the Canada Council for the Arts, the British Columbia Arts Council, and the Government of Canada through the Book Publishing Industry Development Program (BPIDP) for its publishing activities.

04 05 06 07 08 5 4 3 2 1

This catalogue was produced by the Canadian Centre for Architecture, Montréal, and Douglas & McIntyre, Vancouver and Toronto.

Assistant Director, Programs, CCA: Helen Malkin
Senior Consulting Curator, CCA: Mirko Zardini

Exhibition
Curator: André Lortie
Head of Exhibitions: Serge Belet
Exhibition Coordinator: Sophie Lafrance, with the assistance of Darla Der Kaloustian
Designer: Lortie & Schall, architects
Researchers: Claudine Déom, Nancy Dunton, Olivier Filiatrault, Louis Martin, David Rose

Publication
Managing editor: Myriam Afriat
Editors: Usher Caplan, Myriam Afriat
Translators: Marcia Barr, Elaine Kennedy, Donald Pistolesi
Research assistants: Alain Gerbier, Lynne Freeman
Cartographer: Eric Leinberger
Proofreader: Jane Jackel

Design by George Vaitkunas, Vancouver
Typeset in Thesis and printed on Jenson Satin paper
Printed by Friesens in Altona, Manitoba, October 2004

Printed on acid-free paper

Front cover: Olivo Barbieri, *Downtown Montreal seen from the east, with the Maison de Radio-Canada in the foreground*
Back cover: Olivo Barbieri, *Place Ville-Marie*

All photographs by Olivo Barbieri reproduced in this volume are chromogenic colour prints dated 2004. Unless otherwise noted, they are from the collection of the Canadian Centre for Architecture and are a gift of The Sandra and Leo Kolber Foundation. © Olivo Barbieri

The Canadian Centre for Architecture is an international research centre and museum founded on the conviction that architecture is a public concern. Based on its extensive collections, CCA is a leading voice in advancing knowledge, promoting public understanding, and widening thought and debate on the art of architecture, its history, theory, practice, and role in society today.

Contents

Interior Transformations

The extent of Montreal's immense physical transformation during the 1960s must be viewed against the background of social and cultural ferment that permeated the city's public realm in this period. That ferment will be the focus of my preface to this volume, which accompanies *The 60s: Montreal Thinks Big*, an exhibition surveying the profound physical change the city underwent in the extraordinary decade during which innovative transportation infrastructures and major public institutions and buildings were both planned and put in place. The remarkable prescience and universality of the Montreal experience has been captured by Michael Sorkin in "Learning from Montreal," the roundtable discussion published in this volume: "The astonishing thing is that every single standard-issue piece of mid-century modernist strategizing happened here." And all this, Sorkin explains, occurred in advance of typical 1990s urban agendas, where every city strove to use expos, underground railways, and cultural infrastructure as "pump-primers."

It seems highly unlikely that a city long repressed and depressed could have been so dynamically re-imagined, that Montreal could have thought "big" at all in the 1960s, if not for the challenge posed by radical artists who engendered a pivotal cultural revolution. Like all major change, it was heralded in earlier decades, most notably in the *Refus global* (Total Refusal), the manifesto signed in 1948 by Paul-Émile Borduas and more than a dozen other Montreal artists who proclaimed the need to break with prevailing social conventions and oppose the tyranny of the French Catholic Church, which dominated nearly all aspects of everyday life and political thought in Quebec. The big-boss politics of Maurice Duplessis, premier of a poor, rural province for more than twenty years (1936–1959), crushed its citizens in the search for provincial autonomy and foreign investment. Given the absence of a national library in Quebec and the scarcity of locally published editions of literary and critical works by French-speaking Canadians – and all that this implied about the status of francophone culture in Canada at the time – a reaction was inevitable. Already in the 1950s, journals of liberal ideas like *Cité libre* and *Liberté* and the first volumes of Québécois poetry published by Les Éditions de l'Hexagone began to appear. Likewise, new institutions were formed to advance francophone performing arts and film, the earliest being the Théâtre du Nouveau Monde, founded in Montreal in 1951, and the French division of the National Film Board of Canada, instituted in 1958. Québécois nationalist sentiment – expressed by *chansonniers* Félix Leclerc and Raymond Lévesque, who were valorized in France in the early 1950s, and later by Pauline Julien, Gilles Vigneault, and others – spread through the province like wildfire in the 1960s.

Central to national identity in Quebec was the assertion of the French language, bolstered in September 1960 by the founding of a separatist political movement, the Rassemblement pour l'indépendance nationale (RIN). That year, Borduas's manifesto was reprinted in the *Revue socialiste pour un Québec indépendent*, and in 1961 the Mouvement laïc de langue française was founded. In this politicized context, magazines, journals, and local newspapers played a capital role in consciousness raising and in the large-scale mobilization of protest groups. *Our Generation against Nuclear War*, an international journal founded in 1961, was the first English-language periodical to publish left-wing francophone intellectuals. It was followed by French-language journals like *Parti pris* in 1963, *Socialisme* in 1964, *Québec-Presse*, *Noir et rouge*, and *Mobilisation*, all launched in 1969, and the counterculture art journal *Mainmise*, founded in 1970. Reinforced in 1968 by the creation of the Agence de presse libre du Québec (APLQ), which functioned as a news bureau for popular and political action, these publications became the principal outlets for the new dissidents, whose ideas were hotly debated.

Modern Quebec, it can be attested, was born 22 June 1960, with Jean Lesage's election as premier. Lesage's policies were at the heart of the Révolution tranquille, or Quiet Revolution, which constituted a decisive move against the status quo. Although it must be seen in light of the rise of nationalism and anti-colonialism in Third World countries like Algeria, Cuba, Indonesia, Ghana, and Vietnam, the transformation of Quebec was rapid and profound. Within the first five years, Lesage's government moved swiftly to establish new structures. From the outset they revolved around language and the ethos of nationalism, with the creation of the Department of Cultural Affairs in 1961 and the Department of Education in 1964. The election of the first woman to the National Assembly, in 1960, and the passage of the bill giving women full legal rights, in 1964, drastically changed the status of women in Quebec.

In response to an urgent need to stimulate a national art scene, the provincial government funded the Office du film du Québec in 1961 – which, together with the French division of the National Film Board, led to the production of at least thirteen Québécois films over the course of the decade – and in 1964 created the Musée d'art contemporain. That same year, the first international symposium on sculpture in North America took place on Mount Royal in Montreal. In the early 1960s, artists' collectives began to install their works in the streets, and in 1965 and 1966, art students staged strikes to protest the fustian status quo of the École des beaux-arts.

In the same general time frame, major economic infrastructures were initiated by the province, which established agencies intended to strengthen the economy, including the Société générale de financement, which provided development capital to businesses; Hydro-Québec, which nationalized the ten major private hydroelectric companies and thereby capitalized on the key natural resource of the province; and the Caisse de dépôt et placement, the public

At the beginning of the twentieth century the area in question was still known as the "Quartier Saint-Louis," the title of a story by Robert Laroque de Roquebrune that appeared in 1966. It encompasses the "Carré Saint-Louis," which is the name of a 1971 novel by Jean-Jules Richard.

pension fund. The Bibliothèque nationale du Québec was founded in 1967, while the following year the Université du Québec established a network of universities, among them the second francophone university in Montreal.

Intellectual life took off, and Montreal became a crossroads of diverse cultures: Americans objecting to the war in Vietnam sought refuge, intellectuals from Paris were constantly moving back and forth, and Hungarians who had fled the revolution crushed by the Soviet Union in 1956 opened the first cafés in Montreal, places like the Pam Pam, Rose Marie, and Carmen. Dimitri Roussopoulos, a publisher, writer, editor, and leader of the 1960s youth movement, has observed that heated debates also took place in restaurants such as the Swiss Hut and Casa Espagnole, and that while the axis of communications was often Paris, political influences also came from the peace movement in Britain and the civil rights and radical student movements in the United States. This milieu set the tone for public debates and street demonstrations, and in turn influenced the basis of the emerging political parties – the RIN and the separatist Parti québécois (PQ), founded in 1968. Cafés became the haunts of both French- and English-speaking radicals in Montreal. Members of the violent wing of the independence movement, the Front de libération du Québec (FLQ), were also involved – led by Pierre Vallières, author of *Nègres blancs d'Amérique* (*White Niggers of America*), which he wrote between 1964 and 1968 while serving a prison sentence for "subversive activities." The poet Gaston Miron mixed with Nick Auf der Maur, a journalist-activist who worked for the Canadian Broadcasting Corporation (CBC) and the *Gazette*. Also active were Patrick McFadden, an Irish-born editor of the *McGill Daily*, Mark Starowicz, another *McGill Daily* editor who later became a leading CBC personality, and Stanley Gray, an extremist academic activist teaching at McGill University.

It is significant that the first radical public art work in Montreal was the sculpted tree by Armand Vaillancourt at the corner of Hutchison and Sherbrooke across from the Swiss Hut, in the so-called McGill ghetto, lying immediately east of the McGill campus. Just slightly further to the east is the francophone intellectual quarter, a square kilometre within the Plateau Mont-Royal, extending from Saint Lawrence Boulevard eastward to Lafontaine Park and from Sherbrooke Street north to Mount Royal Avenue.[1] Documents compiled by Gaëtan Dostie, an author and collector of Québécois literature, demonstrate that a third of all artists and intellectuals in Quebec lived here. In the 1960s, polyvalent poets, editors, novelists, film and television producers, writers, and activists living in this neighbourhood – including Jacques Godbout, Gaston Miron, Hubert Aquin, Michel Tremblay, Paul Chamberland, Claude Gauvreau, Gérald Godin, and Michèle Lalonde – broke with the past to create a de-ruralized, de-sacralized, de-mythicized modern society.

Although this square kilometre was left unscathed by Montreal's big plans, rash in-town highway building hit the McGill ghetto with the construction of an interchange in the 1950s and the massive demolition in the name of "urban renewal" that followed. Here, on Sainte-Famille and Saint-Urbain streets, the Montreal Peace Centre and the University Settlement welcomed hundreds of young American draft dodgers and deserters, and also provided meeting places for francophone and anglophone community organizers working with the anti-poverty movements, tenant rights organizations, community medical clinics, soup kitchens, and co-ops of various sorts. This kind of activism gave rise at the end of the 1960s to the urban conservation movement in Montreal and to the formidable Milton-Park community protest, which galvanized public opinion and turned the city away from megaprojects requiring demolition and massive rebuilding in favour of projects that addressed the urgent social and urban issues of the city.

As Montreal struggles today with the merger and de-merger of municipalities on the island, new development, and matters pertaining to its charter and to civic democracy, this publication and exhibition are timely reminders of the continuing impact of 1960s initiatives. The emphasis on language and on financial institutions established during the Quiet Revolution had a measurable effect over the following decades. In 1971, for example, French-speaking citizens held only 41 percent of the administrative positions in the Montreal area (a rate lower than anywhere else in the province), as compared with 67 percent in 1991. Similarly, the percentage of companies of at least 100 employees having predominantly French-speaking boards of directors went from 13 percent in 1976 to 43 percent in 1991.

Citizen action and participation forced numerous measures, including the recently legislated Montreal Heritage Council and the Office of Public Consultation, which protect green and blue spaces in Montreal, traditional neighbourhoods, and individual buildings, and also provide public consultation on the appropriateness of proposed new construction. Building development is no longer colonized by foreign capital; instead, the local private sector now productively interacts with government bureaucracy. Most striking in this regard are projects involving buildings for institutions created during the 1960s, which have benefited from such developments. For the Caisse de dépôt et placement, as an example, highly complex and strategic planning was undertaken, starting in 1994, to locate the building and develop its surrounding sector. The instruments for realizing this process simply did not exist when the institution was founded in 1965. Provocative designs for new public buildings under construction throughout Montreal, selected by local and international competitions, are predominantly by Québécois architects. Private institutions have individually and collectively shaped a climate of awareness that has brought Montreal to the point where it now possesses a heightened sense of its built and natural heritage. But this is a work in progress and requires a continually broadening base of citizen participation and local democracy. Taken together, the public and private initiatives that emerged in the 1960s are basic to the responsible development of the city. It took committed citizen action to create them. It will take sustained public collaboration to nourish them, and eternal vigilance to protect them.

The exhibition associated with this volume originated as part of a collaboration among seven museums across the country, with the aim of bringing to light Canada's significant role in advancing innovative social and cultural agendas during the pivotal decade of the 1960s. Under the aegis of this larger project on the 1960s, exhibitions and public programs are also being launched between fall 2003 and winter 2006 by the Montreal Museum of Fine Arts, the McCord Museum of Canadian History, the Vancouver Art Gallery, the National Gallery of Canada, the Canadian Museum of Contemporary Photography, and the Canadian Museum of Civilization. *The 60s: Montreal Thinks Big* is the third exhibition presented by the CCA to draw public attention to formative periods in the history of this city. The first was *Opening the Gates of Eighteenth-Century Montreal*, mounted in 1992, and the second was *Montreal Metropolis, 1880–1930*, mounted in 1998. These projects, as well as *Shaping the Great City: Modern Architecture in Central Europe, 1890–1937* and *The New Spirit: Modern Architecture in Vancouver, 1938–1963*, among others, collectively represent the CCA's continuing commitment to the larger theme of the urban phenomenon – how cities have been imagined and realized over time.

Phyllis Lambert
Founding Director, Canadian Centre for Architecture

Acknowledgments

This work, published in coordination with the exhibition of the same name at the Canadian Centre for Architecture (CCA), is the result of research conducted in a relatively short time with a small but extremely effective team. In contrast to what I had hoped, the project did not allow for bringing together the handful of researchers who specialize in the period, although some of them, including Réjean Legault, Paul-André Linteau, and André Corboz, contributed to the final result with their invaluable advice. In 1998, Michèle Picard began compiling a major bibliography on architecture and urban planning in Canada in the 1960s. In 2000, when the research became focused on Montreal, Louis Martin continued her work and contributed to defining the project as it is today, before leaving the CCA early in 2003. The project would not have been possible without the crucial contributions of Sophie Lafrance, David Rose, and Olivier Filiatrault in Montreal and Gaëlle Ducastain in Paris, whose patient research made it possible to gather an impressive corpus, only part of which is displayed here. Similarly, it would have been impossible without the deep conviction of Mirko Zardini, senior consulting curator at the CCA; the consistent support of Nicholas Olsberg, formerly chief curator and subsequently director of the CCA; the invaluable aid of Helen Malkin, the CCA's assistant director of programs, and Serge Belet, head of exhibitions; logistical support from Nancy Dunton, head of university and professional programs, Alain Laforest, multimedia specialist, and Daria Der Kaloustian; and, first and foremost, the encouragement and enthusiastic involvement of Phyllis Lambert. I must also express my gratitude for the proverbial patience of Myriam Afriat and Usher Caplan, and of my family.

The documents shown here are in most cases from the CCA's archives, curated with passionate commitment by Robert Desaulniers, from its library, which some months ago was still headed by Gerald Beasley, and from its photography collection, under the loving care of Louise Désy. They reveal only a minuscule part of the wealth of the CCA's collections. They have been supplemented by items from various archives in Montreal, other parts of Quebec, and elsewhere in Canada, in particular the archival collection of the City Planning Department of the City of Montreal, as well as from private lenders, including Pei, Cobb, Freed, and Partners in New York, Zvi Hecker in Berlin, and François Dallegret in Montreal, to whom we offer our thanks.

André Lortie

Introduction

The urban planning and architecture of the 1960s have often been disparaged. It is true that they were driven by an irresponsible optimism that left what Lewis Mumford might have termed the living works of more than one city ravaged. In some respects, Montreal was no exception to the rule. And yet, while some consider the legacy of the decade to be catastrophic, they still recognize that it had some outstanding qualities, such as Montreal's underground network of shopping centres, its metro, some remarkable buildings, and the vitality of a city core in which workers and residents from different social classes and cultures all rubbed shoulders. This book is an invitation to experience the decade's complexity. Far from offering a definitive synthesis, it instead provides an exploratory compilation intended to contribute to a broader view of the period. Examining the 1960s, after all, means considering the roots of contemporary urban conditions, so thoroughly do the plans and achievements of the decade continue to impose their logic on today's cities. In this regard, Montreal offers a specific and powerful example through which to approach the general case of the architectural, urban, and social transformations that major Western cities experienced during the second half of the twentieth century. Here, the scale of the plans and achievements and the spatial and social impact of the infrastructure are elements of an exemplary process that invites such consideration.

Nonetheless, describing a metropolis and its transformation is a delicate process. How can we understand its form without investigating the mechanisms that produced it? How can we appreciate its cityscapes without being interested in the perceptions they induced? How can we perceive its evolution without delving deeper into its history? This book looks at the city as a complex cultural phenomenon – as an irregular polyhedron, so to speak, with urban planning and architecture considered as particular facets of it. This type of approach explains the organization of what follows: three articles, complementing one another, explore three different aspects of the period, while a series of vignettes are interspersed among them to provide specific viewpoints on various aspects of the phenomenon.

The first article, written by the sociologist Marcel Fournier, deals with the social and political facets of the Quiet Revolution, providing a historical context essential to understanding the changes in the relationship between society and the urban environment. The second article describes the fabric of urban planning: a social, political, and economic weft woven on the warp formed by the city's physical space. The third, a roundtable discussion between architecture critics and theoreticians Michael Sorkin (American) and Jean-Louis Cohen (European), takes up the more strictly architectural aspects of this slice of history, investigating both the conditions of their emergence and the legacy they represent today.

These essays are interspersed with short, amply illustrated commentaries highlighting specific elements of this metropolitan metamorphosis. Some are related to the major structural realities that imposed constraints on the city and its players, such as demographics, standardization and models, international influences, and social changes. Another set of factors concerns the personalities of the major players on the city's changing stage, describing key individuals, symbolic sites, and archetypical achievements. A third category includes the diverse perceptions that people had of the city, shown in current events, through the eyes of photographers, writers, and technical experts, and in opinions from abroad. The final topic, the 1967 world's fair, Expo 67, in its role as the moving force that turned the city into a gigantic work site during the decade, provides a prism through which the metropolis is diffracted.

A photographic prologue and epilogue feature the work of Olivo Barbieri, whose images of Montreal seen from above allow the city to break free of its own overpowering reality, providing us with a disembodied vision in which only scale, density, and the structure of the metropolis remain.

This is a book that grew out of a strong conviction and guiding principle, namely that it is important to discuss not only what was accomplished, but the totality of the studies and plans drawn up for Montreal, whether or not they were implemented, because each of them in its own way contributed to transforming the mental image of the city and broadening the scope of what seemed possible. This viewpoint is a reminder, on one hand, that Montreal was the stage for ambitious plans whose formulations were sometimes incommensurate with what was actually achieved, and on the other hand, that the city could prove resistant to even the most compelling of plans.

But which Montreal are we talking about? Municipality, district, island, urban area, region: the question, as we know, could provoke endless debate. Given that the technocrats of the day believed the city's vocation was to transcend an administrative division that was too narrow for its dynamic of growth, we have tried not to impose spatial limits that are too restrictive. The question of the metropolis is approached on two different scales: the urban area with its incursions onto the farther shores of the watercourses bordering the island, and the central part lying between the river, the mountain, and the Champlain and Jacques Cartier Bridges. Therein lies one of the characteristics of this dynamic: the combination of consolidation toward the centre with sprawl on the periphery, the outcome being that the economic vitality of the centre did not compromise its social vigour. But the temporal boundaries are clear: they correspond to the fleeting existence of the Montreal Metropolitan Corporation, formed in March 1959 and dissolved on 1 January 1970, to be replaced by the Montreal Urban Community.

André Lortie

The 1960s:
Human Conquest and
Urban Tension

International Events

21 April	1960	Brasília officially declared the capital of Brazil
8 November	1960	John F. Kennedy elected president of the United States
12 April	1961	Yuri Gagarin becomes the first human in space, on board Vostok 1
12 August	1961	Start of construction of the Berlin Wall
4 July	1962	Independence of Algeria and assumption of power by the provisional government in Algiers
22 November	1963	Assassination of President John F. Kennedy in Dallas
7 February	1964	Arrival of the Beatles in New York
21 March	1965	Civil rights march in Selma, Alabama, led by Martin Luther King
27 August	1965	Death of Le Corbusier (Charles-Édouard Jeanneret)
4 April	1968	Assassination of Martin Luther King in Memphis, Tennessee
2 May	1968	Start of the events of May 1968 in Paris
20 August	1968	Warsaw Pact troops enter Prague
26 May	1969	Start of the "bed-in for peace" by John Lennon and Yoko Ono in Montreal
20 July	1969	Neil Armstrong becomes the first human to set foot on the moon
17 August	1969	Death of Ludwig Mies van der Rohe

National Events

22 June	1960	Election of Jean Lesage, start of the Quiet Revolution
3 September	1962	Official opening of the Trans-Canada Highway at Rogers Pass in Alberta
8 March	1963	First attack by the Front de libération du Québec, in Montreal
1 May	1963	Nationalization of electricity in Quebec
10 October	1964	Riots in Quebec City during the visit of Queen Elizabeth II
15 February	1965	The maple leaf flag declared the official flag of Canada
1 July	1967	Centennial of Canadian Confederation
24 July	1967	General de Gaulle's rallying cry of "Vive le Québec libre" during his visit to Montreal
20 April	1968	Pierre Elliott Trudeau becomes prime minister of Canada
24 June	1968	290 people arrested during the Saint-Jean-Baptiste parade in Montreal
12 October	1968	Founding of the Parti québécois by René Lévesque, who is elected party leader
5 October	1970	Kidnapping of British diplomat James Richard Cross in Montreal, which sets off the October Crisis

Local Events

23 January	1960	Opening of Metropolitan Boulevard, Montreal's first expressway
6 April	1960	Arrival of the first tenants of the Jeanne-Mance housing project
24 October	1960	Jean Drapeau elected to second term as mayor
	1962	Opening of the CIL Building
23 May	1962	Start of construction of the Montreal metro system
27 June	1962	Opening of the Canadian Imperial Bank of Commerce Building
29 June	1962	Opening of the Champlain Bridge
10 September	1962	Announcement that the 1967 world's fair is to be held in Montreal
13 September	1962	Official opening of Place Ville-Marie
21 September	1963	Inaugural concert at Place des Arts
27 July	1964	Opening of Place Victoria (Montreal Stock Exchange Tower)
	1966	Start of studies for Complexe Desjardins
	1966	Initial studies for Cité Concordia
14 October	1966	Official opening of the Montreal metro
January	1967	Opening of the Château Champlain Hotel
11 March	1967	Opening of the Louis-Hippolyte Lafontaine Bridge-Tunnel
21 April	1967	Opening of the Bonaventure Expressway
24 April	1967	Presentation of the master plan for the Montreal urban area, *Horizon 2000*, at Place des Arts
25 April	1967	Opening of the Décarie Expressway
27 April	1967	Opening of Expo 67 in Montreal
29 October	1967	Closing of Expo 67 in Montreal
1 December	1967	Opening of the Banque Nationale Building
13 December	1967	Opening of Westmount Square
8 April	1968	Official opening of Place Bonaventure
14 April	1969	Montreal Expos' first home game in Jarry Park
1 January	1970	Establishment of the Montreal Urban Community
12 May	1970	Announcement by the International Olympic Committee that Montreal is to host the 1976 Olympic Games

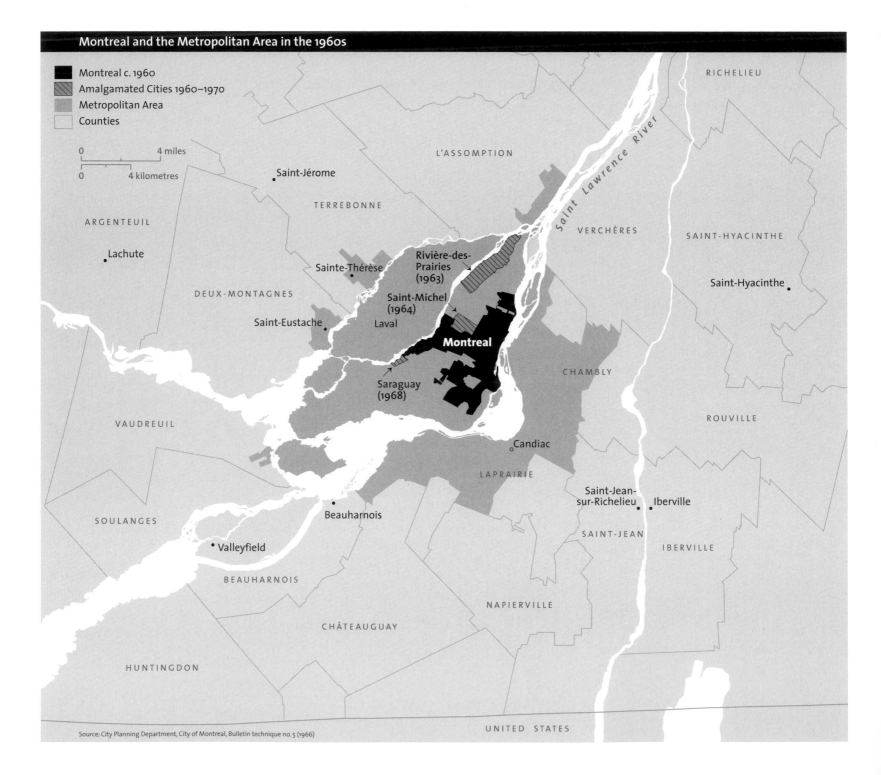

Montreal and the Metropolitan Area in the 1960s

Montreal c. 1960
Amalgamated Cities 1960–1970
Metropolitan Area
Counties

0   4 miles
0   4 kilometres

RICHELIEU

L'ASSOMPTION

Saint-Jérome

TERREBONNE

VERCHÈRES

Saint Lawrence River

ARGENTEUIL

SAINT-HYACINTHE

Lachute

Sainte-Thérèse

Rivière-des-
Prairies
(1963)

DEUX-MONTAGNES

Saint-Hyacinthe

Saint-Michel
(1964)

Saint-Eustache

Laval

Montreal

CHAMBLY

Saraguay
(1968)

Candiac

ROUVILLE

LAPRAIRIE

Saint-Jean-
sur-Richelieu Iberville

VAUDREUIL

SOULANGES

Beauharnois

SAINT-JEAN

IBERVILLE

Valleyfield

BEAUHARNOIS

NAPIERVILLE

CHÂTEAUGUAY

HUNTINGDON

UNITED STATES

Source: City Planning Department, City of Montreal, Bulletin technique no. 5 (1966)

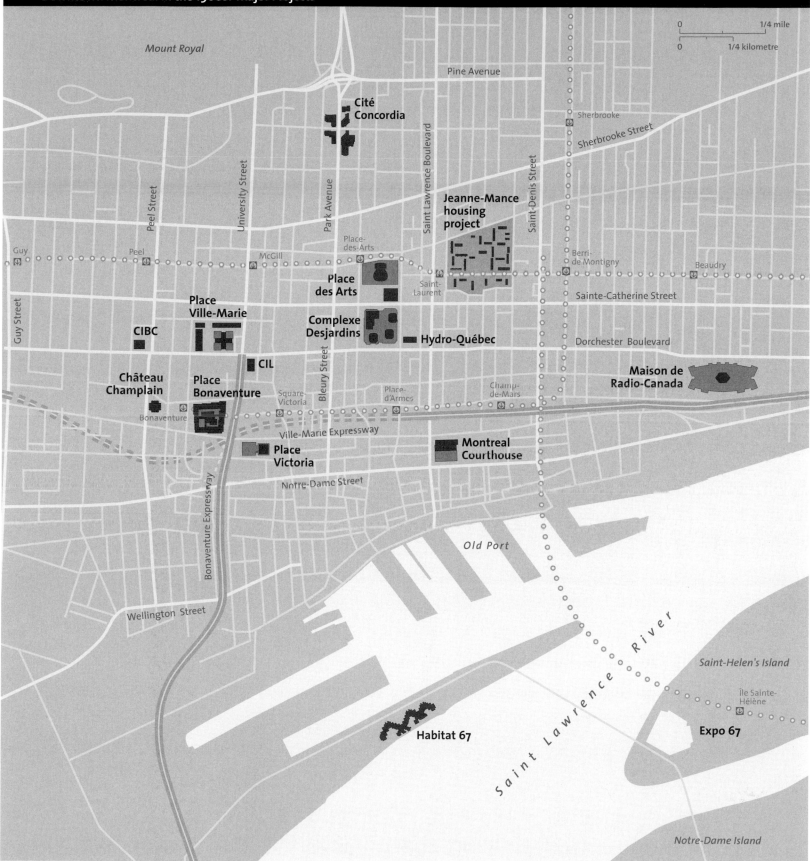

Mount Royal

Pine Avenue

Cité Concordia

Sherbrooke

Sherbrooke Street

Jeanne-Mance housing project

Peel Street

University Street

Park Avenue

Saint Lawrence Boulevard

Saint-Denis Street

Guy

Peel

McGill

Place-des-Arts

Berri-de Montigny

Beaudry

Place des Arts

Saint-Laurent

Sainte-Catherine Street

Place Ville-Marie

Guy Street

CIBC

Complexe Desjardins

Hydro-Québec

Dorchester Boulevard

CIL

Bleury Street

Château Champlain

Place Bonaventure

Square-Victoria

Place-d'Armes

Champ-de-Mars

Maison de Radio-Canada

Bonaventure

Ville-Marie Expressway

Place Victoria

Montreal Courthouse

Notre-Dame Street

Bonaventure Expressway

Old Port

Wellington Street

Saint Lawrence River

Saint-Helen's Island

Île Sainte-Hélène

Habitat 67

Expo 67

Notre-Dame Island

0   1/4 mile

0   1/4 kilometre

**Structure
and Society**

Places and
Players

Perceptions

Expo 67

Master Plan for Metropolitan Montreal

It has been estimated that the population of the Montreal region will be of the order of 4,834,000 persons in 1981, compared with 2,486,902 in 1961.

– Roland Cousineau, City Planning Department, "The Postulates of the Plan," *Métropole: Les Cahiers d'urbanisme*, no. 3 (October 1965): 28

This optimistic estimate went hand in hand with an obvious and seemingly immutable fact: in 1960, Montreal – the second largest French-speaking city in the world, as commentators liked to call it – was the metropolis of Canada. This status, in a voluntarist federal state, promised the city a future of boundless economic and demographic growth.

Given the relative urgency of the situation, Montreal's technical services staff were entrusted with the task of studying how the metropolitan area should develop in order to handle the anticipated growth. What shape should the city take? What new facilities would it require? How should its expansion be managed?

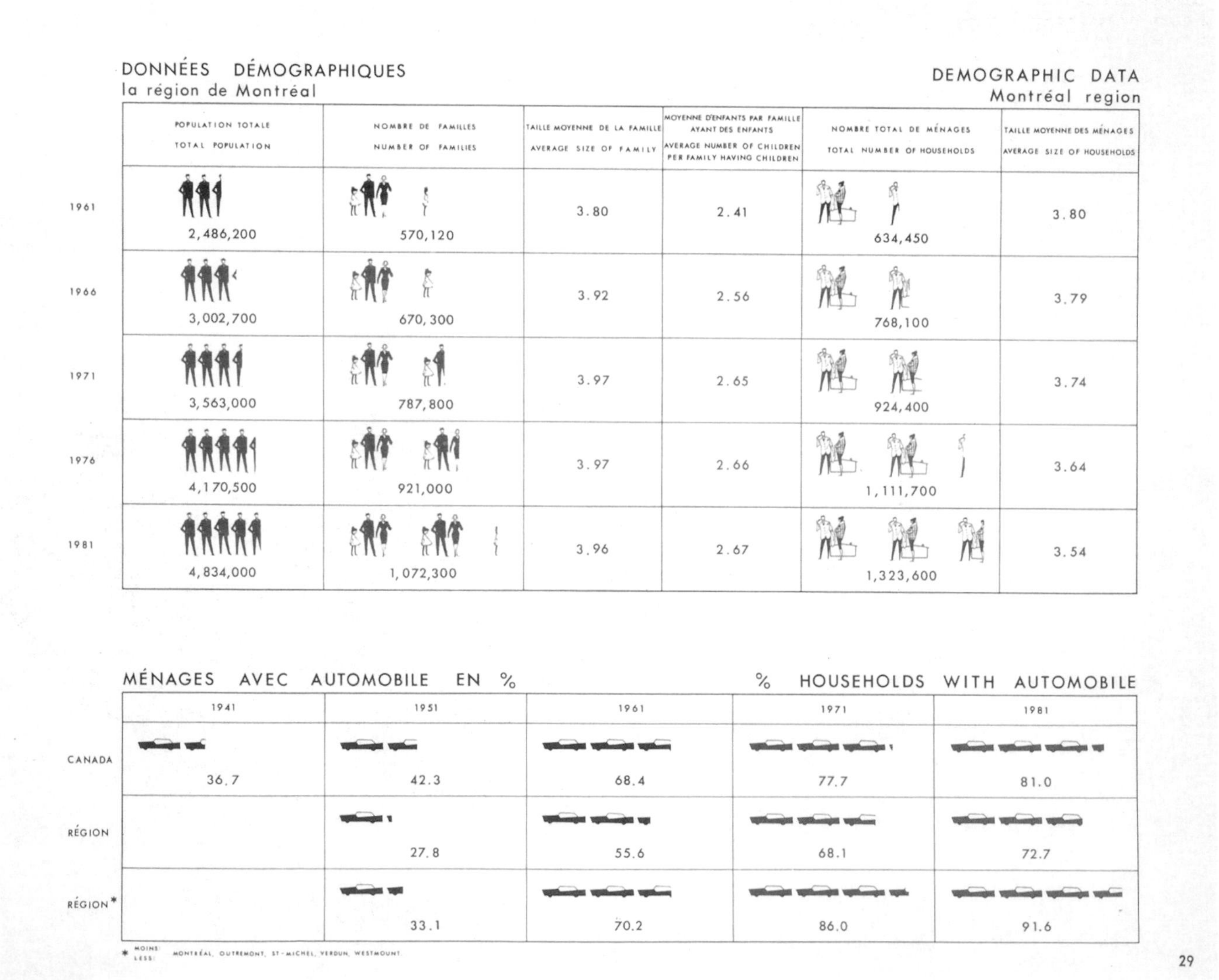

Figure 1
"Demographic Data, Montréal Region." City Planning Department, City of Montreal, *Métropole: Les Cahiers d'urbanisme*, no. 3 (October 1965), 29. Canadian Centre for Architecture, Montréal

DONNÉES DÉMOGRAPHIQUES
la région de Montréal — DEMOGRAPHIC DATA — Montréal region

	POPULATION TOTALE / TOTAL POPULATION	NOMBRE DE FAMILLES / NUMBER OF FAMILIES	TAILLE MOYENNE DE LA FAMILLE / AVERAGE SIZE OF FAMILY	MOYENNE D'ENFANTS PAR FAMILLE AYANT DES ENFANTS / AVERAGE NUMBER OF CHILDREN PER FAMILY HAVING CHILDREN	NOMBRE TOTAL DE MÉNAGES / TOTAL NUMBER OF HOUSEHOLDS	TAILLE MOYENNE DES MÉNAGES / AVERAGE SIZE OF HOUSEHOLDS
1961	2,486,200	570,120	3.80	2.41	634,450	3.80
1966	3,002,700	670,300	3.92	2.56	768,100	3.79
1971	3,563,000	787,800	3.97	2.65	924,400	3.74
1976	4,170,500	921,000	3.97	2.66	1,111,700	3.64
1981	4,834,000	1,072,300	3.96	2.67	1,323,600	3.54

MÉNAGES AVEC AUTOMOBILE EN % — % HOUSEHOLDS WITH AUTOMOBILE

	1941	1951	1961	1971	1981
CANADA	36.7	42.3	68.4	77.7	81.0
RÉGION		27.8	55.6	68.1	72.7
RÉGION*		33.1	70.2	86.0	91.6

* MOINS LESS: MONTRÉAL, OUTREMONT, ST-MICHEL, VERDUN, WESTMOUNT

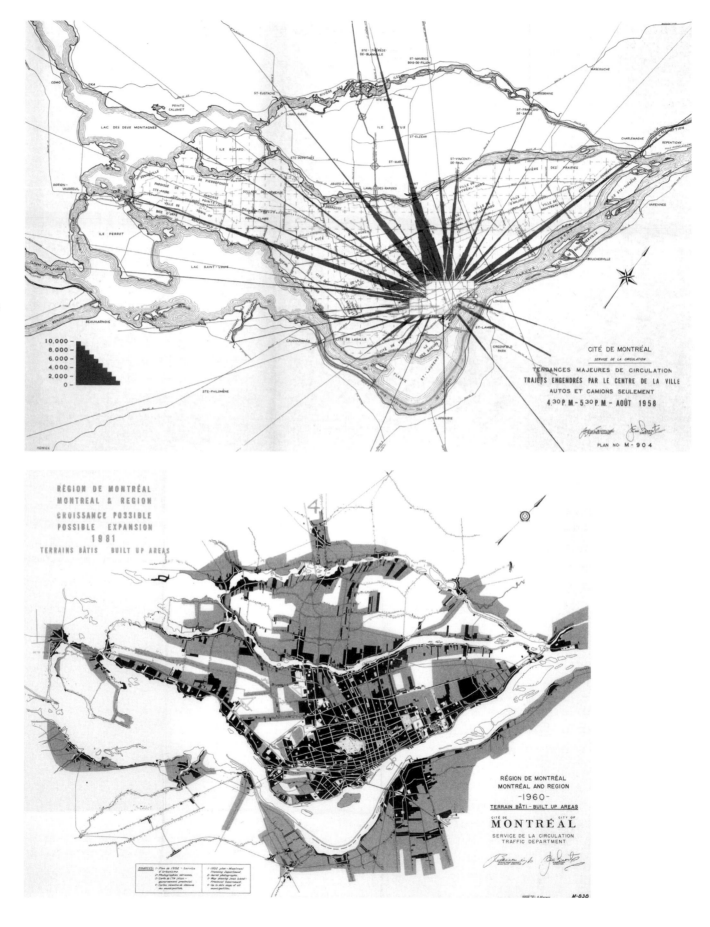

Figure 2
Diagram of traffic flow
from the city centre, August
1958. Montreal City Traffic
Department, *L'artère Décarie:
Realités et perspectives* (May
1961), map 38d. Ville de
Montréal, Gestion de documents et archives

Figure 3
"Montreal and Region, Possible
Expansion, 1981: Built Up
Areas." Montreal City Traffic
Department, *L'artère Décarie:
Realités et perspectives*
(May 1961), map 14a. Ville de
Montréal, Gestion de docu-
ments et archives

Figure 4
Schematic plans comparing
projected growth of Montreal
from 1964 to 2000. Based
on illustrations in "Horizon
2000, Montréal," *Architecture,
bâtiment, construction* 23 (April
1968): 35–36. Canadian Centre
for Architecture, Montréal

Population distribution

1964

2000

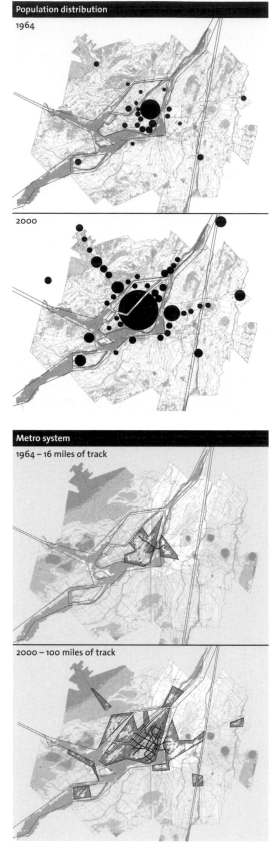

Secondary- and tertiary-sector employment

1964

2000

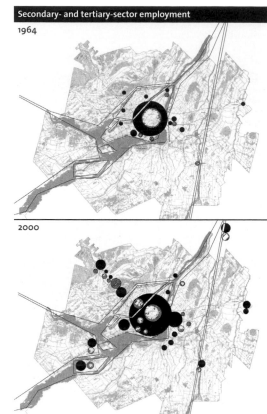

Road network

1964 – 100 miles of roadway

2000 – 500 miles of roadway

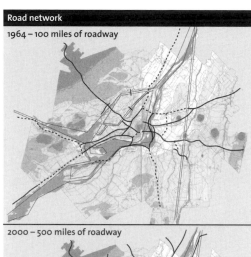
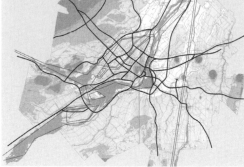

Metro system

1964 – 16 miles of track

2000 – 100 miles of track

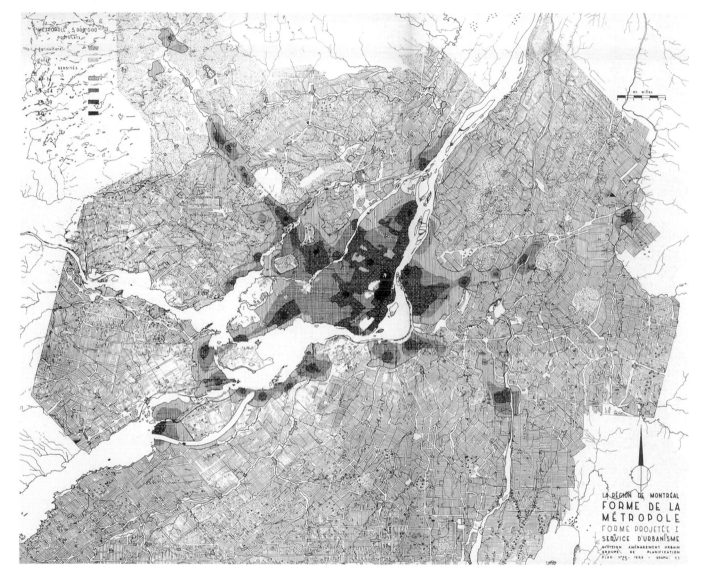

A Society in Motion: The Quiet Revolution and the Rise of the Middle Class

Marcel Fournier

Millions of words have been written since then to explain the underlying factors of the Quebec revolution . . .[1]

1 Peter Desbarats, *The State of Quebec* (Toronto: McClelland and Stewart, 1965), 86.
2 A result of chance because the Liberal Party won by taking only 2 percent of voters away from the Union nationale. Julien Harvey, "Les sources de la Révolution tranquille," in *La Révolution tranquille 30 ans après, qu'en reste-t-il?*, ed. M.R. Lafond (Hull: Éditions de Lorraine, 1992), 81–90.
3 Marcel Rioux, *Un peuple dans le siècle* (Montreal: Boréal, 1990).

The 1960s were a time of great ferment marked by wars, a new geopolitical landscape, remarkable scientific and technological advances, and a revolt of the young. A quick scan of its defining moments sets the entire decade in perspective, with a new American dream and the impotence of an empire facing guerrilla warfare, the rise of nationalisms and increasing struggles for independence, the Arab-Israeli conflict, divisions in the Soviet bloc, and the earliest foreshadowings of the collapse of Communism. In November 1960, John F. Kennedy is elected president of the United States; three years later, he is assassinated in Dallas, Texas. In 1962, Algeria achieves independence. In 1964, the Vietnam War is initiated, continuing until 1973. In 1967, the Six-Day War breaks out. In 1968, France is rocked by major unrest, and Czechoslovakia is occupied. In 1969, Neil Armstrong becomes the first human to set foot on the moon.

And meanwhile in Quebec? For this small society, situated adjacent to the United States and open to Europe – at the crossroads of two worlds, as the American sociologist Everett C. Hughes put it – the 1960s were a decade of change. It was in 1960 that the Quebec Liberal Party, led by Jean Lesage, came into power under the slogan "It's time for things to change." This was the beginning of what would come to be known as the "Quiet Revolution," a term coined by a *Globe and Mail* journalist, referring to the period between 1960 and 1966 when Lesage's Liberal government would introduce a series of sweeping political reforms in Quebec. By some accounts, the revolution had already started in 1959, right after the death of Maurice Duplessis, with the famous "Désormais" ("From now on") speech delivered by his successor, Paul Sauvé. Everything seemed to topple at once – as a result of chance, perhaps,[2] but with what dramatic effect! After a long winter came the spring, and with it a genuine political and intellectual thaw, to quote the sociologist Marcel Rioux.[3] Before, there had been a Great Darkness, a time of introversion; after came Modernity, and an opening up to the world. The poet and McGill University law professor F.R. Scott applauded the

4 Jack Jedwab, "La Révolution 'tranquille' des Anglo-Québécois," in *Traité de la culture*, ed. Denise Lemieux (Quebec City: Institut québécois de recherche sur la culture, 2002), 181–201.

5 David Kwavnick, "The Roots of French-Canadian Discontent," *Canadian Journal of Economics and Political Science* 31, no. 4 (November 1965): 509–523.

6 Craig Brown, ed., *The Illustrated History of Canada* (Toronto: Lester and Orpen Dennys, 1987), 499.

7 Louis Balthazar, "Aux sources de la Révolution tranquille: Continuité, rupture, nécessité," in *La Révolution tranquille 30 ans après*, 91–101.

8 Dorval Brunelle, *La désillusion tranquille* (Montreal: Hurtubise HMH, 1978); Henry Milner, *Politics in the New Quebec* (Toronto: McClelland and Stewart, 1978); Leo Panitch, *The Canadian State: Political Economy and Political Power* (Toronto: University of Toronto Press, 1977).

9 Albert Breton, "The Economics of Nationalism," *Journal of Political Economy* 72, no. 4 (August 1964): 385.

10 Hubert Guindon, "Réexamen de l'évolution sociale au Québec," in *La société canadienne-française*, ed. Y. Martin and M. Rioux (Montreal: HMH, 1971), 149–173; Hubert Guindon, "Two Cultures: An Essay on Nationalism, Class, and Ethnic Tension," in *Contemporary Canada*, ed. Richard H. Leach (Durham, N.C.: Duke University Press, 1967), 33–59.

11 Marcel Fournier, "La question nationale: Enjeux et impasses," in *La chance au coureur: Bilan de l'action du gouvernement du Parti québécois*, ed. J.-F. Léonard (Montreal: Nouvelle Optique, 1978), 177–192; Marcel Fournier, *L'entrée dans la modernité: Science, culture et société au Québec* (Montreal: Les Éditions coopératives Albert Saint-Martin, 1986). See also Marc Renaud, "Quebec's New Middle Class in Search of Social Hegemony," in *Quebec: State and Society*, ed. Alain C. Gagnon (Toronto: Methuen, 1984), 150–185.

end of the Duplessis period and the beginning of what he felt would be Quebec's entry into the modern era.[4] It was in fact the passage from a traditional (or folk) society to a modern (or urban) society. Quebec had finally come of age.

This is the famous "catching up" thesis, which states that Quebec rapidly made up for its "lagging behind" in various areas such as health and education in order to get in step with those Western societies that had already moved into the era of political and social reform and state intervention, and whose baby boomers were now approaching adulthood. Even English Canada was pleased and congratulatory; as David Kwavnick put it, French Canadians had become infected with the Protestant ethic and were adopting the same value system as their English-speaking fellow citizens.[5] In other words, Quebec was apparently becoming more like the rest of the country,[6] a province like all the others.[7]

What was happening was undoubtedly the result of a conjunction of circumstances. First of all, there was a serious recession between 1957 and 1961, with the unemployment rate in Quebec exceeding 14 percent during the winter of 1960. There was a federal election in 1958, which resulted in the ouster of 37 Liberal members of Parliament and brought John Diefenbaker and the Conservatives to power. And there was the death of one Union nationale leader after another – first Maurice Duplessis and then Paul Sauvé. But structural factors also played a role, and these were continental in scope. Some even spoke of a "continental destiny," because of Quebec's dependence on Canada, which was itself dominated economically by the United States. The modernization of commercial enterprises and the introduction of new technologies became imperative. In the perspective of Marxist economics, the Quiet Revolution represented a transition from the growing strength of American multinationals in Quebec's economy to the advent of the monopolistic stage. This transition required a specialized work force, greater investment, and more industrial research. It also created the need for reforms and new initiatives by the Quebec government in the sectors under its jurisdiction.[8]

Social Mobility and Collective Mobilization

Coming at a time of collective mobilization and resurging nationalism, the Quiet Revolution in itself produced a great degree of social mobility that led to a restructuring of social relationships. According to the economist Albert Breton, nationalistic government programs, such as the nationalization of electric power in 1963, could be described as a kind of "public works" for the middle class.[9] The sociologist Hubert Guindon viewed the development of the education, health, and welfare sectors – until then controlled by the Church – in much the same way, maintaining that their "opening up" would prepare the ground for the development of a "bureaucratic middle class."[10] In other words, Quebec's entry into the modern era also meant the "rise of the middle class."[11] Some would speak of "new elites" and of a "new middle class," or a "new bourgeoisie" and "new petty bourgeoisie." All of which overlooks, to some extent, the role of the labour movement, which was a considerable factor in the collective mobilization. The post-war years were marked by major strikes, such as that of the asbestos workers (CCCL-CNTU) in 1949, and by the strengthening of the labour unions, as their memberships

Figure 6
Complexe Desjardins, photomontage with study model, c. 1967. Jean-Claude La Haye and Associates, planning consultants. Canadian Centre for Architecture, Montréal, Fonds Jean Ouellet. Complexe Desjardins is a testimony to the growing power of capitalist institutions in Quebec and the role they played in transforming Montreal's urban landscape. In this study, the group of towers in the complex seems intent on rivalling its counterpart to the west.

12 Marcel Pépin, "Commentaire," in *Georges-Émile Lapalme*, ed. J.-F. Léonard (Montreal: Presses de l'Université du Québec, 1988), 81–83.

13 Pierre Bourdieu, Luc Boltanski, and Monique de Saint-Martin, "Les stratégies de reconversion sociale," *Informations sur les sciences sociales* 12, no. 5 (1974): 61 113.

expanded and their ability to take political action (through cartels and common fronts) increased. The unions were among the most important players in the battle against the Duplessis regime: they represented, as Marcel Pépin described it, a whopping chunk of opposition.[12] The expansion of organized labour during the 1960s, however, was largely due to the unionization of civil servants and highly skilled workers, such as Hydro-Québec's engineers.

The "rise of the middle class" reflected a two-fold movement: on the one hand, the upward mobility of young people out of the working class, and on the other hand, the "social reconversion" of young people from the petty bourgeoisie and bourgeoisie, creating a transformation of economic capital into "cultural capital" through education.[13] Not surprisingly, massive and diversified investments were made in education in the 1960s. People were no longer able to maintain or improve their social status from one generation to the next simply by accumulating some wealth and then passing on their estate. Entire sections of the industrial and commercial fabric disappeared, as craft industries, local shops and businesses, and small-scale farms were swallowed up by large national and multinational corporations. Individuals and families had to then change their economic, social, and political strategies. There was a noticeable shift toward collective undertakings (agricultural and savings cooperatives), more open criticism of the English-speaking competition, a more willing acceptance of state intervention in certain sectors of activity, and finally a degree of political mobilization that was nationalistic in tenor.

Nationalism + Modernization = Nationalization
Social mobility combined with collective mobilization gave rise to an extensive reform movement. The emergence of the new middle class went hand in hand with a renewal of traditional nationalism, not only expressing the middle class's

14 Charles Taylor, "Nationalism and the Political Intelligentsia: A Case Study," *Queen's Quarterly* 72, no. 1 (Spring 1965): 150–168.

15 Brown, *The Illustrated History of Canada*; P.-A. Linteau, René Durocher, Jean-Claude Robert, and François Ricard, *Histoire du Québec contemporain: Le Québec depuis 1930* (Montreal: Boréal, 1986).

16 Balthazar, "Aux sources de la Révolution tranquille," 99–100.

17 William D. Coleman, *The Independence Movement in Quebec* (Toronto: University of Toronto Press, 1984).

18 Brown, *The Illustrated History of Canada*, 471.

19 Dominique Marshall, *Aux origines sociales de l'État-providence* (Montreal: Presses de l'Université de Montréal, 1998), 282.

20 Louis Balthazar, "Quebec and the Ideal of Federalism," in *Quebec Society: Critical Issues*, ed. Marcel Fournier, Michael Rosenberg, and Deena Whyte (Scarborough: Prentice Hall, 1997), 47.

desire for social mobility, but also, as Charles Taylor has pointed out, reflecting a problem of "identity" for a social group that wanted to be the agents of Quebec's modernization.[14] Renewed nationalism and the modernization of the state were so closely intertwined that the history books have been unable to determine which of the two movements was the real driving force behind the reforms.[15]

"The Quebec economy is a dominated economy," proclaimed a headline in *Le Devoir* in 1960. "Maître chez nous" became the slogan of Jean Lesage's "équipe de tonnerre." The new Liberal government's plan was to use the state as a lever of economic development by creating, for example, a savings and investment fund in order to correct the situation and ensure that local savings played a larger role in the development of Quebec's wealth. It was a time of nationalism (which later would be referred to as "neo-nationalism"); the Quiet Revolution bore with it, according to the political scientist Louis Balthazar, the essence of Quebec nationalism.[16]

Quebec's entry into the modern era was closely tied to a process of ever-increasing state intervention and the modernization of the apparatus of government. Quebec was finally and unequivocally becoming a welfare state. There was a desire to introduce a new degree of rationality into political management, while at the same time allowing for the democratization of culture and education. This dynamic was certainly Québécois, but it was also Canadian, since pressure for social and political modernization was coming from that quarter as well; at the national level, the "time for things to change" had come already.[17] All the other provinces, except for the Maritimes, had by now developed their school systems, taken control of hydroelectric power, and eliminated the worst abuses of patronage. All of them, often at the federal government's instigation, had devoted their fast-growing revenues to improving their road networks and opening hospitals and schools to serve mushrooming populations. The province of Saskatchewan, with its socialist CCF government led by Tommy Douglas, had become a veritable laboratory of innovation.[18]

During the period of incredible prosperity following World War II, the federal government adopted a "new national policy" designed to ensure the country's economic stability and the social welfare of all its citizens. A complete system of social security was introduced, including unemployment insurance, a family allowance, and an old-age pension. Canada evolved into a state that was politically unified, highly integrated economically, and led by a strong central government. This Keynesian policy was a response to various pressures and demands – from organized labour, from feminists[19] – and was intended to improve the "welfare of all Canadians," setting the country on the path to becoming a social democracy, with universal social programs, strong unions, and government commitments to create jobs and eliminate regional disparities.

With Louis Saint-Laurent as prime minister from 1948 to 1957, there was every indication that "Canadianism would eventually triumph over provincialism."[20] The federal Liberal Party won massive support in Quebec, and many Quebecers gladly took advantage of new federal programs such as the family allowance payment (a Gallup poll in 1955 showed that over 95 percent of the

21 Marshall, *Aux origines sociales de l'État-providence*, 286. See also Yves Vaillancourt, *L'évolution des politiques sociales au Québec, 1940–1960* (Montreal: Presses de l'Université de Montréal, 1988).

population were benefiting from it). It could be said that for two decades the federal government indirectly paved the way for the emergence of a welfare state in Quebec by providing its reformists with the requisite laws, structures, and expertise. Some have claimed that Lesage's social assistance and education policies were in fact appropriated federal initiatives.[21] Nor should it be forgotten that the principal architects of the Quiet Revolution, Georges-Émile Lapalme and Jean Lesage, both started their careers in federal politics before jumping into the provincial arena.

Lapalme had been elected to the House of Commons in 1945 as the representative for the riding of Joliette-L'Assomption-Montcalm, and was re-elected in 1949. He moved onto the provincial stage in 1950 to become leader of the Quebec Liberal Party, which he thoroughly transformed, setting up the Quebec Liberal Federation, creating a policy commission chaired by Jean-Marie Nadeau, developing new funding rules, organizing party congresses, founding the magazine

Figure 7
Hydro-Québec head office under construction, October 1960. Gaston Gagnier, architect. Photograph: Studio Jac-Guy. Archives Hydro-Québec. Following the nationalization of electricity by the Lesage government, the Hydro-Québec Building came to symbolize the achievements of the state in the service of Quebec society.

22 Marcel Fournier, "Georges-Émile Lapalme: Culture et politique," in *Georges-Émile Lapalme*, ed. Léonard, 159–167; Robert Boily, "La transformation du Parti libéral du Québec sous Georges-Émile Lapalme (1950–1958)," ibid., 222–237.

23 François Aquin, "Jean Lesage, un rassembleur démocrate," in *Jean Lesage et l'éveil d'une nation: Les débuts de la Révolution tranquille*, ed. Robert Comeau (Montreal: Presses de l'Université du Québec, 1989), 41–45.

24 Louis Martin, "Les hommes derrière le pouvoir," *Le Magazine Maclean*, October 1964, 25. The subtitle of the article was "Au Québec, une nouvelle génération de hauts fonctionnaires élabore la 'révolution tranquille': les technocrates" (In Quebec, a new generation of top civil servants is preparing the "quiet revolution": the technocrats).

25 Réjean Landry, "La Révolution tranquille," in *Le Québec en jeu*, ed. Gérard Daigle (Montreal: Presses de l'Université de Montréal, 1992), 609–647.

26 Pierre Elliott Trudeau, "Un manifeste démocratique," *Cité libre* 9, no. 22 (October 1958): 1–31.

27 Charles Taylor, "Le pluralisme et le dualisme," in *Québec: État et société*, ed. Alain G. Gagnon (Montreal: Québec/Amérique, 1994), 61.

28 For example, Michel Bélanger was hired as director general of planning for water power resources, Jean Lessard as president of Hydro-Québec, Josaphat Brunet (an RCMP officer) as director of the Quebec Provincial Police, Jean Fournier as chairman of the Quebec Civil Service Commission, and Jean Chapdelaine as a member of the Délégation générale du Québec à Paris.

29 Paul Gervais, "Les diplômés en sciences sociales dans la fonction publique du Québec" (Master's thesis, University of Montreal, 1970).

La Réforme (edited by Jean-Louis Gagnon), revitalizing constituency associations, and establishing party associations for young people and for women. In his published memoirs, *Le bruit des choses réveillées*, he acknowledged that his goal had been to "slacken the noose that was choking the province."[22]

In the realm of politics, a new type emerged behind the traditional political dignitary: the technocrat with specialized knowledge and training, who produced development strategies, talked about planning, and recommended the rational management of people and things. According to François Aquin, it was under Lesage's Liberal government that the new technocracy and the advancement of the idea of state service appeared in Quebec for the first time.[23] The men behind the power, as they were called in the title of an article by Louis Martin in *Le Magazine Maclean*,[24] were Claude Morin for the area of federal-provincial relations, Arthur Tremblay for education, Michel Bélanger for natural resources, and Jean Deschamps for industry and commerce. In the early 1960s, these men were all in their thirties and possessed university degrees in economics, education, or commerce. Their prime objective was to reform the civil service.

This was the triumph at last of the political over the tribal.[25] A new conception of politics and a new way of doing politics had become essential. Democracy was set against corruption, and at the party level decision-making bodies were established and programs were created. In 1958, Pierre Elliott Trudeau published his democratic manifesto in *Cité libre*, pitting the democratic union (of all reformist forces) against the Union nationale. He argued that the democratic revolution initiated by Papineau, and then pushed forward by Laurier, had become bogged down.[26] Prior to the 1950s, it was assumed that the way to defend liberalism and the democratic heritage was through Ottawa, for at that time Quebec was characterized by a sort of "illiberalism" (as Charles Taylor put it) stemming from its values of traditional and ultramontane Catholicism. After World War II, the forces inside Quebec that were fighting for a liberal society prevailed, just like forces elsewhere in the Western world; in short, French Canada caught up with English Canada.[27] The Quebec Liberal Party, which had gradually detached itself from its big brother in Ottawa, intended to make political life in Quebec more democratic and, once in power, would go ahead with major changes regarding the electoral map, election expenses, fraud, and so on.

To enable the Cabinet to monitor government operations more closely, an Office of the Treasury was created; in 1961, it was turned into a Treasury Board, based on the federal model. Lesage wanted to introduce the taxation methods that he had become familiar with in Ottawa. His model for the role of minister of industry and commerce was C.D. Howe, the "czar of the Canadian economy." Structural renewal depended on the recruitment of highly qualified personnel. Advisors and top-level civil servants were recruited from the universities and the federal civil service.[28] Many of them had university degrees in the social sciences; a number of them had been educated at Laval University.[29] The impact of these "new" experts was particularly decisive, since it was their departments that designed and implemented the most important government reforms: the creation of a Department of Education and regional school boards, the nation-

30 Guy Rocher, "La sécularisation des institutions d'enseignement," in *Jean Lesage et l'éveil d'une nation*, 168–177. The issue of denomination was not resolved: legally, the school boards remained denominational.

alization of electric power, a new social welfare plan, hospital insurance, a new labour code, and the establishment of the Société générale de financement (SGF), Sidbec, and the Caisse de dépôt et placement.

Secularization and Educational Reform

Without a doubt, the "major event" of the Quiet Revolution, arising from the expansion of the Quebec government's role in health and education, was the phenomenon of secularization. The power of the Church was now replaced by that of the state, and public education was brought under state control. Attitudes and practices changed completely – attendance at mass dropped, the number of people entering the religious orders declined – and only the law remained, including the rights of the Catholic and Protestant denominations.[30]

Seemingly by chance, the Quiet Revolution got underway just as the Church in Quebec was beginning to open its doors and windows to the world. Under the banner of freedom, winds of renewal swept through the Church as the Second Vatican Council was held (1962–1965). A popular Sunday television program, "C'est l'heure du Concile," introduced its viewers to the new direction being taken by the Church. Religious rituals were "modernized," the clergy became more community-oriented, and the Church opened itself to new theological currents. *Maintenant*, a progressive magazine published by the Dominican Fathers, appeared in 1962. Secularization began expanding with the creation of the Mouvement laïc de langue française in 1961.

More than any other reform, that of education met the new needs (notably in the training of labour) and reflected the new aspirations of a large part of the population. The saturated market in the liberal professions, the opening up of new careers in science and in administration, the sharp drop in the number

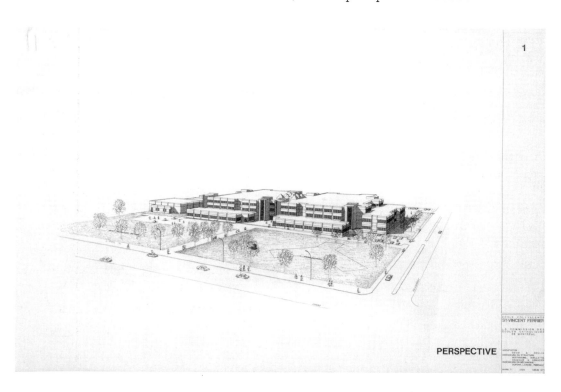

Figure 8
École polyvalente Saint-Vincent-Ferrier, perspective, March 1971. David and Boulva, architects. From a presentation brochure. Canadian Centre for Architecture, Montréal, Fonds Roland Dumais

31   Pierre Dandurand and Marcel Fournier, "Développement de l'enseignement supérieur, classes sociales et question nationale au Québec," *Sociologie et sociétés* 12, no. 2 (April 1980): 104–105.

32   Gérard Pelletier, "Le retour de l'enfant prodigue," *La Presse*, 18 January 1964, 4.

33   Richard Arès, "Le Rapport Parent: Approbations, réserves, et inquiétudes," *Relations*, no. 290 (February 1965): 35.

34   *La Presse libre*, 11 December 1964, 2–3. The editor was Jean-V. Dufresne.

35   Georges Robitaille, "Un grand saut en avant," *Relations*, no. 290 (February 1965): 61.

36   Gérald Godin, "On nous écrit…," *Cité libre* 14, no. 61 (November 1963): 25–26.

of entrants into religious orders, and the huge demand for education created a crisis in the educational system and led to the dissolution of the classical college, which had been a key institution in Quebec. University education and specialized schooling underwent change. The university system became more diversified, with an increased emphasis on the sciences, the social sciences, and commerce. University studies also became more accessible: the rate of attendance among young people between the ages of 19 and 24 rose from 4 percent in 1960 to 9.5 percent a decade later, and the number of full-time students more than doubled, from 26,948 to 54,575.[31]

The era of the classical education was over. The so-called dead languages (Latin and Greek) disappeared, making way for specialization and for a culture of "professionalism," which rejected all forms of traditional authority, denigrated the work of the untrained amateur, and had only contempt for mediocrity and incompetence. Science and "professional" knowledge were pitted against age-old traditions and clerical ignorance. The crucible of knowledge was no longer the salon or the study, but rather the library, the laboratory, and the scientific conference.

When Bill 60 was adopted in January 1964 and the Liberal government, after lengthy negotiations with the bishops, created a Department of Education (with a Superior Council of Education and denominational committees), the editorialist Gérard Pelletier wrote in *La Presse* that the fatted calf had had to be killed.[32] The tabling of the Report of the Royal Commission of Inquiry on Education in Quebec fuelled extensive debate: Father Arès, in the magazine *Relations*, saw this "bold project for educational reform" as "one of the major turning points in our history," marking out a new destiny for the people of Quebec.[33] Monseigneur Parent chaired the commission, and one of its most active members was the sociologist Guy Rocher, who held a Ph.D. from Harvard and taught at the University of Montreal.

The Parent Report was greeted with approval by some and with reservations and concerns by others. The progressive press was almost delirious: the veneration of Latin and Greek was over, technology and mathematical logic would take their place, and free-thinking, child-centred education would become the norm.[34] Everyone applauded the proposals for democratization, liberalization, and decentralization. These were grand, noble, and generous ideas, exclaimed Father Arès, though he also questioned, in the same breath, why it was necessary to rebuild everything from the ground up, and wondered what would become of "our classical humanism" in comprehensive schools. He was equally concerned about the future of private education (primarily the classical colleges), the fate of the confessional school system, and the likelihood of bureaucratic and technocratic *dirigisme* from the new Department of Education. It was a "great leap forward" that, to the most conservative minds, seemed to be a "leap in the dark"[35] and, to the most forward-looking, seemed to be a liberating event. "We are from a generation," wrote the young Gérald Godin in *Cité libre*, "that has seen things being carried out (or certainly appearing to be carried out) expediently. Actions seem to lead to results. It would appear that dawn is breaking, and the darkness is receding."[36]

37 Maurice Lamontagne, *Le fédéralisme canadien: Évolution et problèmes* (Quebec City: Presses de l'Université Laval, 1954). The last sentence of the book reads: "Il ne faut jamais oublier qu'une certaine unification politique est parfois nécessaire pour maintenir et sauvegarder la diversité culturelle" (It must never be forgotten that some political unification is sometimes necessary in order to maintain and safeguard cultural diversity).

38 Peter C. Newman, "The U.S. and Us," *Maclean's*, 6 June 1964, 14.

A Period of Ideological Ferment

The 1960s were a decade marked by two contradictory movements: one that went in the direction of clear-sighted integration with federalism, as it was described by the minister (and later senator) Maurice Lamontagne, who feared that the dream of separatism, if ever realized, might mean suicide,[37] and an opposite movement of nationalistic protest, which, if it were to take a radical turn, might lead to separation. The results of a poll conducted by the Groupe de recherche sociale in the fall of 1963 indicated that 13 percent of Quebecers were in favour of separation, 43 percent were against it, 23 percent were undecided, and 21 percent had never heard of it. It was also found that 78 percent of Quebecers (compared with 57 percent of Ontarians) were in favour of economic union between Canada and the United States.[38]

"Le Canada face à l'avenir" (Canada Facing the Future) was the title given to a 1964 conference of the Canadian Institute on Public Affairs. Its subtitle, "Un pays qui s'interroge," alluded to the uncertainty with which Quebecers in particular were questioning their own future. Jean-Jacques Bertrand, the Union nationale MNA for Missisquoi, felt that finding the right answer would be difficult. Three options were presented: separatism (André d'Allemagne), a new constitution (Pierre Laporte), and "cooperative federalism" (Jean-Louis Pépin). During the discussion period, the topics of "economic decentralization and binationalism," the "special status of Quebec," and "constitutional pragmatism" were addressed. Renewed federalism revolved around three Cs: cooperation, coordination, and compromise. The federal government, for its part, had launched an extensive examination of culture and language through the establishment of the Royal Commission on Bilingualism and Biculturalism – co-chaired by André Laurendeau and A. Davidson Dunton – which issued its preliminary report in 1965.

It was clear, as Dr. Camille Laurin noted in a lecture on the theme of "collective catharsis" in 1965, that Quebecers had not yet made a choice: they were wavering between autonomy within Confederation and complete independence. It was equally clear to Laurin, who was a psychiatrist at the Institut Prévost, that Quebec society had developed a taste for freedom and that nothing would take that away. But along with the wavering, there was also a search for a third way. In his editorial on "the current crisis in Canada" published in *Le Devoir* on 18 September 1964, Claude Ryan advanced the notion of accepting the "Canadian hypothesis" as a framework within which Quebecers could make their case for a reformed federalism. In 1965, the leader of the Union nationale, Daniel Johnson, published a work entitled *Égalité ou indépendance*, and that same year, the government set up a provincial committee on the constitution, before which the Société Saint-Jean-Baptiste de Montréal presented a brief on the idea of "two associated states." The question of Quebec's "special status" was also a central topic of debate. In the provincial election of 1966, the Rassemblement pour l'indépendance nationale (RIN), a grassroots movement led by Pierre Bourgault that had evolved into a political party, fielded 72 candidates. Daniel Johnson won a surprise victory: his party had 55 members elected, with only 40 percent of the vote.

Quebec was certainly in a period of ideological ferment, as Charles Taylor observed in *Cité libre*, and as the following summary of events indicates: in 1960, the RIN, chaired by Marcel Chaput, was founded, and the Action socialiste pour l'indépendance was set up by Raoul Roy; in 1961, the Mouvement laïc de langue française was established, and the daily *Le Nouveau Journal* was founded by Jean-Louis Gagnon; in 1963, the Parti socialiste du Québec was created, following a rift within the Quebec NDP party over the constitutional issue, and the magazine *Parti pris* was launched; in 1964, Marcel Rioux and Jacques Dofny began publishing the magazine *Socialisme*, the Quebec General Student Union was formed, and, in September, *La Presse libre* was published by the CNTU during the strike by three *La Presse* employee unions. Two major events marked the end of the decade: in 1968, René Lévesque left the Liberal Party and founded the Parti québécois, while in the federal election that year Pierre Elliott Trudeau became prime minister of Canada.

These activities all reflect the political and intellectual vitality of the 1960s, but it was a period that also saw a rise in violence. A terrorist movement, the Front de libération du Québec (FLQ), was formed in 1963. Large demonstrations would sometimes culminate in clashes with the police, the most famous example being the "Samedi de la matraque" (riot-baton Saturday), which took place during Queen Elizabeth's visit to Quebec City in the fall of 1964. To borrow the title of an article by Pierre Maheu, there was a shift "from revolt to revolution." "After *Cité libre*, there was *Liberté*. After *Liberté*, we now have *Parti pris*," wrote the Jesuit André Vachon, who saw the new magazine as the last step in a movement that was "destined, from the outset, to always go beyond its own

Figure 9
Sgt. Major Walter Lega injured in explosion of a bomb removed from a mailbox in Westmount, 17 May 1963.
Photograph: Adrien Lunny. Library and Archives Canada, Ottawa, PA-137864

39 André Vachon, "Parti pris: De la révolte à la révolution," *Relations*, November 1963, 326.

40 Charles Taylor, "La révolution futile," *Cité libre* 15, no. 69 (August–September 1964): 10–23.

41 Jacques Lazure, *La jeunesse en révolution* (Montreal: Presses de l'Université du Québec, 1971).

left."[39] *Parti pris* was meant to fight for a "free, secular, and socialist state" and to serve, first and foremost, as an "instrument of demystification," ready to denounce the alienating nature of cultural structures based on religious values. Critical of the totalitarian ideology and "systematic dogmatism" of the new magazine, the philosopher Charles Taylor sarcastically referred to those involved in it as simply "guerrillas from Outremont." He urged his young colleagues to be more rigorous and more realistic in their efforts at constructing a program of social and economic reform.[40]

The Young Generation Enters the Scene

People wanted to "change the world." That, according to Marcel Rioux, was what the cultural revolution was all about. The word "revolution" was on everyone's lips. In Quebec, as the sociologist Jacques Lazure saw it, the young generation was swept up by a triple revolution: a revolution in education (rejecting authority, dropping out of school), a political revolution (reformist, radical, and libertarian trends, along with the independence movement), and a sexual revolution.[41]

Life on college and university campuses across Quebec was bustling. Students demanded educational reforms and a role in school governance. Student newspapers developed and formed links through the organizing of the National Student Press. Student associations were established at every college and university, and they were united in a single federation, the Quebec General Student Union, in 1964. After that, the student movement became radicalized, with increasing strikes, sit-ins, and demonstrations. In the fall of 1965, a strike by students at the École des beaux-arts de Montréal quickly transcended academic issues and internal school matters to call into question the very place of art in society. To calm things down, the Liberal government established a commission of inquiry into art education the following year and asked Marcel Rioux to chair it.

Protests flared up again in the fall of 1968, but this time with greater force. In the wake of the events of May 1968 in France, observers feared the worst. The actions began not at the universities, but at some of the recently created colleges: first at the Lionel-Groulx cégep in Sainte-Thérèse, north of Montreal, and then at some 15 other establishments across Quebec. The strikes and sit-ins paralyzed education for more than two months. The sit-in at the École des beaux-arts de Montréal was the longest and the most radical. The very imaginative and determined art students demanded that the school be self-governing and called for a true democratization of the arts; they questioned not only the role of students in an art school, but also the role of the artist in society.

The number of teach-ins and sit-ins at the universities, primarily in the humanities and social science departments, increased. The debate was raised a notch, from criticism of educational institutions to criticism of the whole of capitalist, bureaucratic, technological society. In the early spring of 1969, the Quebec General Student Union organized a huge demonstration, mobilizing over 10,000 students. It was then that the political and nationalist dimension of the protest movement came into view, on 28 March 1969, when more than 15,000 students

42 Paul-André Linteau, *Histoire de Montréal depuis la Confédération* (Montreal: Boréal, 1991), 487.

43 *150 ans de lutte: Histoire du mouvement ouvrier au Québec, 1825–1976* (Montreal: CEQ-CSN, 1979), 168.

marched through the streets of Montreal shouting "McGill français!" There were three sorts of causes around which the young rallied: the counterculture, with its new values and new lifestyle; the militant agenda of the more populist and far-left political organizations; and the nationalist movement and its newly created Parti québécois.

Protest and militancy were the order of the day. The labour movement, bursting with energy, launched a series of strikes that left a deep mark on the city of Montreal: the "illegal" strike by the nurses at Sainte-Justine Hospital in 1963; the lengthy work stoppage (lasting more than seven months) at *La Presse* in 1964; the Liquor Board strike in late 1964; the many strikes that led to the creation of a united public transit workers front and paralyzed mass transit; the strike by the Syndicat des professeurs de l'État du Québec (SPEQ) in 1966; the strike by Hydro-Québec's engineers and then by its other employees in 1966 and 1967; and the illegal police strike in 1969.[42] The year 1969 was a time of particularly intense social unrest: taxi drivers participated in a wild demonstration targeting the Murray Hill bus company; there were mass protests against Bill 63; and in November a demonstration demanding the release of FLQ members Pierre Vallières and Charles Gagnon escalated into violence.[43] A series of new leaders were at the helm of the labour movement – Louis Laberge from the Quebec Federation of Labour (QFL) in 1964, Marcel Pépin from the Confederation

Figure 10
Debris on MacKay Street during a student demonstration at Sir George Williams University, 11 February 1969. From *The Montreal Star*. Library and Archives Canada, Ottawa, PA-139988

44 Roch Denis, *Luttes de classes et question nationale au Québec, 1948–1968* (Montreal: PSI, 1979), 418.
45 Linteau, *Histoire de Montréal*, 540.

of National Trade Unions (CNTU) in 1965, and Raymond Laliberté from the Corporation des instituteurs et institutrices catholiques du Québec (CIC), which became the Quebec Teachers' Corporation in 1967. It was also a time of labour unity and common fronts. The central labour bodies, led by the Conseil central des syndicats de Montréal, which was chaired by the feisty Michel Chartrand, became radicalized and entered the political arena. It is significant that the celebration of International Workers' Day – May Day – was revived, first in 1965 with a large public meeting organized by left-wing groups, and then in 1970 with a major street demonstration involving all the central labour bodies.

Social Struggles and Intellectual Committedness

Intellectuals, for their part, formed ties with the labour movement: Jacques Dofny, a professor of sociology, served as éminence grise to Marcel Pépin, and the two of them took part in revitalizing – or rather, attempting to revitalize – the Parti socialiste du Québec, created in 1963. Many intellectuals were searching for a new cause to which they might commit themselves.[44] A group called the Mouvement de liberation populaire (MLP) grew up around the magazine *Parti pris*, focusing on propaganda, unrest, political education, and research; in the fall of 1965, *Parti pris* published a manifesto picking up on the thesis of the two-fold domination of Quebec (by the federal government and by the Americans) and the two fold task of liberating it from national oppression and capitalist exploitation. Within the left wing, debates were numerous and divisions frequent. When the MLP disappeared in the spring of 1966, two of its leaders, Pierre Vallières and Charles Gagnon, and a dozen young militants joined the FLQ to wage an underground "global revolutionary battle" against colonialism and imperialism. Others entered the ranks of the Rassemblement pour l'indépendance nationale (RIN) to transform it into a workers party, and later went on to join the Mouvement Souveraineté-Association (MSA), created by René Lévesque in November 1967.

Union leaders, intellectuals, and militants all sought to establish links with social movements and to associate with grassroots organizations. The deterioration in housing conditions, the absence of low-cost housing, and the inadequacy of social services fuelled the discontent that mobilized residents of disadvantaged neighbourhoods and spurred the creation of citizen action groups. Young people with degrees in the social sciences read Marx, discovered the "culture of poverty," moved into neighbourhoods like Hochelaga-Maisonneuve, Saint-Henri, and Pointe Saint-Charles, and became social activists.

The citizen action groups began simply as pressure groups, but then became radicalized – as was the case with the Comité de citoyens de Saint-Jacques – and undertook political action. Through the Front d'action politique (FRAP), they played a role in the 1970 municipal election. Their program, which was socialist in orientation, called for greater citizen involvement in decision-making and proposed numerous reforms in the areas of health, public transportation, culture, recreation, and economic development.[45] It was thus that the first more or less organized opposition to the Drapeau-Saulnier administration

Figure 11
**Milton-Park Citizens' Committee march on City Hall,
24 May 1969.** From *The Gazette* (Montreal). Photograph:
Gerry Bird. Library and Archives Canada, Ottawa, PA-153958

46 Jean Drapeau was first elected mayor of Montreal in
    1954 and was defeated in 1957 by Sarto Fournier, who
    led a new party – the Ralliement du Grand Montréal –
    and was supported by the Union nationale.

47 Claire Helman, *The Milton-Park Affair* (Montreal:
    Véhicule Press, 1986); Phyllis Lambert, "Land Tenure
    and Concepts of Architecture and the City: Milton-
    Park in Montreal," in *Power and Place: Canadian Urban
    Development in the North American Context*, ed. Gilbert
    A. Stelter and Alan F.J. Artibise (Vancouver: University of
    British Columbia Press, 1986), 133–150.

emerged in Montreal. Mayor Jean Drapeau's Civic Party had been in power since
1960.[46] Lucien Saulnier, his right-hand man, was the chairman of the Executive
Committee throughout the entire decade. Their program was to modernize city
management, initiate various reforms, and establish a development strategy
around major projects, including the construction of the metro system, inaugurated in 1966, and the hosting of Expo 67. Several FRAP candidates ran in the 1970
election, held shortly after the events of October, but the results were disastrous:
they were seen as a band of agitators tied somehow to the FLQ.

The impact of the citizen action movement was felt in a number of
sectors: free medical and legal clinics were opened, free daycare centres were
set up, and consumer and housing cooperatives were created. One of the best
examples of this new type of action in the city arose out of the "Milton-Park
Affair." The firm of Concordia Estates had a development project that was to
involve the demolition of houses on Jeanne-Mance. Local residents held repeated
demonstrations in protest and, in 1969, founded the Milton-Park Residents
Association. As in the case of other such groups, the divisions within the association were numerous – there was a "more conservative" wing, a "more radical"
wing, and anarchists. Members were leery of infiltrators. The movement gave
rise to the creation of a family clinic at the University Settlement, which provided
free medical and psychiatric services, as well as a consumer cooperative. Links
were also forged with the universities, and a Community Design Workshop
was set up on Park Avenue, enabling McGill University architecture students
to work with local residents on innovative architectural and urban planning
projects. A large cooperative housing project was launched, to be completed
in the following decade through the determination of two new residents of the
area, Lucia Kowaluk, a community organizer, and her husband, the publisher
Dimitri Roussopoulos.[47]

48 Mordecai Richler, *The Street* (Toronto: McClelland and Stewart, 1969), 53.

49 Cited in Jedwab, "La Révolution 'tranquille' des Anglo-Québécois," 187.

50 Fernand Dumont, *Le sort de la culture* (Montreal: L'Hexagone, 1987), 305.

Figure 12
Liberté, no. 28 (July–August 1963), special issue on Montreal.
Photograph: Denis Vincent. Collection André Lortie

Figure 13
Cité libre 13, no. 57 (May 1963). Collection André Lortie

Culture Comes Alive

In 1960, at the very moment that his "old friends" were about to take power in Quebec City, Paul-Émile Borduas, the author of the *Refus global*, died in Paris. In a letter to Claude Gauvreau written two years before, he remarked that he had been born too soon, in a country too young.

A host of cultural initiatives, events, and achievements testified to the fact that the culture was now truly alive (a magazine put out by the Department of Cultural Affairs in 1966 aptly called itself *Culture vivante*). One could point, for example, to the publication of polemical essays (*Les insolences du frère Untel* by Frère Desbiens, *La ligne du risque* by Pierre Vadeboncoeur), works of fiction (*Le cassé* by Jacques Renaud, *Les contes du pays incertain* by Jacques Ferron), and collections of poetry (*Terre Québec* by Paul Chamberland), the staging of plays (*Les belles-soeurs* by Michel Tremblay), the founding of publishing houses (Boréal Express, Presses de l'Université de Montréal), the launching in 1960 of *Châtelaine*, a progressive magazine that appealed to a wide female audience and showcased literary contributions, the creation of cultural and political reviews (*Liberté* in 1961, *Parti pris* in 1963, *Socialisme* in 1964) as well as scholarly journals (*Recherches sociographiques* in 1960, *Études françaises* in 1965, *Sociologie et sociétés* in 1969), the production of radio and television programs, the hosting of the International Week of Today's Music by Pierre Mercure in 1961, the formation of the Société de musique contemporaine du Québec (through the initiative of Wilfrid Pelletier and Pierre Mercure) in 1966, the setting up of electronic music studios (including McGill University's in 1963), the advent of a new cinema (Claude Jutra, Pierre Perreault, Gilles Groulx, Jean-Pierre Lefebvre), the opening of film theatres, art galleries, and museums, and a growing number of exhibitions. A sort of nationalization of culture was taking place: there was now a Québécois literature, rock music was being sung in French (Robert Charlebois's *Lindberg* in 1967), local films were being seen, joual had acquired the status of a language, and Quebec had found its own bards and minstrels in performers such as Gaston Miron, Gilles Vigneault, and Pauline Julien.

The shift in affiliation from Canada to Quebec could be seen in English-language literature as well, one example being the anthology *English Poetry in Quebec*, edited by John Glassco and published in 1963. Anglo-Québécois intellectuals observed – not without a certain unease – all that was going on, and participated in it. In *The Street*, published in 1969, Mordecai Richler talked about the conflictual nature of the relationship between Jews and French Canadians during the post-war years: "Looking back, it's easy to see the trouble was there was no dialogue between us and the French Canadians."[48] In his novel *Beautiful Losers*, published in 1966, Leonard Cohen included a description of a gathering of French-Canadian nationalists, in a scene that can be interpreted as expressing a certain fear that the rallying victims may breed new victims.[49]

The Quiet Revolution thus seemed, according to Fernand Dumont, to be a cultural revolution,[50] not only involving intellectuals, writers, and artists, but occurring as well in the new mass media of film and television. Beginning in the 1950s, two institutions would pave the way for the Quiet Revolution: the National

51 Balthazar, "Aux sources de la Révolution tranquille."

52 Alain Pontaut, "Les festivals sont fatigués," *Cité libre* 15, no. 69 (August–September 1964): 27.

Film Board (NFB) and Radio-Canada, the Canadian Broadcasting Corporation's French-language network.[51] After the NFB moved to Montreal, it became a hotbed of film production for a new generation of filmmakers. It would become best known for its work in animation: in 1967, one of Norman McLaren's films, *Pas de deux*, was nominated for an Oscar. As well, many documentaries were made by the NFB, including Michel Régnier's *Urbanose* series and numerous films on art, such as Jacques Godbout's *Les Dieux* (1961) and *Paul-Émile Borduas* (1967) and Jacques Giraldeau's *We Are All . . . Picasso!* With the series *Panoramique* in 1958, which included works by Bernard Devlin, Louis Portugais, Claude Jutra, and Fernand Dansereau, a new Quebec cinema emerged, developing all the main themes of the Quiet Revolution, taking a critical look at society, and giving expression to new values (tolerance, openness to the outside world, pluralism, feminism, and sexual freedom). There was an increase in the number of film societies, and the Montreal Film Festival was inaugurated in 1960. In a city that, according to the critic Alain Pontaut, was still "mired in ignorance, mediocrity, and censorship," film had managed to be legitimated as "art."[52]

The production and broadcasting department of Radio-Canada had been set up in Montreal in 1952. In little over a decade, it would alter not only cultural habits – everyone, or nearly everyone, was watching the same program at the same time – but also social values. Radio-Canada brought its viewers closer to North American norms and yet at the same time fostered a new solidarity and a new sense of belonging. This, paradoxically, contributed both to the Americanization of Quebec audiences and to the creation of a "distinct society." Moreover, through its hiring of journalists, script writers, producers, set designers, and researchers, Radio-Canada played a crucial role in what could be termed the "affirmation of modernity." The number of creative people working at the time for this new mass medium was considerable: close to 15 percent of writers from the generation born after 1920 held a position in the broadcasting

Figure 14

Mayor Jean Drapeau and Cardinal Paul-Émile Léger at the unveiling of the project model for the Maison de Radio-Canada, 22 June 1966. Photograph: Le Coz. Archives Radio-Canada

53 Marcel Fournier, "Portrait d'un groupe: Les écrivains," *Possibles* 10, no. 2 (Winter 1986): 129–149.

54 Balthazar, "Aux sources de la Révolution tranquille," 94.

55 Ignace Cau, *L'édition au Québec de 1960 à 1977* (Quebec City: Ministère des Affaires culturelles), 1981.

56 Marcel Dubé, "Dix ans de télévision," *Cité libre* 13, no. 48 (June–July 1962): 24–25.

57 Richard Arès, "Radio-Canada et le Canada français," *Relations* 21 (1961): 325–327.

58 Guy Rocher, *Le Québec en mutation* (Montreal: Hurtubise HMH, 1973), 19.

industry and received remuneration from it.[53] They included not only playwrights (Louis-Georges Carrier, Gilles Derome, Guy Dufresne, Jean-Paul Fugère, Jacques Languirand), but also poets (Fernand Ouellette, Paul-Marie Lapointe, Guy Maufette, Wilfrid Lemoine, Pierre Morency), novelists (Roger Fournier, Jacques Godbout, André Langevin), and people like Jean Le Moyne, the author of *Convergences*, who was a journalist and researcher at the NFB before serving as an advisor and speechwriter for Prime Minister Trudeau.

The first major cultural institution in Quebec to not fall under the control of the clergy,[54] television had a decisive influence on news and public affairs. With programs such as *Les idées en marche* (1954) and *Point de mire* (1956), it offered a window onto the world. Personalities like René Lévesque, Gérard Pelletier, Judith Jasmin, Wilfrid Lemoine, Pierre Elliott Trudeau, and André Laurendeau could be seen on Quebec television, spreading the call for social change, modernization, and critical thought. According to Fernand Séguin, Radio-Canada was the most extraordinary thing ever to happen to French Canada since the days of Jacques Cartier.[55] Assessing the achievements of Radio-Canada in its early years, the playwright Marcel Dubé declared that the publicly owned network was responsible, directly or indirectly, for Quebec's intellectual awakening, its flourishing arts and letters, and its ideological revolutionism.[56] In effect, it hastened the disintegration of French Canada's traditional culture and contributed to the development of a new culture based on democratic and secular humanism.[57]

Quebec's television landscape was soon transformed by a "liberalization of the airwaves" that led to the introduction, in 1961, of two privately owned stations – CFTM and CFCF. In response to this new competition, Radio-Canada was forced to modify its programming, which until then had been elitist. Culture now evolved into "mass culture" and became a kind of industry, as seen, for example, in the establishment of the Canadian Film Development Corporation (CFDC) in 1967. The following year, the Quebec government decided to set up its own television network, Radio-Québec, which would begin broadcasting in the mid-1970s.

The work of Radio-Canada, along with that of the universities, publishing houses, and print media (such as *Le Devoir*), led to the creation of an intellectual and artistic community on the one hand and a cultivated audience on the other. The encounter between these artists and this audience in turn fostered a cultural resurgence that resulted in the founding of intellectual journals and the formation of theatre companies that were to be the seedbeds of the Quiet Revolution.[58] The creative and dynamic new "cultural elite" that grew up around these institutions spearheaded the opposition to the Duplessis government. These were the people who would be reading *Cité libre*, or publishing their own views in it. Many of them would attend the CIPA (Canadian Institute on Public Affairs) conference, held annually in the Laurentians, initially under the chairmanship of Léon Lortie, a chemistry professor at the University of Montreal. Adding to the impact of the CIPA conferences was the open-line broadcast that the publicly owned television network devoted to it each year. Its participants included the people whom Duplessis called "pelleteux de nuages" (dream chasers) – intellectuals whose expertise in the social sciences and the humanities was enlivened by a critical spirit.

59 Marcel Rioux, *Jeunesse et société contemporaine* (Montreal: Presses de l'Université de Montréal, 1971).

60 Marcel Fournier, *Les générations d'artistes* (Quebec City: Institut québécois de recherche sur la culture, 1986); Marcel Fournier, "L'artiste en jeune homme et jeune femme," in *Déclics: Art et société, le Québec des années 1960 et 1970* (Quebec City: Musée de la civilisation; Montreal: Musée d'art contemporain / Fides, 1999), 90–116.

61 Yvon Lussier, "La division du travail selon l'ethnie au Québec, 1931–1961" (Master's thesis, University of Montreal, 1967).

Smoking his Gitane cigarettes, and sporting a beret and tinted glasses, with *Le Monde* tucked under his arm, the anthropologist and professor of sociology Marcel Rioux embodied the new intellectual – one who challenged religious and political authority, defended secularism, socialism, and independence, called for emancipation and creativity, and was open to all possibilities. Rioux contributed articles to *Cité libre* and participated regularly in the CIPA conferences (of which he became chairman). After the Liberals were elected, he moved beyond the ideology of "closing the gap" and sought to advance the causes of emancipation and development. The future, he asserted in a booklet titled *Jeunesse et société contemporaine*, belonged to the young. From his point of view, intergenerational conflicts were to contemporary society what class conflicts were at the beginning of the Industrial Revolution. Young people were more than an age group: they were a veritable political force, an engine of change.[59]

Artistic Life

The younger generation of artists was in the vanguard of the cultural revolution.[60] Art was, more than ever, synonymous with freedom – freedom of thought, freedom of expression. Québécois artists in the 1960s led a bohemian life. Existentialism was in the air. People frequented cafés, spent long evenings in bars and intimate music venues, and went to parties at friends' places. They tried to solve the world's problems, listened to Brassens and Ferré, read Camus and Sartre, watched Truffaut and Godard films, and tuned in to Guy Maufette's "Cabaret du soir qui penche" on Sunday nights. They dreamt of Paris and went to New York. They let their hair grow long and smoked pot. An underground world was formed, and new trends in food and clothing emerged. Many fled from the consumer culture altogether, in order to get closer to nature.

The population of artists and art teachers increased significantly, climbing from 683 in 1951 to 2,340 in 1961.[61] At the École des beaux-arts de Montréal, the number of students registered full-time jumped from 279 in 1964–1965 to 600 in 1967–1968. The artistic community became organized: in 1961, the Association des sculpteurs du Québec was formed, with Yves Trudeau as its first president, and in 1966, the Société des artistes professionnels du Québec was established. The status of the artist changed as a result of the rise of professionalism, the advent of a labour market for art graduates, the development of "integrated art," and the inclusion of the arts in the curriculum of educational institutions. The art world benefited from new institutional and financial support, first from the Canada Council for the Arts, created in 1957, and then from the Quebec government's Department of Cultural Affairs, created in 1961, with Georges-Émile Lapalme at the helm. The Department of Cultural Affairs was very active from the start: it subsidized cultural organizations such as Arts et métiers graphiques, the Montreal Museum of Fine Arts, and the magazine *Vie des Arts* (created in 1954 by Andrée Paradis), set up assistance programs for artists, opened a museum of contemporary art in Montreal (directed by the art critic Guy Robert), and funded a large sculpture symposium on Mount Royal as well as an exhibition in Spoleto, Italy, devoted to contemporary French-Canadian painting.

62 See the two volumes of *Les arts visuels au Québec dans les années 1960*, ed. Francine Couture: *La reconnaissance de la modernité* (Montreal: VLB, 1993) and *L'éclatement du modernisme* (Montreal: VLB, 1997).

63 Suzanne and Laurent Lamy, *La renaissance des métiers d'art au Canada français* (Quebec City: Ministère des Affaires culturelles, 1967).

By the early 1960s, the growing number of interesting artists in Montreal made it possible to speak of a "Montreal school."[62] The more prominent among them included the painters Guido Molinari, Charles Gagnon, Rita Letendre, Yves Gaucher, Jacques Hurtubise, Jean McEwen, Claude Tousignant, Denis Juneau, and the sculptors Henry Saxe and Ulysse Comtois. Many of the artists of this generation were associated with the Plasticien movement, and a number of them were also teachers. The École des beaux-arts de Montréal alone hired 15 new teachers between 1962 and 1969, including Yves Trudeau, Ulysse Comtois, Giuseppe Fiore, and Pierre Ayot. Styles and techniques became more varied; etching and lithography began to flourish. The old opposition between art and craft, or between the pure and the applied arts, was called into question. In Montreal, competition arose between the École des beaux-arts "up" on Sherbrooke Street and the École des arts appliqués "down" on Saint-Denis. With Julien Hébert and Michel Robichaud, design acquired the status of art. In addition, a growing body of work by ceramists and weavers emerged as part of an "arts and crafts" revival.[63] During this time, the number of women artists increased, though people were not yet talking about "women's art" or "feminist art." Betty Goodwin's print series of 1969 titled *Vest* sparked controversy and eventually came to be seen as a major landmark in Canadian art.

The artist was no longer someone alone and on the margins. New galleries opened – Agnès Lefort, Denyse Delrue, Galerie Libre – and new studios

Figure 15
Alexander Calder's sculpture *Man* at the symposium on sculpture, Expo 67, March 1967. Photograph: Gilles Lortie. Collection André Lortie

64 The expression "artiste animateur" was used by Francine Couture in "Identités d'artiste," in *Déclics: Art et société*, 50–90.

65 See *Québec Underground*, ed. Yves Robillard (Montreal: Médiart, 1973).

and group exhibition venues were set up, such as Atelier libre de gravure in 1964 (which two years later became La Guilde graphique, headed by Richard Lacroix), Atelier Graff in 1966, and Galerie Média in 1969. Through symposia (in 1964 on Mount Royal, in 1965 at the Musée d'art contemporain, and in subsequent years at Alma and Parc du Champ de Bataille in Quebec City) and through murals in public buildings (including the luminous fibreglass mural by Jean-Paul Mousseau created in 1961 for the head office of Hydro-Québec, and Jordi Bonet's 1969 mural for the Grand Théâtre de Québec), art ended up becoming public art, and artists such as Serge Lemoyne, Armand Vaillancourt, and André Fournelle in their various ways entered the public space, the space of political debate. Every sculpture created by Vaillancourt (for example, in Asbestos and Montreal in 1963, and in Toronto in 1966) sparked controversy.

Formed shortly before the 1967 world's fair, the group Fusion des arts (1965–1969), led by Yves Robillard, gave early expression to the issue of "art and society," and did so through a multidisciplinary perspective and groundbreaking techniques. Expo 67 turned out to be a catalyst for the entire community of artists. It was there, at the Youth pavilion, that Fusion des arts presented a performance/environment titled *Les mécaniques* that drew spectators into a real "happening." This was the era of the artist as *animateur*,[64] the artist who, driven by the ideal of the democratization of art, wishes to get out of the studio and have direct contact with the public. Opération Déclic, a series of public events (exhibitions, discussions, performances) held in 1968 at the Bibliothèque nationale on Saint-Denis, was designed to close the gap between artists and the public and to demystify art. Some artists, like Serge Lemoyne, were determined to create nothing less than a "total art." A "Quebec Underground" emerged: the concepts of "festival, cultural event, and alternative information network" were debated, and attempts were made to establish a new relationship between art, science, and technology and between art and politics.[65] Urban planning became a matter of concern to artists like Melvin Charney, who published *Architecture et urbanisme au Québec* (with Marcel Bélanger) in 1971 and conceived the exhibition *Montreal: Plus or Minus?* for the Montreal Museum of Fine Arts in 1972. The Rioux Report on art education, made public in 1969, went far beyond administrative issues and gave serious thought to its subject: it called for the democratization of art, and for each and every citizen to become a "creative being" – in short, for the revitalization of society through art. A utopian dream?

A Society in Motion

Two undoubted facts remain, and with them two questions that arise. First of all, there were certainly a great many movements, and indeed a lot of "movement." There was social mobility, collective mobilization, the reform movement, and the cultural revolution, all of which came together to set Quebec society "in motion." Social movements were the very epitome of the 1960s: from the labour movement to the nationalist movement, by way of the grassroots movements, not to mention the terrorist movement, everything was moving. And yet, did anything really change in the end? Inequalities only became more pronounced, and

66 Fernand Dumont, "Quelle révolution tranquille?" in *La société québécoise après trente ans de changements*, ed. Fernand Dumont (Quebec City: Institut québécois de recherche sur la culture, 1990).

poverty did not go away. Secondly, it has always seemed that the artists, writers, and intellectuals constituted the driving force – they were the spark, were they not? A connection is often posited between the rise of neo-nationalism and the fact that writers (especially poets) and intellectuals, who constituted a sort of vanguard, were speaking out. It was, to borrow the title of a poetry collection by Roland Giguère, "l'âge de la parole." But was it really so?

Throughout the many analyses that have been made of the 1960s, the importance of the changes that occurred and the crucial role played by the artistic community are two of the more persistent "myths." The Quiet Revolution is subject to more debate now than ever before. "What quiet revolution?" asks Fernand Dumont, who has emphasized the ad hoc nature of many of the institutional changes and has pointed to the numerous failures.[66] Some try to glorify it and defend its gains. Others refer to it when criticizing the "Quebec model" – characterized by state intervention and a pervasive bureaucracy – supposedly imposed since then. To today's younger generation, that era of excitement and turmoil is so closely associated with the baby boomers that it has become synonomous with bourgeoisification.

One has to be careful, then, in talking about the 1960s. Nevertheless, beyond all the theories that have been propagated, a few things are clear: first, not everything having to do with modernization owes its start to the Quiet Revolution, and second, genuine changes of a structural and cultural order are achieved only over the long term, and on a level that is at one and the same time local and (increasingly) global. In brief, the Quiet Revolution was not the "end of history." Or, to put it more plainly, it was not the be all and end all.

Structure
and Society

**Places and
Players**

Perceptions

Expo 67

The Players

A number of factors were responsible for Montreal's metamorphosis during the 1960s. There was a broad consensus on projects involving renovation (for example, between Bleury and de Lorimier), rebuilding (the Central Station area), major road construction (the east-west expressway), and the metro. The projects, which had in some cases been under discussion for several decades, were implemented in the context of a favourable political and economic situation that allowed them to be merged into planning measures in which the various levels of government all played a part. Such cohesion was critical in the case of a major event like Expo 67, which turned out to be the catalyst in the development of Greater Montreal.

This process would not have been possible without the contribution of a number of strong personalities who would be key players in Montreal's destiny. There were certainly social, economic, political, national, and international forces acting on these individuals, but it was through their vision that such forces took form in the city's spatial and temporal reality. At the risk of oversimplification, it may be said that this moment in time allowed two generations to meet. One generation, older, who occupied the decision-making positions, had acquired their expertise through practice and action. The other generation, with more extensive academic training, some of it acquired abroad, were very young when they acceded to the positions of responsibility that gradually emerged as the Quiet Revolution progressed and expanded the potential for action. Thus the long-term commitment of an experienced generation was joined with the theoretical knowledge and enthusiasm of youth. This scenario was found not only in the technostructure, where managers were supported by young graduates who took the helm of newly created technical departments, but also in the private sector, where senior staff were spurred on by co-workers whose broader vision extended even beyond provincial and national boundaries.

Among these personalities, some were true visionaries who saw Montreal as fertile ground for making their dreams reality. One of them was Mayor Jean Drapeau, who envisaged Canada's metropolis as a chance to realize his complex ambitions, with their sometimes paradoxical effects

The Politician: Jean Drapeau

Jean Drapeau (1916–1999) was mayor of Montreal from October 1954 to October 1957, in tandem with businessman Pierre Desmarais, chairman of the Executive Committee, and then again from November 1960 until 1986, initially with Lucien Saulnier and then with Yvon Lamarre. He first came to notice in municipal politics in 1950, leading a public inquiry on behalf of the Committee on Public Morality, together with the crusading lawyer Pax Plante. Drapeau's political ambitions were never in doubt, but rather than positioning himself in a complex landscape where federal and provincial nationalists of varying degrees of social and economic liberalism were going head to head, he preferred the office of mayor of Canada's great metropolis, discovering that it offered him a field of action with international scope: Expo 67, Man and His World, the Floralies, the Olympics, and even a major-league baseball team.

Figure 16
Jean Drapeau, December 1962.
Photograph: Armour Landry.
Centre de Montréal des Archives
nationales du Québec

on French-Canadian society in Quebec (Brian McKenna and Susan Purcell, *Drapeau* [Toronto: Clarke Irwin, 1980]). He was supported by another, more discreet politician, a pragmatic foil to the public figure: the chairman of the Executive Committee, Lucien Saulnier, who gave substance to the mayor's schemes. Individuals like the American real estate developer William Zeckendorf on the one hand and architects and urban planners like Daniel van Ginkel and his wife, Blanche Lemco, on the other typified the period with their uncompromising involvement in their respective areas of action and expertise. The question remains as to who was the real author, or at least the real developer, of the plans for a future city of 5 million inhabitants (see pages 26–29). Was it the director of the City Planning Department, Claude Robillard? Was it the international consultant Hans Blumenfeld? Or was the project the result of a kind of social imperative, such as the one described by the sociologist Maurice Halbwachs in his analysis of the reconstruction of Napoleon III's Paris under the capitalistic pressure of the Second Empire?

The Civil Servant: Lucien Saulnier

The mayor would not have been able to implement his plans without a pragmatic partner like Lucien Saulnier (1916–1989), who had a gift for organization. Saulnier was a businessman when he was first elected in 1954. After serving continuously as chairman of the city's Executive Committee from 1960 to 1970, he left that position to become the first chairman of the Executive Committee of the new Montreal Urban Community, created on 1 January 1970 — a post he held until 1972, when he left municipal politics.

The Technocrat: Claude Robillard

Claude Robillard (1911–1968) belonged to the upper echelons of a municipal civil service whose know-how had been forged in the heat of action. He joined the city's Public Works Department in 1945. He became head of the new Parks Department in 1953 and increased its scope significantly. In 1961, he accepted the directorship of the City Planning Department, which was in a state of total disorganization, and he led it successfully into the age of the metropolis, until his premature departure from the position at the end of 1964.

Figure 17
Lucien Saulnier, March 1959.
Photograph: City of Montreal Photographic Services. Ville de Montréal, Gestion de documents et archives

Figure 18
Claude Robillard. Photograph: City of Montreal Photographic Services. Ville de Montréal, Gestion de documents et archives

The Developer: William Zeckendorf

Taking on a project like Place Ville-Marie in Montreal in 1956 would have been impossible without a vision. The visionary in this case was William Zeckendorf (1905–1976), the head of Webb and Knapp, which had already developed gigantic real estate projects in Denver, Washington, Dallas, and New York; the power of this real estate empire was such that its declaration of bankruptcy in 1965 shook Wall Street. It is often the lot of visionaries to bear the brunt of start-up problems; the Montreal operation wound up in serious financial difficulty, which led to the founding of Trizec, a company that would be very active in the Canadian real estate market in the 1960s and 1970s.

The Architect: André Blouin

A collaborator of Auguste Perret in the rebuilding of the city of Le Havre, and winner of an American Institute of Architects bursary in 1951, André Blouin (born 1920) moved to Montreal in 1952 and opened an office in 1954. With an attitude uncommon among local architects, he did not hesitate to combine professional practice and teaching; in his academic role, he explored the potential of Montreal's urban space by authoring theoretical projects that included plans for a "Place de la Confédération" south of Place des Arts (see page 178). The variety of areas to which Blouin contributed – architecture, urban planning, architectural criticism, theoretical studies – made him atypical among his Quebec colleagues.

Figure 19
William Zeckendorf, c. 1959.
Archives of Pei, Cobb, Freed, and
Partners, Architects

Figure 20
André Blouin, c. 1955. Canadian
Centre for Architecture,
Montréal, Fonds André Blouin

The Urban Planners: Van Ginkel Associates

Daniel van Ginkel (born 1920) and Blanche Lemco van Ginkel (born 1923) represented Montreal's own link with the major forums of modern architecture and urban planning. Dutch by origin, and a member of CIAM and later of Team X, Daniel van Ginkel extended his activities well beyond Montreal; in New York, for example, he worked on the plan for movement in midtown Manhattan, and also became an international expert on airport planning. His wife, Blanche Lemco, was a graduate of McGill (1947) and Harvard (1950). Hired by Le Corbusier in 1948, she worked on the "Unité d'habitation" in Marseilles. Like her husband, she devoted part of her career to teaching (at the University of Pennsylvania, the University of Montreal, McGill University, and the University of Toronto, among other places) and to supporting professional institutions and organizations (founder of GIA, member of the Philadelphia CIAM group, 1952–1957).

The Engineers: Lalonde and Valois

Complementing one another in temperament and skills, the engineers Jean-Paul Lalonde and Roméo Valois initially excelled in the field of structural analysis, then in public works. When their usual work ground to a halt during World War II, they turned to road-building. In the early 1960s, the two founders of the firm gradually handed their affairs over to Valois's son, Jean-Pierre Valois, and son-in-law, Bernard Lamarre; the versatility of the organization that had been formed during those difficult years enabled the heirs to conquer the international market and take their place among the foremost purveyors of technical skills to clients of the World Bank.

Figure 21
Daniel van Ginkel and Blanche Lemco van Ginkel, 1962. Collection Blanche Lemco van Ginkel

Figure 22
Jean-Paul Lalonde and Roméo Valois with their wives. From Lavalin Inc.'s 25th anniversary publication, 1986. Collection Bernard Lamarre

**Structure
and Society**

Places and
Players

Perceptions

Expo 67

A Collective Vision (The Quebec Pavilion Competition)

Figure 23
**Pavilion of Quebec, Expo 67.
Papineau, Gérin-Lajoie, Le
Blanc, architects; Luc Durand,
associate architect.** Photograph: Deidi von Schaewen.
Collection Deidi von Schaewen

*Quebec expresses itself. In the context of a world's fair, like a
country in its own right, Quebec vigorously makes its presence felt ... And it does so in a manner that is consciously
open and assertive, clear and light, independent and original.*

– Papineau, Gérin-Lajoie, Le Blanc, and Luc Durand, architects, draft
   (in French) for the presentation of their project for the Quebec
   pavilion, Archives nationales du Québec, P193: S1/46

In the 1960s, Quebec opened up to the world and stepped
onto the international stage, with Montreal leading the
way. Its self-image, evidently shared by the majority of
Quebecers, was reflected in both the form and content of
the Quebec pavilion at Expo 67.

According to Sibyl Moholy-Nagy ("Expo 67, Montréal,"
L'Architecture d'aujourd'hui, no. 133 [September 1967]:
ix–xi), Quebec's was one of three sophisticated Canadian
pavilions, each of which showed, in its own way, that form
and structure can complement and complete one another
through new, truly progressive means. Without reaching
the level of enthusiasm of the *New York Times* architecture
critic who called it "the Barcelona pavilion of Expo 67,"
Peter Blake affirmed that "the mirror-faced, 1.5-million-cu.-
ft. showcase for the Province of Quebec is, by all odds, the
most suave pavilion constructed at Montreal." He snidely

noted that "the one probably unintentional touch of
humor will be found *out*side the pavilion: its mirror surfaces
so distort the preposterous French Pavilion next door as
to make that absurdity look almost intriguing" ("Quebec's
Shimmering Vitrine," *The Architectural Forum* 126, no. 5
[June 1967]: 31, 34).

The strong impression made by the pavilion was due
to both the clearly modernistic signature of its façade
and its bold technical design: the concrete floors and
Vierendeel steel façade were supported by four hollow
steel towers that accommodated elevator shafts and
emergency stairs. Also noteworthy was the design integrity of the building: it was devoted entirely to the content
it housed. The architects Papineau, Gérin-Lajoie, Le Blanc,
and Durand were responsible for the interior as well as
for the envelope, and the two were therefore seamlessly
integrated throughout the process. The decision to grant
one firm sole responsibility for the entire building made
the Quebec pavilion significantly different from most of
the other pavilions, which were built as temporary, multifunctional shells. In light of this notable feature and the
monumental quality of the pavilion, Peter Blake expressed
the hope that it would not be demolished after the closing
of Expo 67. In fact, the major constraint imposed on participants in the competition launched by the Quebec government was that the building would be able to remain
in use afterwards as a cultural complex, with a museum, a
restaurant, theatres, and a conservatory.

Apart from a few general remarks from the premier
of the province, Jean Lesage, calling the pavilion a unique
opportunity for Quebec to assert its economic and cultural
vitality and show itself in an ennobling and yet accurate
light, the competition program said nothing about the
message the pavilion was to convey. It was up to the architects to express Quebec's image in a register that was
unquestionably monumental and contemporary, and to
ensure that the materials and treatment of the façade
would serve as the architectural prologue and epilogue to
an imposing display representing the power of a surging
metropolis and the drive of a people advancing together
toward the year 2000.

Figure 24
Pavilion of Quebec by day, photograph of perspective, c. 1965. Papineau, Gérin-Lajoie, Le Blanc, architects; Luc Durand, associate architect. Library and Archives Canada, Ottawa, 1970-019

Figure 25
Pavilion of Quebec by night, photograph of perspective, c. 1965. Papineau, Gérin-Lajoie, Le Blanc, architects; Luc Durand, associate architect. Library and Archives Canada, Ottawa, 1970-019

Figure 26
Pavilion of Quebec, photograph of schematic plans of four levels. Papineau, Gérin-Lajoie, Le Blanc, architects; Luc Durand, associate architect.
Centre de Montréal des Archives nationales du Québec

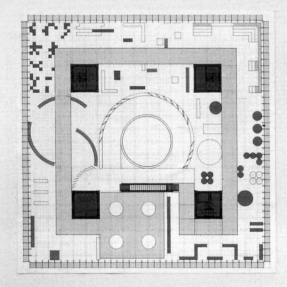

plan du deuxième étage

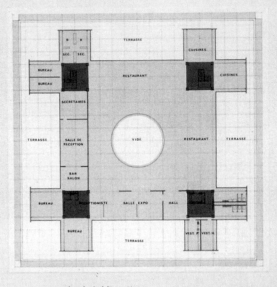

plan du troisième étage

plan du premier étage

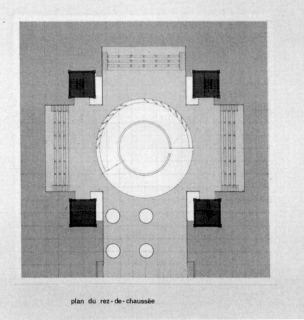

plan du rez-de-chaussée

The mirrored glass walls were illuminated at night, revealing the seemingly weightless exhibits inside, which visitors to the pavilion could enjoy viewing all along the suspended ramp that ran from the top level to the bottom. Visitors were able to get a sense of the vastness and harshness of a territory ("Challenge") that was tamed by force of will, labour, and inventiveness ("Struggle"), out of which a people emerged ready to face the challenge of the approaching millennium ("Drive"). The themes were expressed through audiovisual media (soundtracks, films, still photographs, transparencies) and through metaphoric sculptures based on coloured cubes, some of them static and others in motion. In this heroic account, the metropolis – Montreal – constituted the interval between the ordeal of the struggle and the emancipation of a French-speaking community on North American soil, ready to brave the future.

The future of modern-day Quebec was resolutely industrial and urban. That was the message conveyed by the steel and glass façade subtly sloping inward toward the top, even though, paradoxically, the changing metropolis of Montreal was the product of international capital, the sources of which were increasingly unclear. Quebecers seemed to recognize themselves in this prism of international accents and, like the jury, adopted it unanimously (*The Gazette*, 7 November 1964, section 4).

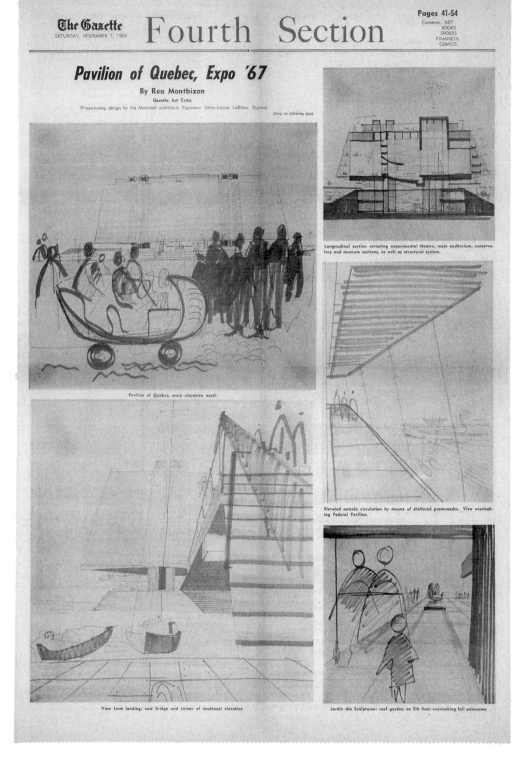

Figure 27
The Gazette (Montreal),
7 November 1964. Canadian
Centre for Architecture,
Montréal, Fonds Ernest Cormier

Figure 28
Pavilion of Quebec under construction, 20 May 1966. Papineau, Gérin-Lajoie, Le Blanc, architects; Luc Durand, associate architect. Photograph: Gabor Szilasi. Centre de Montréal des Archives nationales du Québec

Figure 29
Pavilion of Quebec, interior view. Papineau, Gérin-Lajoie, Le Blanc, architects; Luc Durand, associate architect. Photograph: Deidi von Schaewen. Collection Deidi von Schaewen

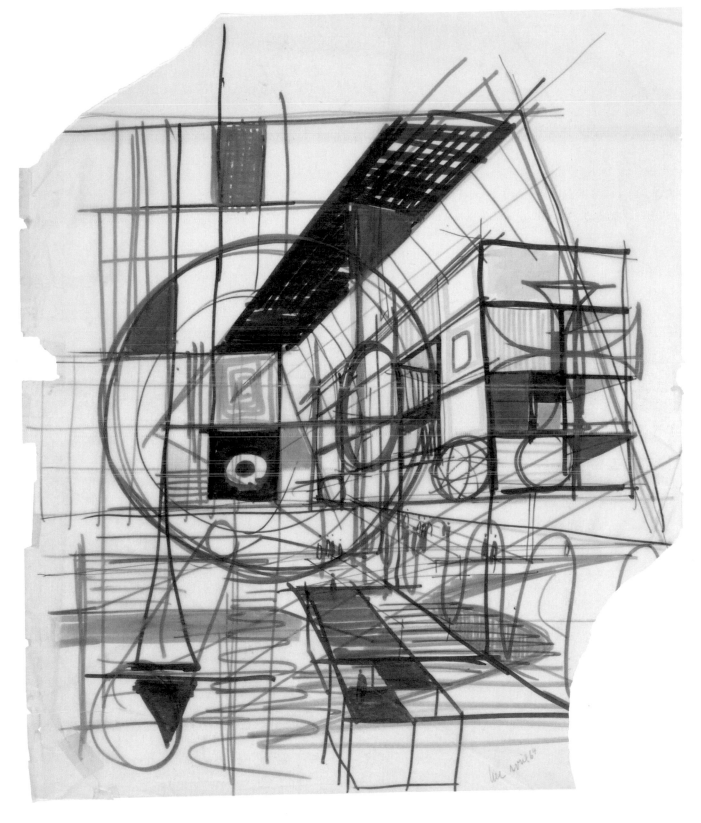

Figure 30
Pavilion of Quebec, perspective sketch of interior, April 1964. Papineau, Gérin-Lajoie, Le Blanc, architects; Luc Durand, associate architect. Fibre-tip pen, ink, and graphite on tracing paper, 40 x 34 cm. Canadian Centre for Architecture, Montréal, Fonds Luc Durand

Structure
and Society

Places and
Players

Perceptions

Expo 67

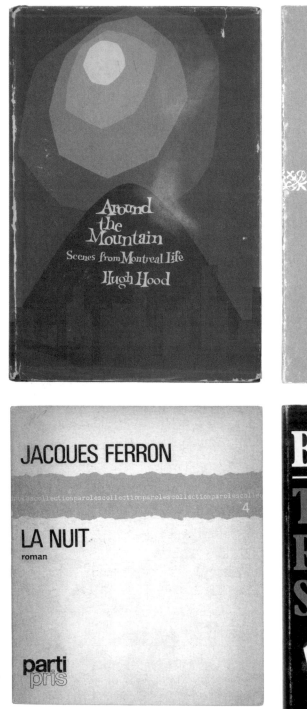

Quebec literature set in Montreal in the 1960s portrays the slow appropriation by French Canadians of an urban space whose horizons gradually broaden to the outermost edges of the metropolitan area. Novels such as Gérard Bessette's *La bagarre*, set within the limits of the streetcar lines, and Jacques Godbout's *Salut Galarneau!*, criss-crossed by highways, depict not only geographic and economic conquest, but also cultural and social emancipation: the people of Quebec become free as they move beyond the boundaries to which they had often been confined by their circumstances.

English-speaking authors of the period seemed readier to explore this complex space, judging at least from the works of the more prolific among them, such as Mordecai Richler and Hugh Hood. In *Around the Mountain: Scenes from Montreal Life*, Hood sets out not only to discover the French-speaking working-class neighbourhoods in the east end, but to investigate the farthest reaches of the city and its suburbs, including the area around Dorval Airport and the Trans-Canada Highway construction site, places where the big city was whittling away at the island. Hood's scenes of Montreal are quite different from those offered by certain French-language writers. In *La nuit*,

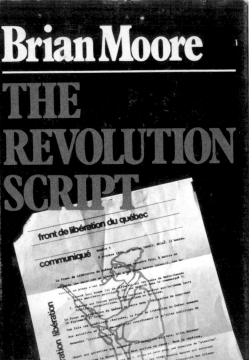

Figure 31
Hugh Hood, *Around the Mountain: Scenes from Montreal Life* (1967). Collection André Lortie

Figure 32
Pierre Gravel, *À perte de temps* (1969). Collection André Lortie

Figure 33
Jacques Ferron, *La Nuit* (1965). Collection André Lortie

Figure 34
Brian Moore, *The Revolution Script* (1971). Collection André Lortie

It was a small, wooden building, covered with sooty, peeling paint that gave the impression of an alligator's skin. The pinewood balcony was rotten and the creaking stairs leaned a good fifteen degrees. Pieces of cardboard replaced the glass panes on the front door ... He found himself in a corridor with yellowish walls, dimly lit by a small bulb which hung from the ceiling. At the far end, there was a stairway leading to the second floor. The first room on the right was empty ... They walked toward the back into the kitchen. There the door was blocked by a cast-iron stove. Everything seemed to indicate that this was the only occupied room in the house.

– Gérard Bessette, *La bagarre* (Montreal: Cercle du livre de France, 1958), quoted from the English translation, *The Brawl* (Montreal: Harvest House, 1976), 204

Marc's taxi turned off the boulevard now, going down towards the waterfront, moving through the residential slum streets of French Montreal, old streets of uneven little redbrick houses with small windows, double-paned to keep out the terrible winter winds ... streets in which many and multifarious families are crammed into airless, pokey Dickensian warrens which remain unchanged amid the fine false fronts of the Expo 67 years ... It is a street of People's Credit Jewellers, and Bagues de Mariage, et Fiançailles; it is Caisse Populaire banks on the corner, and the one building which has size, stature, and some sense of graystone grandeur is, you can be certain, called The Church of the Sacre Coeur, or Visitation, or St. Jean Baptiste.

– Brian Moore, *The Revolution Script* (Toronto: McClelland and Stewart, 1971), 30–31

Figure 35
House in the "Molasses" district, 1963. Photograph: Michel Saint-Jean. Library and Archives Canada, Ottawa, PA-147526

Figure 36
Church steeple and Saint-Urbain Street, 11 June 1964. Photograph: Jeremy Taylor. Collection Jeremy Taylor

Jacques Ferron shows a city split between the centre (on the island) and the suburbs (on the South Shore), a rift that corresponds to the duality of his main character. In *À perte de temps*, Pierre Gravel, through his character Robert D., describes the city as a "big, huge, monstrous thing that had never been given a name."

The terrorist activities of the 1960s very likely fed into the image of the city that Gravel's novel projects. This aspect of the period is vividly conveyed as well by Brian Moore in *The Revolution Script*, which ventures into the French-speaking working-class neighbourhoods of that terra incognita, the east end. Both authors bear witness to the obliteration of the working-class city, which technical experts had cast an assessing eye on and declared obsolete, dooming it to destruction and laying the ground for its replacement by a modern city that could on occasion prove fascinating, such as the one that rises up, at a bend in the road, in Gilles Carle's 1965 film *La vie heureuse de Léopold Z.*

But the attractiveness of the new scale, standing out sharply against the old scale of the industrial city born of history, was outweighed by the drastic nature of the destruction. That certainly is what caught the attention of many photographers, including Brian Merrett, David Miller, and Jeremy Taylor. Only the tourist guides, who became increasingly numerous as the world's fair approached, managed to find soothing rhetoric to mask the disparities, praising the city's large tertiary sector, its dual role as an industrial centre and port, its historic monuments, and what would soon be called its "biculturalism."

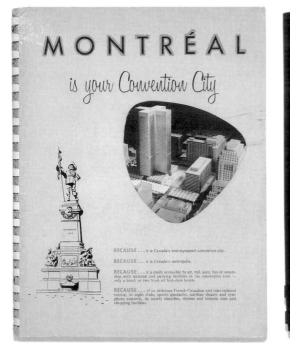

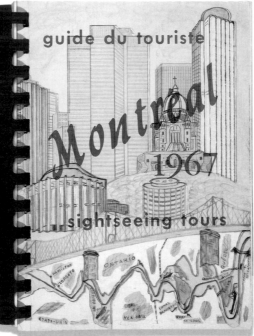

Figure 37
Montreal Tourist and Convention Bureau, *Montréal Is Your Convention City* **(c. 1962).** Canadian Centre for Architecture, Montréal

Figure 38
Montréal 1967: Sightseeing Tours **(c. 1967).** Canadian Centre for Architecture, Montréal

Figure 39
Montée Saint-Léonard (Anjou) Interchange ramps, 15 August 1965. Photograph: Armour Landry. Centre de Montréal des Archives nationales du Québec

The most arresting of these desert monuments is the Montée de Saint-Léonard *interchange on the east-island section of the Trans-Canada highway ... The sides of the ramps, and the retaining walls, have running patterns like those on the borders of carpets, pleasant but repetitive. But the monolithic ramp-supports have distinct and individual semi-abstract, semi-representational figures on them, many of great beauty, others purely grotesque.*

None of the ramps, none of the criss-crossing roadways, one on top of another, go anywhere, and their roadbeds are filled with great lumps of damp mud. The connecting roads haven't been built, so that this piece of architectural triumph is at the moment an exercise in design without function, of the most alarming kind. If you look at it long enough, it starts to scare you ...

– Hugh Hood, *Around the Mountain: Scenes from Montreal Life* (Toronto: Peter Martin Associates, 1967), 132–133

Before the first street corner, I looked back. I could no longer distinguish my house from the row of other castles, which were all alike except for the colours and materials of the façades – a difference which, at that hour, was hardly striking. But I did not have to get closer: all that humbly pretentious, proudly shabby architecture remained blind and sullen. Had my departure been noticed, one of those houses, probably the eleventh or twelfth, if not the ninth or thirteenth, would have turned on a light: my own would have become a beacon in the night ...

– Jacques Ferron, *La nuit* (Montreal: Parti pris, 1965), 31

Figure 40
Development of the suburbs, single-family houses, 11 July 1951. Centre de Montréal des Archives nationales du Québec

Figure 41
City Planning Department,
City of Montreal, *Métropole:
Les Cahiers d'urbanisme*, no. 1
(January 1963). Canadian Centre
for Architecture, Montréal

Figure 42
Robert Robert, City Planning
Department, City of Montreal,
*La vague d'expansion métro-
politaine*, Bulletin technique
no. 1 (January 1964). Cana-
dian Centre for Architecture,
Montréal

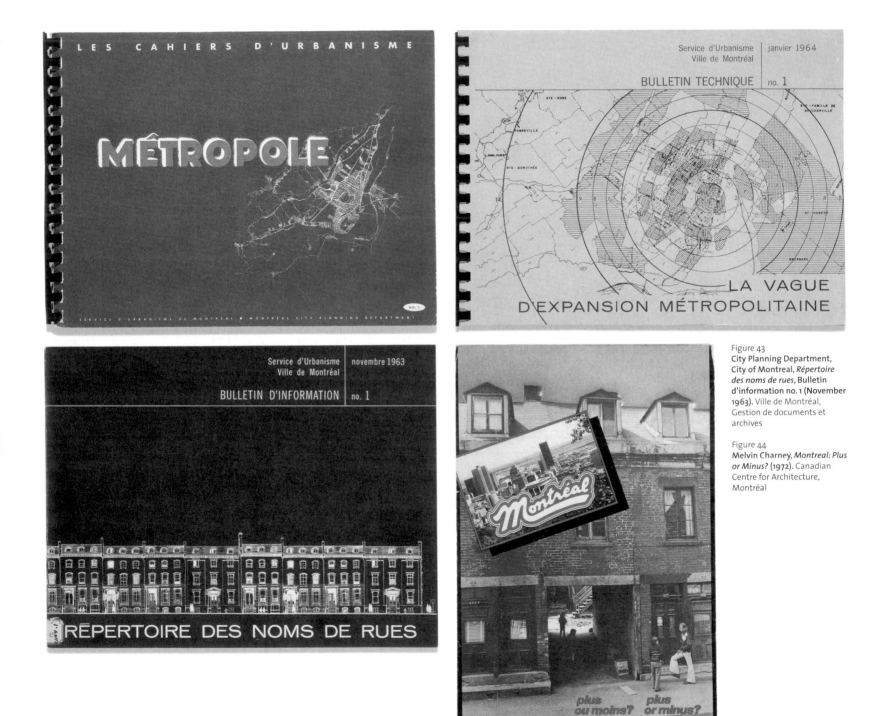

Figure 43
City Planning Department,
City of Montreal, *Répertoire
des noms de rues*, Bulletin
d'information no. 1 (November
1963). Ville de Montréal,
Gestion de documents et
archives

Figure 44
Melvin Charney, *Montreal: Plus
or Minus?* (1972). Canadian
Centre for Architecture,
Montréal

Concrete, glass, and steel girders. Twenty, thirty, fifty stories high. To tell the truth, the city didn't exist. In its place, a big, huge, monstrous thing that had never been given a name sprawled around a mountain and ended by dwindling into suburbs: east, west, north, a few scattered slums ... In the centre, glass and girders.

– Pierre Gravel, *À perte de temps* (Toronto: Anansi; Montreal: Parti pris, 1969), 26

Meanwhile, in the heart of uptown Montreal, old buildings, sometimes streets of them, came tumbling down as the wreckers went to work. Corner lots were piled high with carved wooden doors, marble mantels, iron chandeliers and window railings, and ancient bathtubs, once the pride of Montreal's gentry. Victorian mansions and block-long Edwardian terraces became piles of rubble until stark, oblong skyscrapers rose in their places.

– Leonard L. Knott, in *Montreal: The Golden Years* (Toronto: McClelland and Stewart, 1965)

Figure 47
Poster for the film *La vie heureuse de Léopold Z*, 1965.
Cinématheque québécoise

Figure 48
Milton-Park project: Looking north on Hutchison Street between Milton Street and Prince Arthur Street, 14 July 1971. Photograph: David Miller. Canadian Centre for Architecture, Montréal

Age of buildings	Metropolitan area		Metropolitan area (excluding Montreal)		Montreal	
	Number	%	Number	%	Number	%
under 19 years	278,639	50.7	147,178	67.0	131,461	39.8
19 to 44 years	131,009	23.8	44,300	20.2	86,709	26.3
over 44 years	140,083	25.5	28,230	12.8	111,853	33.9
Total	549,731	100.0	219,708	100.0	330,023	100.0

It is generally agreed that the fundamental causes giving rise to the need for urban renewal are two-fold: obsolescence, which means there is something that no longer serves its intended purpose, or no longer meets the requirements of a modern society ... [and] physical decay, which refers solely to the quality of the buildings.

The useful life of an ordinary residential building, with a wooden frame and outside walls clad in brick or stone, is a maximum of 55 years (Manuel d'estimation des biens fonds, 3rd ed. [Montreal: City of Montreal, 1954]). The oldest group – over 44 years –

includes the majority of the buildings to be redeveloped, since they have reached or will soon reach the end of their useful life (55 years).

– J.J. Delvaux and Pierre Lett, City Planning Department, "Rénovation urbaine à Montréal," *Métropole: Les Cahiers d'urbanisme*, no. 3 (October 1965): 44, 47 48.

Dorval could not believe that such destruction was occurring in his own neighbourhood, where he had lived ever since he had decided that he had to live somewhere. They were demolishing the houses of the only people he knew in the whole world and the bulldozer was just waiting to knock down his house too. They would crumble it into dust, into fragments of brick where he had lived for more than twenty years. And yet it all seemed to him like an echo of something that was happening far

away or the dream of a man who is too much alone ... It stinks. The smell of misery is coming out of all the holes those machines are making in the walls and roofs. Rich peoples' houses must stink when they're demolished too. But they never demolish the goddam capitalists' houses.

– Roch Carrier, *Le deux-millième étage* (Montreal: Éditions du Jour, 1973), quoted from the English translation, *They Won't Demolish Me!* (Toronto: Anansi, 1973), 32–33

Figure 49
Milton-Park project: Demolition of Hutchison Street and Park Avenue below Prince Arthur Street, 30 October 1972. Photograph: David Miller. Canadian Centre for Architecture, Montréal

Structure
and Society

Places and
Players

Perceptions

Expo 67

The Impact of Multimedia

Some architecture critics, like Reyner Banham ("L'uomo all'Expo," *Casabella*, no. 320 [November 1967]: 48–50) and Sibyl Moholy-Nagy ("Expo 67, Montréal," *L'Architecture d'aujourd'hui*, no. 133 [September 1967]: ix–xi), had a difficult time deciding what the major legacy of Expo 67 would be. The truth is that the architectural display was disappointing for anyone who might have looked forward to seeing an avant-garde pavilion of the kind designed by Mies van der Rohe for the Barcelona fair in 1929 or by Le Corbusier for the Brussels fair in 1958.

The innovation at Expo 67 lay elsewhere. It was to be found in the general organization of the fair, especially its transit system, and in the multimedia spectacles that drew huge numbers of visitors. The critics were alternately frustrated and fascinated by the way in which the architectural spaces had been eclipsed by the programming in them, and by how sound and image had been deployed in the creation of a new kind of "total environment." The *New York Times* film critic Bosley Crowther noted in reference to Labyrinth, a pavilion designed entirely around the audiovisual presentation it hosted, that the nature of the architectural environment was becoming more and more of a factor in the combination of elements that made up this unfamiliar medium. The architecture critic Jeremy Baker observed that a conventional space, however well designed, could not compete with the thrilling effects of its audiovisual program ("Expo and the Future City," *The Architectural Review*, no. 846 [August 1967]: 154). The focus on content was the result of an agreement between the National Film Board (NFB) and the Canadian Corporation for the 1967 World Exhibition guaranteeing that the architectural design of the pavilions would be subordinated to

the technical requirements of the audiovisual productions being managed by the NFB (Gerald G. Graham, *Canadian Film Technology, 1896–1986* [Toronto: Associated University Presses, 1989], 215).

The Czechoslovak, Italian, and British pavilions, as well as the Kaleidoscope pavilion, presented shows ranging from sophisticated slide presentations to multi-projector screenings. Many of these shows were genuinely artistic, and because of how intensely they involved the spectator they were more informative and more powerful than any other mode of presentation. The pavilion that drew the most enthusiastic response was Labyrinth. Here, as in many of the other pavilions, the simultaneous display of still images and moving images required the development of extremely complex equipment for filming and screening, and for the synchronization of images to sound and images to other images. The experiments in this field carried out by the NFB for Expo 67 led to the development of the IMAX process, used for the first time by Fuji in its pavilion at Expo 70 in Osaka, Japan.

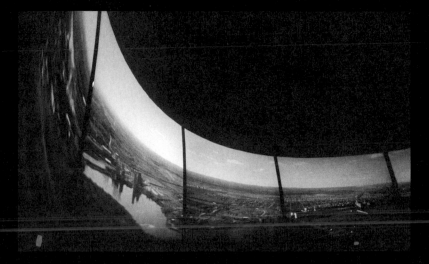

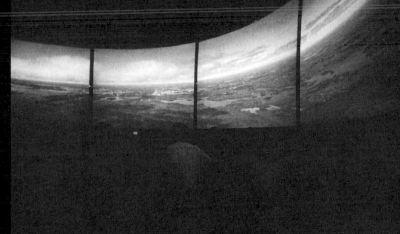

Figure 50
Diapolyecran presentation, consisting of 15,000 slides projected onto 112 sliding cubes, pavilion of Czechoslovakia, Expo 67. Photograph: Geoff Winningham. Collection Gerald O'Grady

Figure 51
Canada 67, **film produced in Circle-Vision 360° by Walt Disney, pavilion of the Telephone Association of Canada, Expo 67.** Photograph: Geoff Winningham. Collection Gerald O'Grady

Figure 54
Polyvision presentation, pavilion of Czechoslovakia, Expo 67. Photograph: Geoff Winningham. Collection Gerald O'Grady

Figure 55
Multi-screen film presentation, Labyrinth pavilion, Expo 67. Photograph: Geoff Winningham. Collection Gerald O'Grady

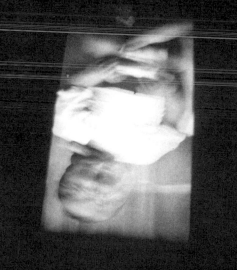

Figure 54
Polyvision presentation, pavilion of Czechoslovakia, Expo 67. Photograph: Geoff Winningham. Collection Gerald O'Grady

Figure 55
Multi-screen film presentation, Labyrinth pavilion, Expo 67. Photograph: Geoff Winningham. Collection Gerald O'Grady

Montreal 1960: The Singularities of a Metropolitan Archetype

André Lortie

Flying into Montreal nineteen years later, in the summer of 1967, our very golden Expo summer, coming from dowdy London, via decaying New York, I was instantly struck by the city's affluence . . . I rode into the city on multi-decked highways, which swooped here, soared there, unwinding into a pot of prosperity, a downtown of high rise apartments and hotels, the latter seemingly so new they could have been uncrated the night before. Place Ville Marie. The metro. Expo. Île Notre Dame. Habitat. Place des Arts. This cornucopia certainly wasn't the city I had grown up in and quit.[1]

The Decade of Unlimited Possibility

The decade to which this publication is devoted was a time of upheaval. This was true not only of Montreal, but of cities in general, and of Western society as a whole, whose essential nature was, so to speak, given spatial expression in them.[2] In the wake of the Depression, followed by World War II, and then the circumstances of an arduous rebuilding process for some nations and the difficult conversion of a wartime economy back to a peacetime economy for others, the 1960s turned out to be a time of endless challenges and unlimited potential. The crises in housing, sanitation, traffic, and urban renovation, all the projects discussed, planned, and even scheduled between the two world wars, but never implemented because the means were lacking, suddenly seemed within reach and amenable to action. In most Western countries, ambitions – often of long standing – were overtaken by new dynamics that transcended or ultimately reshaped them, broadening their scope and giving them a new rationale. Considering the amount of time required after 1945 to develop the major projects characteristic of the period, it seems natural that the decade in which changes seemed most abundant, in North America as in Europe, was the 1960s.

    Voluntarist planning policies such as urban planning and especially Keynesian state planning were among the new dynamics that fostered radical changes in thought and action in relation to cities, especially large cities. Another force probably driving these changes was the internationalization of the economy, which increased both the number of players and their strength. Canada was not immune to this phenomenon. It is enough to look at the large tertiary-sector

1 Mordecai Richler, *The Street* (Toronto: McClelland and Stewart, 1969), 5.
2 Guy Burgel, *La ville aujourd'hui* (Paris: Hachette, 1993); Marcel Roncayolo, *La ville et ses territoires* (Paris: Gallimard, 1990).

3 Paul-André Linteau, *Histoire de Montréal depuis la Confédération* (Montreal: Boréal, 1992), 429ff.

developments, from Toronto's Eaton Centre to Vancouver's Bentall Centre, and the great cultural achievements of the period such as Place des Arts in Montreal and the Confederation Centre of the Arts in Charlottetown, or at the underpinnings of road, port, and airport infrastructure, to be convinced that a change of scale had occurred that was not without its effect on the urban space and on the perceptions of those who dwelled in it.

In Canada, as in North America generally, the 1950s and 1960s were years of significant growth, despite the ups and downs of the international economic situation. Carried along by this favourable dynamic, successive federal governments decided to reinforce the nationalist sentiment revived by World War II and launched programs to strengthen Canadian unity. Planning was to be the new panacea. Paradoxically, it contributed to the blinding of Montrealers to the fate of their city: they were less sensitive to current economic conditions than to the long term, and the curve of future projections seemed to promise them irresistible growth, even as the power of Toronto, and also of Calgary and Vancouver, had already begun to increase. Montreal had been the uncontested metropolis of Canada in the nineteenth century, and its apogee continued into the first half of the twentieth. The opening of the Saint Lawrence Seaway in 1959, which allowed large ships to bypass the Lachine Rapids, and the acceleration of trade in the direction of the Pacific, contributed to the inexorable decline of Montreal. The city lost its status as a major industrial centre, which had been linked to its role as the hub of continental commerce and communication and as the centre of Canadian investment activity. From that point on, Montreal essentially entered a period of transformation from an industrial city into a city dependent on the tertiary sector, losing its status as the metropolis of the entire country and becoming instead the metropolis of its region.[3]

Planning, as it applies to cities, means regulating market forces in order to control anarchic development at the periphery as well as the harmful effects of real estate and land speculation in the centre. In an earlier era, controlling urban organization meant chasing after urban development and trying to correct its mistakes by intervening in the public domain through costly expropriations or, in Montreal, through the approval procedure. It is easy to understand that such urban-planning-by-regularization gave way to a process of forecasting and anticipation, this being the means by which political power could force private real estate developers to respect rules that could serve as guidelines for land use and architectural and urban forms. Because saving public money is always an issue, urban planning also means giving priority to the public interest (namely, a functional and healthy city) over the private interest (the absolutely unconstrained right to buy and sell property).

During World War II, Montreal acquired the tools to implement such a policy. The first significant decision came in 1941, and consisted in the creation of a City Planning Department, a prerequisite for the switch from corrective planning, which was suitable for public works, to a system of urban planning based on prediction. The department grew rapidly during the 1950s and 1960s, like the city it served, which seemed to have embarked on the conquest of its island site,

Figure 56
"Urbanized Land, Metropolitan Area." City Planning Department, City of Montreal, *Urbanisation: Étude de l'expansion urbaine de la région de Montréal*, Bulletin technique no. 5 (November 1966), map 2. Canadian Centre for Architecture, Montréal

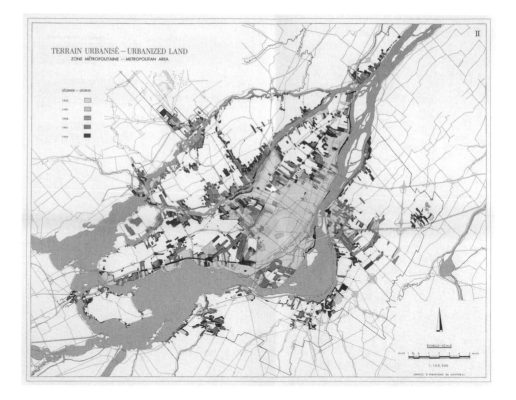

4 The island's population grew from 1.32 million in 1951 to 1.75 million in 1986. See Linteau, *Histoire de Montréal*.

5 City Planning Department, *Urbanisation de Montréal, plan directeur, rapport préliminaire* (Montreal: City of Montreal, 1944).

6 "Horizon 2000, Montréal," *Architecture, bâtiment, construction* 23 (April 1968): 32–38.

7 Pierre-Yves Denis, "Conditions géographiques et postulats démographiques d'une rénovation urbaine à Montréal," *Revue de géographie de Montréal* 21 (1967): 153.

8 Jean Drapeau was mayor from October 1954 to October 1957, with the businessman Pierre Desmarais serving as chairman of the Executive Committee, and then from November 1960 until 1986, first with Lucien Saulnier and then with Yvon Lamarre.

with its urbanized area growing much faster than its population (fig. 56).[4] Study of an overall plan was begun during the war, and an initial version was published in 1944.[5] This first effort posed no opposition to urban expansion, which demographers foresaw as a powerful trend that promised an urban area with 7 million inhabitants by the end of the twentieth century.[6]

And that is undoubtedly one of the most fascinating items of data in our study of the 1960s in Montreal, since it determined all the studies, projects, and decisions of the decade – a period in which major achievements in public infrastructure and facilities went from idea to inception to completion.

We have chosen to base our approach to the decade on these aggregate data. We examine the intersection of the long span of time during which local plans for land use were being elaborated by Montreal experts and/or civil society with the specific political and economic situation at the time, including national planning and internationalization of capital. Using this approach, we can observe Montreal in various ways. On a local scale, the area was the site of an astonishing urban plan. The forecast of 4.8 million inhabitants by 1981[7] (the area had a population of 2.11 million in 1961 and would actually number 3.3 million in 2000) not only led to thinking big, but gave a specific, clearly designed form to the spatial organization. It also represented a major political challenge that was taken up by Mayor Jean Drapeau, whose longevity in power extended far beyond the decade.[8] And it provided a playing field with large stakes to be won in real estate investment – a factor that would exert its own influence, both political and technical.

In addition, Montreal provides an interesting picture of national land use policies (fig. 57) as they relate to major infrastructural elements: the road system, of course, but also sea and river routes (the Saint Lawrence Seaway) and airports (Dorval and later also Mirabel). National policies even extended to housing, in the centre as well as on the periphery of cities (through the Central Mortgage and Housing Corporation, or CMHC), and to industry (the post-war reconversion) and culture (the imminent celebration of the centennial of Confederation). Montreal is a focal point for observing the local effects of these federal policies, whether they were accepted as is or adapted. Montreal can also be compared with other Canadian cities and their specific responses to the same forces, which in a sense ultimately determined their transformation too.

Finally, Montreal invites comparison on an international scale, given the universality of the situation in which Western countries found themselves at that time. Montreal's particular dynamic acts as a prism to diffract this universality, breaking it down into its components and revealing the spectrum of forces at work, here as in other cities, including a technical project, a political plan, a specific national and international conjuncture, and committed participants. Local, national, international: these are the three levels at which the findings of this study are significant, since Montreal seems archetypical of the dynamics at work after World War II in all major cities of the West.

But the interest of this research does not reside in some merely abstract description of these major transformative forces, in the manner of an economic, sociological, or geographic survey, but rather in the way it looks locally for the tangible effects of these forces, on a human scale and in real space. Such is the intent of this essay, which examines the conditions under which the urban plan emerged (section 2) by observing its consequences on a large scale (section 3) and

Figure 57
Turcot Interchange, 12 November 1967. Photograph: Jeremy Taylor. Collection Jeremy Taylor

9 Craig Brown, ed., *The Illustrated History of Canada* (Toronto: Lester and Orpen Dennys, 1987).

10 These are the four major categories defined by the Congrès internationaux d'architecture moderne (CIAM) and set forth in the Charter of Athens, and they correspond in general to the actual divisions in a technocratic society.

11 T.M. McGrath, *History of Canadian Airports* (Toronto: Lugus, 1992).

12 Kates, Peat, Marwick, and Company, "Notes on Location Study, Montreal International Airport, February 1968," Canadian Centre for Architecture, Montréal, Fonds van Ginkel, 27-A34-37.

13 André Lortie, "Paris-CDG, l'aeroporto e la città," *Casabella*, no. 604 (September 1993): 22–31.

14 Many notable films about this major project were produced in the 1950s and 1960s by the National Film Board.

Figure 58
Main passenger terminal, Dorval Airport, 1965. Archibald, Illsley, and Templeton, architects; Larose and Larose, associate architects. Photograph: Armour Landry. Centre de Montréal des Archives nationales du Québec

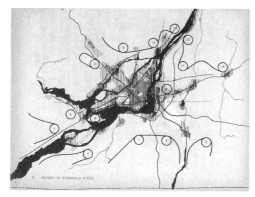

Figure 59
"Zones of Possible Sites." Kates, Peat, Marwick, and Company, *Notes on Location Study, Montreal International Airport* (February 1968). Canadian Centre for Architecture, Montréal, Fonds van Ginkel

at its centre (section 4), and considers Montrealers' receptiveness to the transformation of their city (section 5). But the first step is to describe more fully the national context surrounding Montreal's development.

Centralized Thinking and Action

A basic fact about the transformation of Montreal (and of urban Canada in general) in the 1960s is that it was driven, at least to some degree, by centralized thinking that reflected a desire to reduce regional imbalances and disparities,[9] based on the premise that all regions of the country should be on an equal footing in terms of meeting the requirements of modern life – mobility, work, housing, and recreation.[10]

Mobility

The years following World War II saw the emergence of a new equation for continental and international transportation and travel, in which the ships and trains that had made Montreal's fortune in the system of trade linking the urban centres of northeastern North America, the hinterland, and Europe were gradually supplanted by two other modes: air and road transportation. Even before the rapid rise of commercial air transportation, the standardization and construction of airports seemed an effective way to alleviate regional disparities. Moreover, Canada's vast territory necessitated a rational deployment of airports, or else the entire system might prove impracticable. These facilities were required to meet international air transport standards; the government monitored compliance with these standards through the Canadian Department of Transport.[11]

Standardization of Dorval Airport was the first instance of Montreal's adaptation to these requirements. With its wide glass façade and its two-level vehicle access (for arrivals and for departures), the new airport compared favourably with others inaugurated in that era next to major European and North American cities (fig. 58). Barely had the airport opened in 1960 when it was necessary to consider doubling its capacity in order to keep the facilities at a level appropriate to the metropolis of 5 million inhabitants anticipated by the technical departments. Kates, Peat, Marwick, and Company were mandated to conduct a study in 1967,[12] resulting in the identification of various sites commensurate with the future megalopolis. The final selection, the Mirabel area (which we will not discuss, given the complexity of that political and financial imbroglio), can be understood only in relation to the growth forecasts (fig. 59). The choice is symmetrical with that made at the same time for Paris's urban area: in 1965, a decision was taken to increase the capacity of Orly Airport (which dates from 1961) with a new facility at Roissy-en-France, inaugurated in 1974.[13]

For all that, if the great national work project of the nineteenth century was the transcontinental railroad, in the twentieth century it was the Trans-Canada Highway, far more than air transport, that symbolized unification of the territory.[14] For the major cities of the Western world, the advent of the train and subsequently the superhighway represented breaks with what had gone

15 André Lortie, "Grandes voiries: Permanence des tracés et fluctuation des écritures," in *Infrastructures, villes et territoire*, ed. Claude Prélorenzo (Paris: L'Harmattan, 2000), 155–160.

16 Larry McNally, "Roads, Streets, and Highways," in *Building Canada: A History of Public Works*, ed. Norman R. Ball (Toronto: University of Toronto Press, 1988), 51.

before. The first break, between industrialization and rail transport, changed the relation of cities to their territories: the railroad station usually remained close to the downtown, and transhipment led to the creation of a powerful hierarchy that included the centre, secondary industrial terminals, and inner and outer suburbs. In the case of the second break, the automobile and the major infrastructures that served it, by their ubiquity, destroyed the relation of scale between the city and the greater territory. In Canada, the Trans-Canada Highway, extending from one ocean to the other, crossed the built-up sections of major cities, which suffered the effects of the traffic even though they were not its destination. This phenomenon is identical to what occurred at the same time in the United States, for example, where cities such as Philadelphia were crossed by national highways like Interstate 676, which today splits the city right down the middle to connect the Benjamin Franklin Bridge over the Delaware River to the east with the expressway along the Schuylkill River to the west.[15]

More difficult to implement than the links of the air transport system, the lines of the highway system required negotiations with numerous parties: provincial, regional, and municipal. To that end, the Trans-Canada Highway Act of 1949 provided for government participation at a level of 10 percent of the investment. In reaction to the rate at which Canadians used motor vehicles, which grew rapidly in the 1950s and 1960s, an amendment increased the level of support to a limit of 90 percent of expenditures for new construction.[16]

Work

Just as the railroads served industry in the nineteenth century, so the major road and highway infrastructures played a part in the reorganization of production facilities. Trains and ships tended to concentrate exchange points near the centre;

Figure 60
City Planning Department, City of Montreal, land-use map, 1949, section 56-68. Canadian Centre for Architecture, Montréal, courtesy Ville de Montréal, Gestion de documents et archives

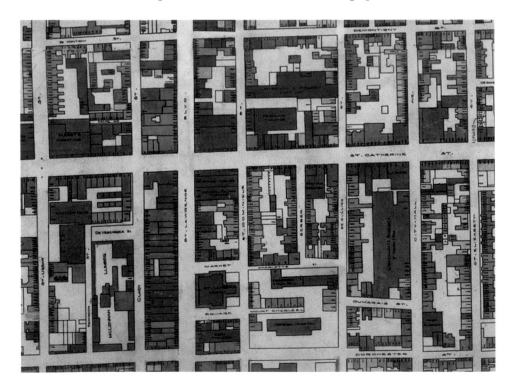

17 Brown, *The Illustrated History of Canada*; Linteau, *Histoire de Montréal*, 44off.

18 William Zeckendorf with Edward McCreary, *The Autobiography of William Zeckendorf* (New York: Holt, Rinehart and Winston, 1970), 167.

19 The first version of the Eaton Centre can be attributed to the same American group, Webb and Knapp, under the name of their Canadian subsidiary, Trizec.

20 Henry Aubin, *City for Sale* (Montreal: Éditions l'Étincelle; Toronto: J. Lorimer, 1977), 65.

superhighways and, even more so, airplanes were clearly dissociated from the centre, and industry became less localized as a consequence. The deindustrialization of Canadian urban centres was not the goal of any concerted policy, but rather a by-product of government actions that accompanied a trend toward industrial concentration, as an extension of the war effort.[17] This movement tended to absorb craft industries, shops, and small or medium-size family businesses, which used to be situated close to the centre and could draw on the local labour pool (fig. 60). Encouragement of industrial consolidation led to a change of scale that caused industry to move outside centres and relocate along new major infrastructures, far from workers' traditional housing.

The government was not the only force whose actions had direct and indirect consequences for the spatial organization of large cities. While the movement toward industrial relocation was unprecedented, the concentration of tertiary industry in the city centre, in specialized buildings, continued a trend that had been underway since the end of the preceding century. It reached unforeseen levels in Montreal, however, with the construction of 150,000 square metres of office space in Place Ville-Marie. This project by the developer Webb and Knapp had a stimulating influence, as evidenced by two major skyscrapers that followed in its wake (fig. 61). The first of these was the Canadian Imperial Bank of Commerce tower, whose president chose to locate the bank's head office in the same vicinity – his ambition was to have a building that would be higher than the headquarters of the rival Royal Bank. The second, for Canadian Industries Limited (CIL), was built by Lionel Rudberg, a local real estate developer who had been "galvanized by this entry into his town."[18]

The trend toward real estate concentration in complex projects that consolidated one or more blocks of urban land was not a new idea in North America, Rockefeller Center in New York being the obvious example. It was, nonetheless, an innovation for Montreal, and it raised the city to the level of other major centres. It was soon imitated elsewhere in Canada, particularly in Toronto,[19] and caused investors as far away as Vancouver to dream.[20] Operations on such a scale

Figure 61
Office tower construction, 23 April 1961.
Photograph: Jeremy Taylor. Collection Jeremy Taylor

21 For a more thorough study of this topic, see Marc H. Choko, "Dossier habitation," University of Montreal, 1974, and the report by Melvin Charney, *The Adequacy and Production of Low-Rental Housing* (Ottawa: Central Mortgage and Housing Corporation, 1971).

22 *Journal of the Royal Architectural Institute of Canada* 36 (January 1959): 21, and 37 (August 1960): 330.

23 *Housing and Urban Growth in Canada* (Ottawa: Central Mortgage and Housing Corporation, 1956).

required huge amounts of capital, and the sources for such capital broadened to include the United States and England in the case of Place Ville-Marie, and also Germany, Italy, and Switzerland. Whereas economic activity in Canada was generally quite regulated, the new foreign investment in Canadian real estate was unregulated, and it took the place of whatever financing might have been provided by investors on the scene who would have been able to monitor the results from close up.

Housing

Government planning also concerned itself with housing. The flight of industry left urban centres devitalized and drained of the sources of employment that supported social diversity. This loss of value in the centre lent plausibility to the plan for separation of uses that had been demanded for decades by social and health reformers. Federal policies adapted relatively quickly to these changes. Instituted by the 1938 National Housing Act, they evolved from managing demobilization (using the lessons learned after World War I) to responding to the housing crisis, to the renovation of slum neighbourhoods. At first, such neighbourhoods were redesigned exclusively for housing, but starting in 1956, aid began to be directed toward purposes other than residential.[21] A few years later, the pattern of demolition and reconstruction gave way to mixed development that combined new construction with restoration of the traditional habitat, as in the Milton-Park neighbourhood.

Each municipality had its own response to the standardization of aid, which suggests that the aid was gradually being appropriated in a manner that did not involve a policy based on models. In Halifax and Vancouver,[22] CMHC managed development, adapting the model buildings designed by the chief architect Ian MacLennan (see pages 120–124). In Toronto, however, it was the firm of Page and Steele that designed the highly publicized Regent Park project, for which the architect, Peter Dickinson, had envisioned towers with innovative two-level L-shaped apartments. In Montreal, the Jeanne-Mance housing project clearly restored the stages of the critical process, since MacLennan's high-rise buildings were in part abandoned in favour of row housing on three levels, as we will see below. From then on, the municipality would guide housing policy, while renovators would look for models and forms better suited to the Montreal environment.

During the same period, CMHC promoted single-family dwellings and produced models for units and subdivisions (see pages 120–124). If industry was indeed deserting the city centre, it was important to ensure that the labour force it required was available nearby. In the 1956 speech by the chairman of CMHC to the Royal Commission on Canada's Economic Prospects, we can hear the more planning-friendly tone of a country like France: "Because of its fundamental place in a modern industrial economy and because of its deep social implications, housing is a matter in which governments at all levels are inevitably and intimately involved. The provision of housing has some of the aspects of a public service."[23] The concomitant urbanization of the periphery must also be under-

24 Marc H. Choko, Jean-Pierre Collin, and Annick Germain, "Le logement et les enjeux de la transformation de l'espace urbain: Montréal, 1940-1960," *Revue d'histoire urbaine* 15, no. 2 (October 1986): 127–136, and 15, no. 3 (February 1987): 243–253.

25 Brown, *The Illustrated History of Canada.*

26 Hans Elte, "Cultural Centres," *Journal of the Royal Architectural Institute of Canada* 42 (May 1965).

27 In 1961, Drapeau submitted to Prime Minister Diefenbaker a dossier outlining a series of large-scale projects aimed at bolstering Montreal's status as a major Canadian city: "Mémoire du Comité exécutif de la cité de Montréal, soumis au très honorable John D. Diefenbaker, premier ministre du Canada." This very political approach can be seen as a rebuff of the provincial government's interference in municipal affairs; Drapeau was fiercely opposed to the power-sharing being imposed on Montreal at the time.

stood in this sense, and not exclusively as encouragement for the construction of ideal communities.[24] But the project was also economic and technical insofar as "the construction and maintenance of housing is in itself a major national industry." And national planning was clearly intertwined with the issue of housing, which brought together large-scale industry, the transportation infrastructure, and the organization of a territory's communities: "The creation of residential areas involves the design of street systems, public services, and the siting of shopping centres, schools, and churches. The building of houses is therefore the initial step in shaping the patterns of communities which will influence the lives of many generations."

Recreation

With the centennial anniversary of Confederation looming on the horizon, the federal government emphasized a new mode of intervention already undertaken in the late 1950s, which consisted in providing financial support for local projects,[25] in particular those involving cultural and performance-related industries. The Confederation Centre in Charlottetown was evidence of this policy, as was the new Winnipeg Art Gallery.[26] This is the context in which the very large involvement of different levels of government in Expo 67 should be understood. And it is the yardstick by which Mayor Drapeau's great skill in acquiring funding from all those different sources must be measured. The strategy can be better appreciated if we realize that in 1961, a year before Montreal's candidacy as a world's fair site was approved, the city had already made its case to the prime minister of Canada.[27]

The 1960s are the story of Montreal's acceptance of these forces, which transcended the wishes of the municipality and were placed, more or less successfully, at the service of a powerful collective project, to which many parties would contribute, each in its own way, although it seemed there was no one who held the key to it or who was able to describe it clearly.

Planning and Infrastructure

Nonetheless, such a collective project did exist, even if it could be deemed at first glance more technical or technocratic than political. Evidently, it was no longer in the cards to abandon the major city in Canada to its endemic housing crisis, unhealthy living conditions, and obsolescent industry. At the local level, the creation of the City Planning Department was evidence that matters were being taken in hand, while other signs were perceptible at the provincial level, such as the establishment of a commission to study city-related problems. This shift in level was indicative of a concomitant broadening of the issues with which planning was concerned. It can be seen in the technical approach to these questions, which were themselves in line with certain political concerns that lie outside the scope of this article. First we must look at the evolution of the technical approach, which changed from correction to prediction, before observing its large-scale effects, which were the subject of an ambitious urban development plan.

28 On this subject, see the work of Jeanne M. Wolfe and Hannah P. Shostack.

29 An exhaustive master plan for undeveloped areas was published by the department in 1954. Collection of the City Planning Department, no. 08829.

30 See "Plan d'aménagement de la partie centrale de Montréal (du port jusqu'à la rue Dorchester environ)," dated 30 September 1952 and signed by the consultant, Gréber; "Plan d'aménagement du quartier de l'hôtel de ville," dated 25 September 1953 and signed by the consultant, Gréber.

31 City Planning Department, *Études de circulation, été 1945* (Montreal: City of Montreal, 1946); City Planning Department, *Études de circulation, été 1946* (Montreal: City of Montreal, 1946), arguing the merits of widening Dorchester Street; City Planning Department, *Études de circulation* (Montreal: City of Montreal, 1949).

From Correction to Prediction

Between 1941 and 1944, the new City Planning Department drafted a master plan for the central portion of Montreal Island (fig. 62), impelled to some extent by the need for geographical coherence. This document was based on broad theoretical principles of urban land use and summarized the main modes of action in use at the time. The built-up areas of the city were linked by a string of parks and public gardens and surrounded by major thoroughfares from which a number of segments opened out into extended diagonals connecting the centre to the rest of the island. The long lines of these diagonals seem to reflect an effort to complement and at the same time transcend the web of local streets.[28] On a larger scale, the plan did not extend beyond the limits of the island, and on the east and west remained well inside them. Development of parks and gardens,[29] establishment of road and highway departments, and zoning were the tools used to correct the imperfections of a general organization deemed to be deficient. No measures were taken on a regional scale, however; links with the rest of the region were barely considered.

This overarching plan was implemented by real action on the ground. Local corrective measures were envisaged, in particular around Central Station and in the neighbourhood of City Hall.[30] On a more general level, the adaptation of the road system was designed on the basis of a vehicle count.[31] Undoubtedly one of the most spectacular measures was the widening of Dorchester Street (today known as René-Lévesque Boulevard), completed in the mid-1950s, which met a variety of objectives (fig. 63). It created a major artery in and out of the city, which relieved traffic in the section of the centre devoted to business, while greatly increasing the potential value of land all along this new monumental space, on which the buildings had been demolished.

Figure 62
"Master Plan, Preliminary Study." City Planning Department, City of Montreal, *Planning for Montreal: Master Plan Preliminary Report* (1944), 48. Canadian Centre for Architecture, Montréal

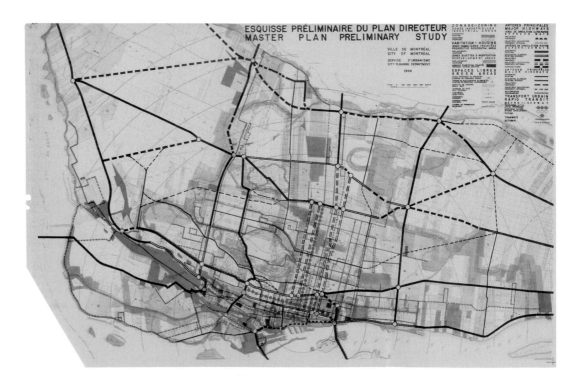

32 Cliff Ellis, "Professional Conflict over Urban Form: The Case of Urban Freeways, 1930 to 1970," in *Planning the Twentieth-Century American City*, ed. Mary Sies and Christopher Silver (Baltimore: Johns Hopkins University Press, 1996).

33 It is sufficient to consider the southern part of Paris's peripheral boulevards, begun in 1958. See Jean-Louis Cohen and André Lortie, *Des fortifs au périf* (Paris: Picard / Pavillon de l'Arsenal, 1992).

34 Surveyer, Nenniger, and Chênevert, Engineers, *Cité de Montréal: Projet autostrade nord-sud à proximité du boulevard Saint-Laurent* (Montreal, May 1959).

35 City Planning Department, *An East-West Expressway* (Montreal: City of Montreal, 1948).

Added to this type of transformation, which involved the widening of roads (something that had been going on for decades), was a new kind of intervention: the ordinary network of streets was to be paralleled by high-speed roads, elevated or depressed, that would be separated from the regular street grid and unaffected by the traffic on the streets they crossed. Models for this approach were already known. Such thoroughfares had been advocated since the late 1930s by the United States Bureau of Public Roads[32] and had been proposed in Europe during the same period.[33] The appropriately named Metropolitan Boulevard belongs to that generation (fig. 64). Its route was congruent with the street grid of a sector that was still relatively undeveloped at the time the roadway was built. Planning for a north-south artery to run over Saint Lawrence Boulevard dated from the same time;[34] it was intended to increase the capacity of that axis, which was saturated by local traffic (fig. 65). It would eventually be abandoned, in contrast to the east-west artery in the port area, which was considered as early as 1948, in imitation of the highway over Manhattan's docks (fig. 66).[35] The actual construction of this expressway in the early 1970s belonged instead to a third generation, more overtly superhighway-oriented, which was not constrained by the geometry of the streets and the volume of the inhabited areas over which the expressways passed (see pages 136–141).

Figure 63
Widening Dorchester Street to create Dorchester Boulevard, 31 March 1955. From *The Gazette* (Montreal). Library and Archives Canada, Ottawa, PA-119875

Figure 64
Construction of Metropolitan Boulevard, c. 1958. Centre de Montréal des Archives nationales du Québec

Widening through expropriation and paralleling by viaducts or trenches were two approaches that suffered from the same major flaw: in a city already densely developed, as in east-end Montreal, they were costly and complicated to implement. For this reason, the rapid growth of the urbanized areas of the large cities of the Western world motivated technical experts and reformers to develop means of predicting and orienting private urban development instead of lagging behind development and then assuming the task of correcting it through heavy public investments. Henceforth the challenge in Montreal was to take advantage of the dynamic of the anticipated growth and incorporate it into a predesigned program that could point the way to new development as well to the renovation of old neighbourhoods.

However, this program coincided with a number of others: that of economic players who saw Montreal as an important arena for profitable development, of the federal government – whose plans included the completion of the Trans-Canada Highway and placed a strong emphasis on the construction of single-family dwellings – and of provincial authorities seeking to regulate Montreal's expansion. All these programs together resulted in an explosion of images of a metropolis that was now turning into a major urban centre, indeed a region, and that would henceforth be conceived of on this geographical scale. Before examining the impact of the economic players and of federal policy on the ambitious Montreal plan, we need to look at the provincial political context.

Figure 65
Project for a north-south expressway along Saint Lawrence Boulevard, aerial perspective of the interchange at Dorchester, May 1959. Surveyor, Nenniger, and Chenevert, engineers; Hanno Compus, renderer. Ville de Montréal, Service de la mise en valeur du territoire et du patrimoine

Figure 66
"The Modern Expressway," nine international references. City Planning Department, City of Montreal, *Une autostrade est-ouest* **(1948), 9.** Published in English as *An East-West Expressway.* Canadian Centre for Architecture, Montréal

36 Robert Rumilly, *Histoire de Montréal*, vol. 5 (Montreal: Fides, 1974), 175.

37 Jean-Pierre Collin and Gérard Divay, *La Communauté urbaine de Montréal: De la ville centrale à l'île centrale* (Montreal: INRS Urbanisation, 1977), 42ff.

38 It would be superseded a decade later by the creation of the Montreal Urban Community. The period of the 1960s therefore coincides exactly with this episode.

In November 1952, at the request of Montreal's elected officials, the Government of Quebec appointed Judge Roland Paquette to serve as chairman of a commission of inquiry into the problems of the metropolis. His report, which was submitted to the government of Maurice Duplessis in January 1955, recommended the creation of a 29-member agency that would include, alongside the representatives of the provincial government, an equal number of representatives appointed by the suburban municipalities and the City of Montreal. Among other things, the agency was supposed to arbitrate conflicts and administer intermunicipal services.[36]

As soon as the recommendations were presented, the Drapeau-Desmarais administration expressed its opposition to "any metropolitan structure that would not recognize the effective preponderance of Montreal over the suburbs."[37] For the city administration, the solution to municipal problems would be Montreal's annexation of the other municipalities: "One Island, One City!" With Drapeau defeated in 1957, the Metropolitan Montreal Corporation was created by legislation in March 1959.[38] Under the new law, Montreal's City Planning Department was charged with managing a project that encompassed the entire urban area.

An Ambitious Urban Plan

There was a clear-cut break between the plans of the 1960s and those of a decade earlier, which had been designed in Paris in the offices of the urban planning consultant Jacques Gréber (fig. 67) and had presented a metropolis relatively modest

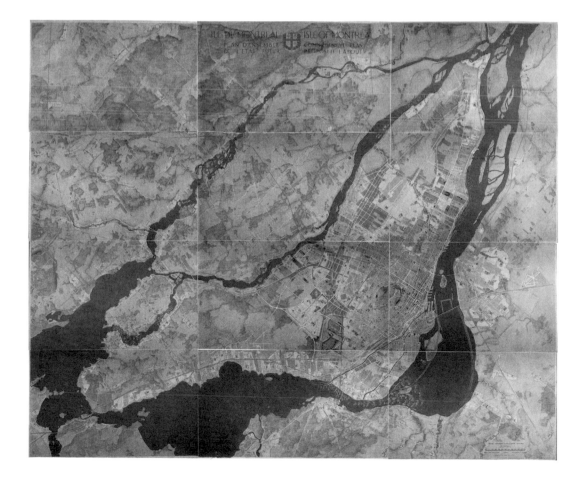

Figure 67
**"Isle of Montreal: Comprehensive Plan, Proposed Layout,"
1951. Jacques Gréber, urban planner.** Photograph: Alain Laforest, CCA. Canadian Centre for Architecture, Montréal, courtesy Ville de Montréal, Gestion de documents et archives

39 José M'Bala, in a highly questionable study, suggests
that this plan was designed for a city of 5 million
inhabitants. Given the urbanized area it covered, the
density would have been nearly double that of Paris,
which was the highest in Europe. José M'Bala, "Prévenir
l'exurbanisation: Le plan Gréber de 1950 pour Montréal,"
Revue d'histoire urbaine 29, no. 2 (March 2001): 62–70.
I continue to consider this plan to be a simple illustration
of a project designed by municipal departments;
see André Lortie, "Jacques Gréber et l'urbanisme: Le
temps et l'espace de la ville" (Ph.D. diss., Université de
Paris XII, 1997).

40 It should be noted that in traffic studies from the 1940s,
the "red dots" are essentially in the city centre, while
entrances to bridges are points of minor congestion.
See City Planning Department, *Études de circulation, été
1945* (Montreal: City of Montreal, 1946).

41 *Circulation à Montréal*, directed by Bernard Devlin (NFB,
1955).

42 Today the population is just under 10.9 million.

43 See Hans Blumenfeld, *The Modern Metropolis*, ed. Paul D.
Spreiregen (Cambridge, Mass.: MIT Press, 1967).

44 City Planning Department, *Étude de la forme: Région de
Montréal*, no. 2 (Montreal: City of Montreal, 1966).

in size and under control, enlarging on principles already elaborated in the 1944 plan.[39] In contrast to the 1944 plan, the hinterland was at least mentioned in the new plan, but was frozen in its rural state, without any new connection to the island.[40] This representation made no changes to the vision still prevailing in 1957, when Mayor Drapeau presented his highway development plans before the cameras of the National Film Board using a map that still did not cover Montreal Island in its entirety.[41]

In the early 1960s, the political organization, and the technocratic organization that resulted from it, contributed to changes in the way the urban area was represented. But demographic predictions also encouraged a change of scale: a population of 4.8 million by 1981 and of 7 million by 2000. It was the era for rationales of that type, all based on similar predictions. At the same time, in the Paris region, a choice was made to build new cities to house a regional population that was supposed to reach 14 million by the year 2000.[42]

In Montreal, the outcome was an astonishing study of metropolitan morphology of a sort ordinarily left to academics. With advice from the renowned urban planner Hans Blumenfeld,[43] and referring to the work of such theorists as Gaston Bardet, Yona Friedman, and Kevin Lynch, the Urban Development Division pondered the most auspicious form to give the urban area. Star-shaped, dispersed, linear, concentrated, galactic: plans for the use of space were drawn up in reference to specific examples, such as Saint Petersburg for the linear city and Paris for the concentrated version (figs. 68, 69, and 70).[44]

This debate, which went far beyond the group of technical specialists in the City Planning Department, was enriched by a variety of contributions that confirmed professional planners' interest in these questions. Evidence of this can be seen in the articles in the magazine *Architecture, bâtiment, construction* devoted to the subject, such as the article by Claude Beaulieu, recently returned from Paris, who had collaborated with the urban planner Jacques Gréber in several

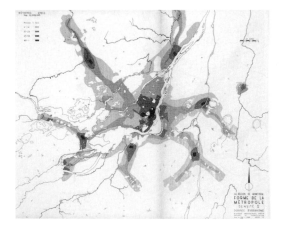

Figure 68
Star-shaped metropolis, hypothetical plan for the Montreal region with a population of 10 million inhabitants. City Planning Department, City of Montreal, *Étude de la forme: Région de Montréal*, no. 2 (1966), plan no. 20. Canadian Centre for Architecture, Montréal

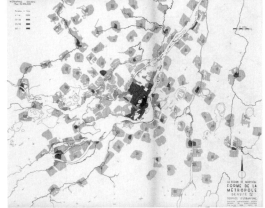

Figure 69
Galactic metropolis, hypothetical plan for the Montreal region with a population of 10 million inhabitants. City Planning Department, City of Montreal, *Étude de la forme: Région de Montréal*, no. 2 (1966), plan no. 22. Canadian Centre for Architecture, Montréal

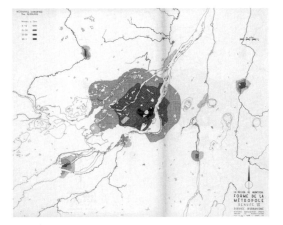

Figure 70
Concentrated metropolis, hypothetical plan for the Montreal region with a population of 10 million inhabitants. City Planning Department, City of Montreal, *Étude de la forme: Région de Montréal*, no. 2 (1966), plan no. 24. Canadian Centre for Architecture, Montréal

45 Claude Beaulieu, "De la nécessité de bien organiser les villes," *Architecture, bâtiment, construction* 10 (April 1955): 38–41.

46 André Blouin, "De l'urbanisme, de l'Homme et de l'architecture," *Architecture, bâtiment, construction* 12 (April 1957): 58–61.

47 See especially the articles by R.W.G. Bryant in the December 1962, October 1964, and November 1965 issues.

Montreal studies and who advocated the creation of a green belt and satellite cities,[45] or the one by André Blouin, an architect originally from France, who would have liked to see Montreal become a demonstration site for the application of the Charter of Athens (figs. 71 and 72).[46] But this question also interested the public in general, and the magazine *Cité libre*, not to be outdone, opened its pages to architects and urban planners.[47]

On the basis of these studies, the City Planning Department made a well-defined and well-argued choice that subsequently guided major decisions, whether of a general order, like zoning regulations, or ad hoc, like the specific route of a major highway or the construction of a large-scale facility. The choice was to combine a dense centre, modelled on Paris, with a periphery in the form of a four-pointed star, of which two of the points would be predominantly industrial, following the line of the river, and two, toward the Laurentians and the Eastern Townships, would be residential in character (see pages 26–29). This plan served as a guide for consolidation of the core through architectural projects on an unprecedented scale, while at the same time the city spread out to fill its geographic site. Clearly, there was an understanding of the importance of both the business centre and development of the periphery.

One of the factors that made possible the paradoxical dual dynamic of sprawl and centralization was the implementation of a large-scale transportation infrastructure to support both individual transport and mass transit. As the highways and expressways were designed and implemented, they had a dilating and expansive effect on land occupancy throughout the territory, since they made it possible to reach distant destinations without adding to the total travel time. Within the built-up sections of the urban area, the metro ensured unlimited mobility that was both fast and economical.

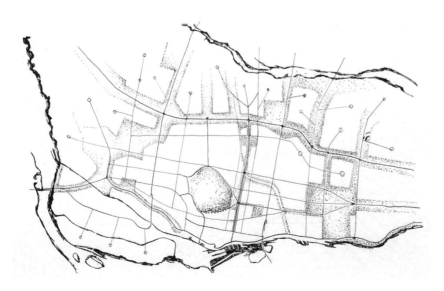

Figure 71
Schematic plan for Metropolitan Montreal. Claude Beaulieu (architect and planner), "De la nécessité de bien organiser les villes," *Architecture, bâtiment, construction* 10 (April 1955): 39. Canadian Centre for Architecture, Montréal

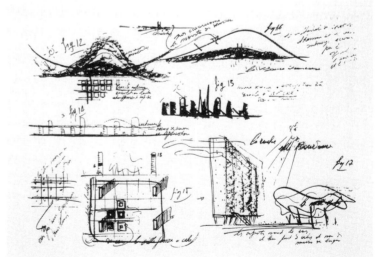

Figure 72
Conceptual sketch from the drawings series "The Application of Sound Planning." André Blouin (architect), Blouin, "De l'urbanisme, de l'Homme et de l'architecture," *Architecture, bâtiment, construction* 12 (April 1957): 61. Canadian Centre for Architecture, Montréal

48 "Proposed Subway Plan for Montreal," *Canadian Engineer* 59 (16 December 1930), 721.

49 Typically this represented the thinking of the urban planners of the Chicago Plan, Burnham and Bennet, to whom the study for the City of Ottawa was entrusted: Sir Herbert Holt (Chairman), *Report of the Federal Plan Commission on a General Plan for the Cities of Ottawa and Hull*, Sir Herbert Holt, A. Lacoste, H. Smith, F. Darling, Mayors of Ottawa and Hull, Commissioners, 1915.

50 J.A. Lalonde, L. Girouard, L. Letendre, Engineers, *Plan directeur: Routes à caractère métropolitain* (Montreal: Corporation of Metropolitan Montreal, 1961).

51 City Planning Department, *Métropole: Les Cahiers d'urbanisme*, no. 3 (Montreal: City of Montreal, October 1965), 34.

This dual dynamic resulted from the conjunction of widely differing rationales. The long-term rationale was the effect of a sort of social inertia, which meant that planning projects discussed and approved between the two world wars, but never applied because of lack of funds and/or political will, were recycled after World War II without being re-examined. This was the case with the metro, whose route remained essentially unchanged from the 1930 plan[48] to the plans adopted in 1944 and later. A project like the metro was a response to theories that, while dating from the early twentieth century, were based largely on the experience of the nineteenth, and in Europe as in America recommended fluidity and density in the centre, supported by mass transit (tram, metro, railway station, etc.), the widening and creation of roads, and the construction of buildings that would accommodate the various economic, political, and other functions, both essential and symbolic.[49] This long-term logic encountered another rationale, based on the current economic situation, namely the voluntarist national planning we have already mentioned, in particular the Canada-wide highway system, which ran into Montreal's urban space and impinged on corridors already envisaged before World War II (fig. 73).

If it seems clear in retrospect that expressways were the vectors of the extensive urbanization of Montreal's periphery, nothing predestined them to extend into the area that was already built up. In 1961, the objective of the master plan for road development proposed by the engineers Lalonde, Girouard, and Letendre to the Metropolitan Montreal Corporation was still to provide solutions for local problems.[50] But the necessity of preparing Montreal to receive Expo 67 and the subsidies offered for building the Trans-Canada Highway pushed forward construction of the Metropolitan Boulevard extensions, the Décarie Expressway, the Louis-Hippolyte Lafontaine Bridge-Tunnel, and Montée Saint-Léonard, followed early in the next decade by the Ville-Marie Expressway. Each of these segments meant that national and provincial highways were crossing the urban area (figs. 74 and 75).[51]

By making these old road projects possible through subsidies that covered most of the investment, government intervention ensured that the road system would have the character of an expressway, and defined its scale, thus

Figure 73
Network of the major arteries. Montreal City Planning Commission, *Plan de l'Île de Montréal* (1935). Ville de Montréal, Gestion de documents et archives

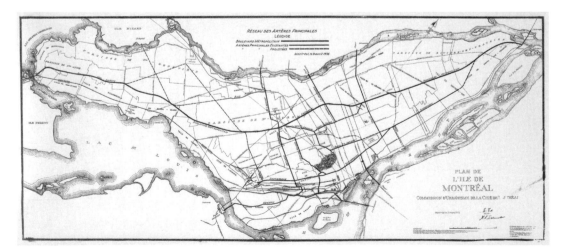

Figure 74
"Master Plan – Metropolitan Roads Network." Lalonde, Girouard, and Letendre, engineers, *Plan directeur: Routes à caractère métropolitain* (1961), plan no. 52. Ville de Montréal, Service de la mise en valeur du territoire et du patrimoine

Figure 75
"Limited Access Expressways." City Planning Department, City of Montreal, *Métropole: Les Cahiers d'urbanisme*, no. 3 (October 1965), 40. Canadian Centre for Architecture, Montréal

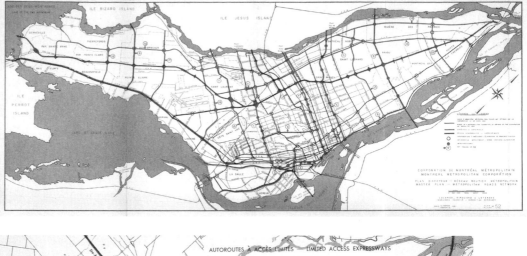

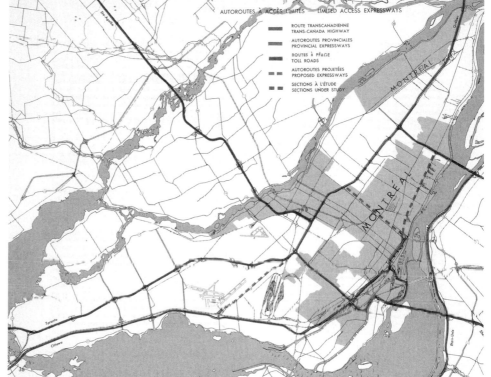

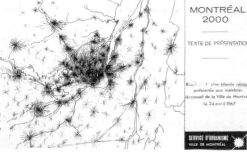

Figure 76
City Planning Department, City of Montreal, *Montréal 2000* (24 April 1967). Ville de Montréal, Service de la mise en valeur du territoire et du patrimoine

52 City Planning Department, *Montréal 2000: Esquisse du plan témoin régional présentée aux membres du conseil de la Ville de Montréal* (Montreal: City of Montreal, 24 April 1967).
53 City Planning Department, General Studies Division, "Rôle potentiel des villes satellites" (Montreal: City of Montreal, 1966).

causing changes in the relation of the city to its territory. That relation would never be the same. Henceforth traversed by a great many vehicles that did not stop in it, the city took on a flow of traffic that was not actually coming into it but which it had to put up with anyway. At the same time, major road projects that were originally intended to serve the organization of the city core in its relations with the different parts of the urban area became instead the means by which the city overflowed its site, so to speak, both on and off the island, onto the South Shore, and north onto Île Jésus and beyond.

This massive project for the urban area had the year 2000 as its horizon (fig. 76),[52] and optimistically provided both for renewal of the city centre and for something like satellite cities on the periphery.[53] Under study during the first half of the decade, it was partially implemented in preparation for the world's fair but

54 Don Mills, in suburban Toronto, was a precursor. See Desmond Morton in Brown, *The Illustrated History of Canada.*

55 Ludger Beauregard, "Les centres d'achats de Montréal," *Revue de géographie de Montréal* 27, no. 1 (1973): 17–28.

56 Hugh Hood, "A Green Child," in *Around the Mountain: Scenes from Montreal Life* (Toronto: Peter Martin Associates, 1967), 132–137.

57 Bernard Vachon, "La création de Candiac en banlieue de Montréal: Essai d'analyse spatiale et financière d'une trame d'appropriation du sol en milieu péri-urbain," *Revue de géographie de Montréal* 27, no. 1 (1973): 29–39.

was made public only in 1967. While decisions affecting the municipality of Montreal were consistent with it, as we will see in terms of the centre-city zoning, the political status and technocratic structure of the Corporation did not allow it to impose its policies outside that perimeter. Added to the weakness of the means of action was a painful review of the objective data: by the end of the decade, the demographic projections on which the planning was based were found to be unrealistic in regard to the growth curves. From then on, the time-lines were split: on the one hand, infrastructures launched for a city of 5 million to 7 million inhabitants, and on the other hand, urban expansion that was thought to be just the beginning of a phenomenon for which one had to make preparations so that its extreme phase could be more manageable – a phase that essentially would never arrive.

The New Periphery

The emergence of residential suburbs consisting of single-family houses was not a new phenomenon in the 1960s.[54] What was new was the intense functional and spatial segregation induced by their relation to major highways. Concomitantly with these new roads, large shopping centres like Galeries d'Anjou (400,000 m²) and Carrefour Laval (100,000 m²) were built, directly connected to their own highway interchanges.[55] These new cathedrals of consumption were indissociable from the single-family housing developments encouraged by CMHC, a favoured area for real estate investment that took advantage of public policies on transportation. The transformation was observed at the time by the short-story writer Hugh Hood: "These and other similar buildings, finished and half-finished, are apt to be set down in fields of solid mud, with a hundred feet of open dumping ground between them and their neighbours . . . The way the city grew and spread fascinated him. It sprouted like something alive. This month there were dozens of families living on crescents where last month there had been nothing."[56]

A bedroom community like Candiac was made possible only by the opening of the newly built Champlain Bridge, which constituted a vital section of the highway leading to the American border. It opened up that part of the South Shore to urban development, and developers acquired agricultural land near the river in hopes of profiting from the existence of the Seaway and setting up industrial facilities (see pages 124–131).[57] But while industries were leaving the city centre, where they had been part of an urban fabric in which habitat and activities intermingled, it was not so as to be closer to river and maritime transportation, but to move to sites along the major roads. The dispersion of industry was part of the dynamic of renewal of the city core at the same time that it fostered urban sprawl, which in its conquest of the territory was characterized by a very strong separation of uses.

Nuns' Island took part in this expansion related to the construction of the Champlain Bridge (which was completed in 1961). Like Candiac, it was an urban creation underwritten entirely by private enterprise. Unlike Candiac, which gained territorial autonomy at the expense of the municipalities in which the land it acquired was located, Nuns' Island was annexed to the municipality of Verdun.

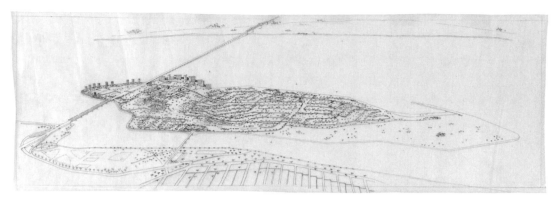

58 City Planning Department, Urban Development Division, *Remembrement du territoire: Aménagement de Rivière-des-Prairies*, vol. 1 (Montreal: City of Montreal, c. 1968).

59 Hugh Hood, "The Village Inside," in *Around the Mountain*, 115.

Figure 77
Nuns' Island, aerial perspective, c. 1958. Harold Ship, architect. Pen and black ink, coloured pencil, and graphite on tracing paper, 32.3 x 95.8 cm. Canadian Centre for Architecture, Montréal, Fonds Harold Ship

The skill of the developers, Quebec Home and Mortgage Corporation, lay in creating a diversity of real estate possibilities, to allow for a population density that could support the creation of public facilities and businesses (which was not the case in Candiac, despite the predictions of its designers; see pages 124–131). High-rise buildings, row houses, small multi-unit buildings – this complementarity already existed in the initial sketches by the architect Harold Ship (fig. 77), who was succeeded by a multidisciplinary team that included Mies van der Rohe and the Montrealer Philip Bobrow. The image of mixed use and diversity that resulted from this urban development in a natural setting soon convinced prospective residents, all the more because Nuns' Island had all the advantages of an exceptional site, and was only a stone's throw from downtown without having any of its drawbacks.

The City Planning Department envisaged a project of the same type on land newly annexed from Rivière-des-Prairies, on the north shore of Montreal Island. Looking to the new English and Swedish towns and to France's top-priority urban development zones, and more specifically to the Hook Hampshire project in England, the department's planning group designed a new neighbourhood for 100,000 residents that would receive the population affected by centre-city urban renewal.[58] Town houses were planned that would look out onto gardens and be clustered around a few high-rise buildings (fig. 78). The project was probably rendered obsolete by societal pressure to keep those displaced by urban renewal in the same neighbourhood, and by the revised demographic forecasts. Eventually, houses arranged around gardens would be built some years later in Little Burgundy by the architect Jean Ouellet (the "Îlots Saint-Martin").

These all-of-a-piece creations were not the rule, however. New urban development was also grafted onto historical development as an extension of it, manufacturing syncopated continuities in which Hugh Hood unearthed layers of exquisite urban remains that he took pleasure in deciphering, as he bicycled around and came upon them: "True enough, it's no more than five miles from the centre of town, but you can detect the ancient village inside the suburban growth, like an attenuated ghost, traceable by houses spotted along the street as you ride north, interrupted by modern installations of a qualified beauty and utility."[59]

The same logic of territorial conquest prevailed when it came time to select a site for Expo 67. It was initially thought that the event would be held in Pointe Saint-Charles, Maisonneuve, Saint-Léonard and Anjou, Lasalle, or Mercier, and that the adjacent neighbourhoods would be renovated and any spaces

Figure 78
City Planning Department, City of Montreal, *Remembrement du territoire: Aménagement de Rivière-des-Prairies*, vol. 1 (c. 1968). Canadian Centre for Architecture, Montréal

60 Letter from Daniel van Ginkel to Colonel E. Churchill, 26 October 1963, Canadian Centre for Architecture, Montréal, Fonds van Ginkel, 27-A21-01, and "Professional Opinion on Choice of Site for the Canadian World Exhibition, Montreal 1967," 14 March 1963, Fonds van Ginkel, 27-A21-12.

61 Édouard Fiset, in *Expo 67: The Memorial Album* (Toronto: Thomas Nelson and Sons, 1968), 39.

filled in. Daniel van Ginkel, the architect hired as a planning consultant by the Canadian Corporation for the 1967 World Exhibition, believed it should be the moving force behind an ambitious program of urban development.[60] His preference was for the site nearest the city centre, where it would function as an extension of the downtown area toward Pointe Saint-Charles and the port, while the other sites would have extended the mental image of the city toward the east, as the Olympic Games would do in 1976.

It is in this context that the final choice can be appreciated. For Édouard Fiset, Expo 67's chief architect, the idea of developing Saint Helen's Island was an extension of Frederick G. Todd's 1937 project to create a major city park on this spot.[61] This was the inspiration that guided Fiset in his overall design, which preserved the original island in the form of a park and strengthened the relation of the landfill to the adjacent water and rock in the portions wrested from the river. The result was a large area for leisure and entertainment that recalled Coney Island and Flushing Meadow in New York (the latter the site of earlier world's fairs) and the Bois de Vincennes in Paris (where the Colonial Exhibition of 1931 had been held). The unusual nature of the site contributed to these perceived resemblances. The metro being built at the same time, in addition to providing excavation debris that could be used as the raw material for the artificial landfill, confirmed that the site was an extension of the city centre and was both close to it (a few minutes' ride) and far away from it (given the distant view of the downtown skyline and the totally different feel of the site).

Figure 79
Place Frontenac, perspective, c. 1971. Gagnon, Archambault, and Durand, architects. Black pencil, graphite, and self-adhesive plastic film on tracing paper, 86 x 103 cm. Centre de Montréal des Archives nationales du Québec

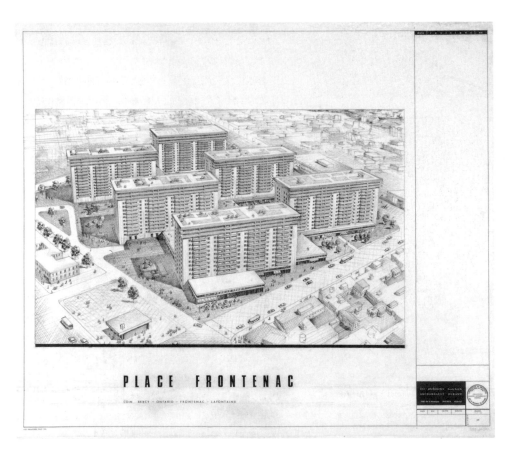

PLACE FRONTENAC

62 Benoît Clairoux, *Le Métro de Montréal, 35 ans déjà* (Montreal: Hurtubise HMH, 2001), 139.

63 At that time, Pei was head of the architectural division of Webb and Knapp, which formed the kernel of the Pei agency that would be founded some years later.

64 Isabelle Gournay, "Manifestation du gigantisme au centre-ville," in *Montreal Metropolis, 1880–1930*, ed. Isabelle Gournay and France Vanlaethem (Montreal: Canadian Centre for Architecture, 1998), 169–199.

65 Peter Blake, "Vincent Ponte: A New Kind of Urban Designer," *Art in America* 57, no. 5 (September–October 1969): 62–67.

The metro was also a vector for the conquest of urban space. Not only was it a moving force behind the densification of the city core, as we will see below, but it also allowed points of density, modelled on the centre, to be exported to the end of the line. That was the reason behind the sharp increase in land values in the area of Longueuil that was served by the metro, which within a few years saw a large open parking lot transformed into a dense, dynamic centre.[62] The effect was similar in the eastern part of the city, where ambitious real estate development projects were flourishing in just a few years near the Frontenac station, the terminus of the original Number 1 line, running from there as far as Atwater (fig. 79).

Consolidation of the Centre

While expressways were doing their part to empty the city's built-up areas of a share of their economy and population, the metro had the reverse effect. The fact that it consolidated urban development along its route was nonetheless not without consequences for the urban fabric. As an example, it is sufficient to recall the construction of the characterless rental properties atop the downtown stations before they were even in service, like the building put up by the developer David Bloom on the corner of Guy and de Maisonneuve. Nevertheless, the metro opened up unprecedented possibilities in the city core by becoming an underground branch of the shopping centres that were an inevitable part of any major undertaking in the tertiary sector (see pages 164–167).

The Business Centre and Private-Sector Initiative
Among these new-style ventures, the large-scale project with which Montrealers most identified was indisputably Place Ville-Marie, built by the American real estate developer William Zeckendorf with the architect Henry N. Cobb (a collaborator of I.M. Pei),[63] the urban planner Vincent Ponte, and the local architectural firm of Affleck, Desbarats, Dimakopoulos, Lebensold, Michaud, and Sise. Though radical in its urban stance and unique in its architectural forms, it was not without its antecedents; here, once again, was an original formulation of old objectives that had been kicking around since the turn of the century, when the major railway companies were rivalling one another with huge projects located close to where their infrastructure crossed the city centre.[64]

Place Ville-Marie filled a gaping hole in the urban fabric that had resulted from the excavation of the railway tunnel under Mount Royal. Far from proving destructive to the old city, as other subsequent ventures would be, it remedied the side-effects of the railway while amply profiting from it, since the 45-storey building was adjacent to Central Station and the Queen Elizabeth Hotel and connected to them by an underground shopping promenade – the original exemplar of a network of shopping centres that continued to grow over the years, and which Vincent Ponte promoted indefatigably.[65]

This venture cleverly combined the symbolic register with innovative implementation, and took full advantage of the proximity of the new metro. Something as basic as the choice of name was typical of Zeckendorf, who was shuttling back and forth between the mayor and the cardinal on the one

Figure 80
Aerial view of downtown Montreal, 18 July 1961. From *The Gazette* (Montreal). Photograph: Gar Lunney. Library and Archives Canada, Ottawa, PA-129265

Figure 81
William Zeckendorf with Jean Lesage, premier of Quebec, and Donald Gordon, president of Canadian National Railways, 13 September 1962. Photograph: Associated Commercial Photographers Ltd. Archives of Pei, Cobb, Freed, and Partners, Architects

66 Zeckendorf, *Autobiography*.

67 Hubert Aquin, "Essai crucimorphe," *Liberté*, no. 28 [vol. 5, no. 4] (July-August 1963), 323–325.

hand (representing the French-speaking population) and the English-speaking bank owners and industrialists on the other, and understood immediately the unique character of Quebec culture (fig. 81).[66] Not only did the cruciform building plan incorporate symbolism that referred back to Quebec's origins, as Hubert Aquin noted in 1963,[67] it also made reference to the avant-garde's imagined architecture and rationalist discourse: the "Cartesian building" beloved of Le Corbusier, in detailing that could have come from the pen of Mies van der Rohe. The main plaza, around which the entrances of the different buildings in the complex were distributed, was certainly a large empty space, given the high density the surrounding structures created, but above all it represented a pertinent strategic decision: the open space, level with Dorchester but higher than Cathcart Street, was initially occupied by users of the tertiary-sector complex, who encountered one another there from morning to night. The topography allowed for the insertion of a layer of small shops under the plaza, opening out onto Cathcart Street and extending down toward the metro and Central Station. From the plaza, broad stairwells (now filled in) gave access to the underground level, flooding the corridors and shops with natural light. The gradual emergence of this podium can be viewed as a combination of individual objects rather than the excavation of a foundation; even the earliest sketches indicated the square as a collection of different venues, each with its own theme, without any real unity (fig. 82).

Place Ville-Marie prepared the ground for a hitherto unimagined urban layout based on megastructures that would follow the path of the railway as it

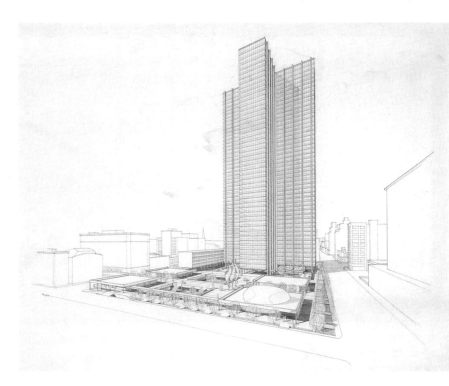

Figure 82
Place Ville-Marie, perspective, 1956. I.M. Pei and Associates, architects and planners; Henry N. Cobb, partner-in-charge; Robert Regala, draftsman. Graphite on illustration board, 50.5 x 76 cm. Archives of Pei, Cobb, Freed, and Partners, Architects

Figure 83
Re-development scheme for McGill College Avenue, photograph of massing plan, 1962. I.M. Pei and Associates, architects; Henry N. Cobb, architect-in-charge. Archives of Pei, Cobb, Freed, and Partners, Architects

68 "A Sense of Place," *Progressive Architecture*, February
    1966, 186–189.
69 Daniel van Ginkel, "Central Area Circulation Study,"
    fig. 8 (Le Centre Hochelaga), Canadian Centre
    for Architecture, Montréal, Fonds van Ginkel, 27-A13.

entered the city. Toward the north, in the years following the inauguration of Place Ville-Marie, Zeckendorf suggested redesigning McGill College Avenue by widening it in accordance with the 1953 study by Gréber (fig. 83).[68] Ordinary urban renewal finally brought about this widening in the 1990s.

The railway's tract of land south of Central Station was the subject of a number of studies that followed one another in quick succession. At the request of Lionel Rudberg, in collaboration with the architecture professor John Bland, the architects André Blouin and Victor Prus investigated covering the railroad tracks completely with an artificial flooring that would extend all the way from the station to an overhang over the Lachine Canal and the port. This "Confederation Promenade," inspired to a large extent by Brasilia (fig. 84), was intended to house an auditorium and offices. From the esplanade, a rail shuttle would link the downtown with the world's fair.

This proposal was in line with the general traffic organization study carried out by Daniel van Ginkel at the request of the city. In that case, too, a large empty plaza above the tracks was to contain buildings with a variety of purposes, arranged like pieces on a chessboard: "A major commercial development at the hub of transportation . . . the proposed Centre Hochelaga would result in a new commercial complex based around facilities for conventions, trade fairs, and other related uses."[69] This study sealed the fate of the east-west expressway, which from then on was destined to run underground through the centre of the city. The municipality retained only the part of the concept that located the metro and the roadway in a single trench that would be buried under the artificial floor of very large buildings (see pages 168–173).

It was in Place Bonaventure that the "Centre Hochelaga" program was finally implemented, with all the components brought together in one building – programmatic diversity at its most extreme. Designed by Affleck, Desbarats, Dimakopoulos, Lebensold, Michaud, and Sise, this powerful ziggurat combines, in a single edifice constructed over the Central Station railroad tracks, access to a metro station, parking for 1,000 vehicles, offices, galleries of boutiques, and a huge exhibition hall with its loading docks, the whole surmounted by a 400-room hotel with three restaurants, a swimming pool, and a rooftop garden. The post-and-beam structure is made of reinforced concrete, and its exhibition hall

70 Norbert Schoenauer, *Architecture Montréal* (Montreal: Southam Business Publications, 1967), 22.

71 A 1962 graduate of McGill University, Morris Charney was first involved in the initial design phase for Place Bonaventure, before accepting a bursary to travel in Europe, then joining Jean-Claude La Haye and Associates when he returned.

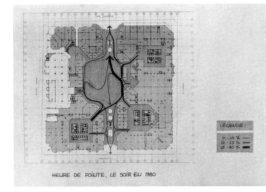

Figure 85
Complexe Desjardins, traffic study for evening rush hour, 1980. Jean-Claude La Haye and Associates, architects and planners. Collection André Lortie

rises to a height of 15 metres. The experimental façade, made up of panels of precast bush-hammered concrete with insulation material incorporated in them, was developed in collaboration with the National Research Council.[70]

This strategy was characteristic of an entire generation of projects that tended to subordinate aesthetics to design, with the form of the whole deriving from proper arrangement of its constituent parts. Alexis Nihon Plaza, Place Dupuis, and, somewhat later, Complexe Desjardins are typical examples. In the case of Place Desjardins, the location of bus termini on the east and west sides, the link to the metro and Place des Arts on the north, and the old historical part of the city on the south, as well as the position of the passages to the batteries of elevators, determined the general form (fig. 85). This clever design was the work of Morris Charney, head of the planning and major projects division that the urban planner Jean-Claude La Haye had set up in his agency to meet this new type of demand.[71]

Some of these high-density projects were implemented under Amendment 2887 (of 9 September 1963) to the regulation respecting municipal construction, allowing construction that exceeded the land occupancy coefficient – which was twelve times the area of the lot in this sector. Insofar as an empty space, open or roofed, was preserved within the precincts of the project, the area of the project could be increased by six times the surface area of that empty space. It was probably under this regulation that Alexis Nihon Plaza was allowed to grow from two to three buildings as long as it included the central atrium that has remained its distinguishing characteristic (fig. 86).

Opportunities were created by the fact that regulations allowed developers to build private underground passages across public rights-of-way. This helps explain how something like the Bonaventure station could be built outside any

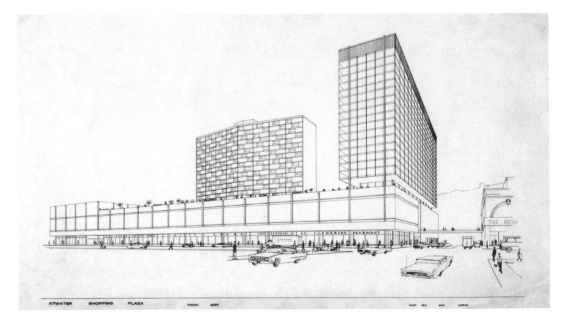

Figure 86
Atwater Shopping Plaza (Alexis Nihon Plaza), preliminary-scheme perspective, 1963. Harold Ship, architect. Photostat, 35.5 × 71 cm. Canadian Centre for Architecture, Montréal, Fonds Harold Ship

72 City Planning Department, *Zonage du flanc sud du Mont Royal* (Montreal: City of Montreal, 1962).

73 François Rémillard and Brian Merrett, *Demeures bourgeoises de Montréal: Le mille carré doré, 1850–1930* (Montreal. Méridien, 1986).

Figure 87
Bonaventure metro station, perspective of the platforms, c. 1963. Victor Prus, architect. Photostat with graphite, 45.5 x 65 cm. Collection Victor Prus

major project and yet serve as a hub for some of the largest of them – Place du Canada, Château Champlain, Place Bonaventure, and Central Station (fig. 87).

Another regulatory provision specifically concerned the zoning of the south slope of Mount Royal. It allowed construction of residential buildings with a total surface area more than five times that of the lot, limited to a height by taking into account the outline of the mountain.[72] Such buildings as the Port Royal, Le Cartier, and Mountain Place are the result of this rule (figs. 88 and 89). They were the most deluxe buildings among the constellation of apartment buildings of ten or more storeys that ate away at the swanky residential fabric of what in the preceding century had been the Square Mile of Montreal's upper crust.[73] These apartment buildings differed from office buildings in their slender silhouette. Unlike office buildings, they did not require a large lot in order to be profitable and could be built simply as a replacement for a single-family dwelling. The neo-Brutalist tendency in architecture that emerged during the 1950s,

Figure 88
Proposal for Port Royal Apartments, elevation, c. 1962. Attributed to André Blouin, architect. Photocopy mounted on foamcore, 40 x 29.5 cm. Canadian Centre for Architecture, Montréal, Fonds André Blouin. Subsequently designed by Ian Martin, architect.

Figure 89
Proposal for Mountain Place, photograph of presentation model, 1961. Office of Mies van der Rohe, architect. Canadian Centre for Architecture, Montréal, Fonds Peter Carter. Project not realized.

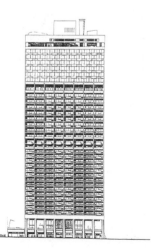

74 *Projet de rénovation d'une zone d'habitat défectueux et de construction d'habitations à loyer modique* (Montreal: City of Montreal, 1954). The source of this report is the work done by the consultative committee, chaired by Paul Dozois.

which advocated the use of raw materials in their rough state, allowed these structures of precast concrete to be even more profitable for their developers. The coexistence of contrasting architectural types, in which a landscape of stone or brick houses is interspersed with apartment towers made of concrete with a rough surface or showing the form marks, is the image we consider characteristic of the business district's immediate periphery.

"Development of the south slope of Mount Royal took place during a period when there was a change of scale," observed the City Planning Department. This change, as the reader will have understood, is the physical outcome of the urban planning undertaken in response to the demographic projections, which anticipated a "Parisian" density in the city centre (fig. 90).

Social Housing and Public Intervention

To the west, at the bottom of the McGill College axis that followed the railroad tracks, Place Ville-Marie increased the value of land that until then had been neglected even though it lay at the downtown's edge (which was now moving up from Saint James Street to the newly widened Dorchester Street). In contrast, other projects necessitated major demolition. This was the case in the section between Bleury and Saint-Urbain, which was the eastern, and institution-filled, response to the western north-south axis. Here, as in other cities, it was for reasons of hygiene and sanitation that the destruction of this remaining layer of the original urban fabric had been planned as early as the 1950s. But the debates raised by this renovation brought to light a second line of reasoning, in this case economic in nature. The real estate tax on neighbourhoods deemed obsolete, in which housing, small businesses, craft industries, and small manufacturing enterprises were intermingled, was not as high as what could be generated by rational land use, governed by the principle of separation of uses. East of Bleury, however, as south of Saint-Antoine, there was reason to fear that market forces alone would not be sufficient to generate urban renewal.

The 1944 map already identified a broad "zone subject to modification" that was bounded by Bleury, Sherbrooke, de Lorimier, and Craig (Saint-Antoine). Within this perimeter lay 5 of the 13 renovation sectors identified in the report submitted to the Executive Committee of the City of Montreal in 1954 by Paul Dozois, a city councillor.[74] In 1959, the City Planning Department published the results of a study of potential urban renewal in the rectangle bounded by Craig, Bleury, Sherbrooke, and Saint Lawrence, opening this axis to a cycle of projects that has continued uninterrupted ever since, its latest phase being the new concert hall complex (the competition for it was adjudicated in 2003).

Plans for a concert hall on the site of present-day Place des Arts were announced in 1955. The decision to build it was arrived at under pressure from Montreal's elite and was made possible in part through a public subscription campaign. At that time, the need for a performance hall that could accommodate large-scale events was beginning to be felt, probably reflecting the opening of Lincoln Center in New York (fig. 91). The agency of the world-renowned industrial designer Raymond Loewy was given a mandate for a design study, which was

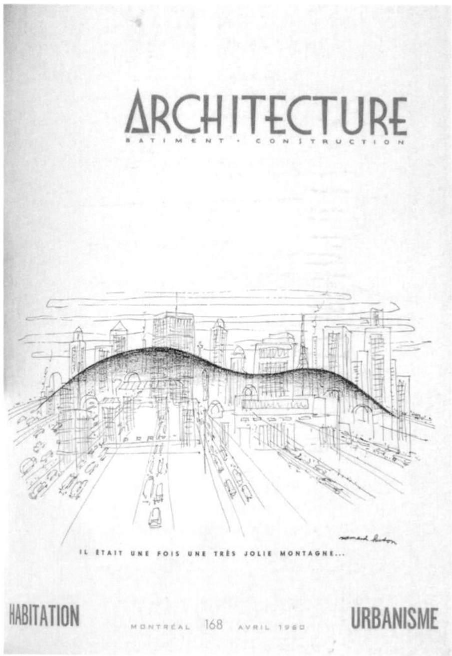

Figure 90
Architecture, bâtiment, construction 15, no. 168 (April 1960). Normand Hudon, artist. Canadian Centre for Architecture, Montréal

75 Mina Hamilton, "Designing a Cultural Center," *Industrial Design*, September 1964, 56–61.

considered by some to be exemplary.[75] The design envisaged by Loewy and his team was both ambitious and pragmatic. Since, given the high cost of expropriation, it was impossible to use the entire area bounded by Saint-Urbain, Sainte-Catherine, Jeanne-Mance, and de Maisonneuve, they organized the complex of three concert halls to incorporate the buildings that could not be removed. Part of the project's originality was that, like Place Ville-Marie, it contained a promenade of shops, in this case located under the raised central area by which concert-goers reached the individual concert halls, and these shops had entrances on Sainte-Catherine, forming a continuity with the street's vibrant commercial orientation. In the end, this option was not pursued when the plan was implemented by the architectural firm of Affleck, Desbarats, Dimakopoulos, Lebensold, Michaud, and Sise.

The transparent façades that give passers-by a view of the colourful crowd of concert-goers during intermission was reminiscent of Lincoln Center. The shape of the 3,000-seat concert hall was more like that of the new theatre in Münster, West Germany, by the architects Deilmann, Hauser, and Rave, which had an exterior peristyle that echoed the curved tiers of seats. But it may be that the shape really referred to the imagery of the Congrès internationaux d'architecture moderne (CIAM), so symbolic was it of the ultimate conquest to which this organization aspired, the conquest of the "heart of the city." At the time, the implementation of this cultural project catapulted its creators onto the national scene. Place des Arts reflected the experience they had acquired in their Queen Elizabeth Centre in Vancouver (1955–1959) and, at the other end of the country, contributed to their success in the competition for the Confederation Centre in Charlottetown (1961–1964).

Project followed project along this axis during the entire decade. In 1960, the architects André Blouin and Jean Gareau were dreaming of building a "Place de la Confédération" continuous with Place des Arts, an immense administrative, cultural, sports, and tourism complex set on an artificial floor raised above street level. There was even a short-lived plan to combine the services of the Canadian Broadcasting Corporation in that location. Finally, the Desjardins Group commissioned the urban planner Jean-Claude La Haye to study the site for a tertiary-sector complex, in partnership with the federal government. Construction started in 1972, with the provincial government but without the federal government, which was planning to invest in the Guy Favreau project just to the south. To the north, projects took shape more slowly, with studies by the architect Jean

76 On this subject, see the excellent dossier put together by Marc Choko and published under the title *Les Habitations Jeanne-Mance: Un projet social au centre-ville* (Montreal: Éditions Saint-Martin, 1995).

77 Irving Layton, "De Bullion Street," in *Collected Poems* (Toronto: McClelland and Stewart, 1965). See also Daniel Proulx, *Le Red Light de Montréal* (Montreal: VLB, 1997).

Michaud for the Institut de technologie de Montréal, undertaken in 1964, followed by a study for the Université du Québec, which was made public in May 1968 and concluded that there was good reason to implement the Place des Arts/Place d'Armes axis.

In a 1981 interview, La Haye said that he had had to convince the Quebec government ministers Paul Gérin-Lajoie and René Lévesque of the benefits of keeping the Université du Québec and Hydro-Québec in the city centre rather than exporting them to the periphery. It is true that this decision ensured a vital density and level of activity for the sector, which had already been cited by Daniel van Ginkel as a major point of concentration (fig. 92). This density would not have had the same quality if, as in certain American cities, it had excluded all forms of housing. The polemics surrounding the social mission of the Jeanne-Mance housing project, between Sanguinet, Ontario, Saint-Dominique, and de Maisonneuve, focused in part on the desirability of maintaining low-cost housing in the city centre.[76] Reactions to this housing project were mixed, and are a microcosm of the complexity of the relationships that were formed among the various protagonists on the municipal, provincial, and federal levels in regard to subsidized housing, and of the tensions that resulted on the ground.

There was basically a consensus on the choice of area. Identified by the Dozois Report, the neighbourhood was marked by run-down buildings and public spaces, low-income residents, and the tacitly acknowledged presence of a network of prostitution: "Rouged whores lean lips to narrow slits . . . Here private lust is public gain and shame," wrote the poet Irving Layton about de Bullion Street in the 1940s.[77] Criticism concentrated on the use for which it was destined, and included the financial stability of the project, the urban form chosen, and especially the timeliness of implementing a social program that would produce so little economic value in immediate proximity to the city's business centre.

Figure 92
Central area concentration plans, photograph, c. 1962. Van Ginkel Associates, architects and planners. Canadian Centre for Architecture, Montréal, Fonds van Ginkel

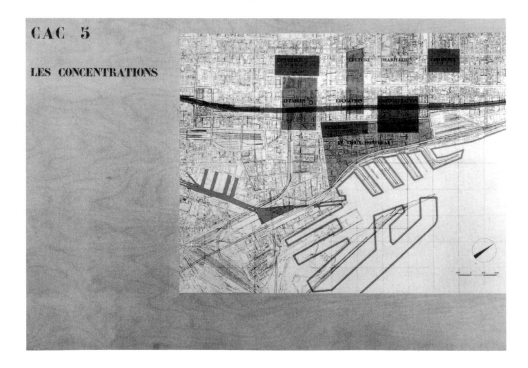

78 See the article "Le plan Dozois, coup de force contre l'Est" in *Le Devoir*, 27 June 1958, and the magazine editorials of Gaston Chapleau, "Le projet Dozois, progrès ou recul," *Architecture, bâtiment, construction* 12, no. 130 (January 1957): 15, and "Cité-Ondes, Cité-Familles," *Architecture, bâtiment, construction* 12, no. 138 (October 1957): 33.

79 Jean Drapeau, *Cité-Famille, un projet d'habitation et de relogement conçu d'après les besoins et les habitudes des familles de Montréal; Cité des ondes, un projet de suppression des taudis et de rénovation du coeur de Montréal* (Montreal, 1957).

In the late 1950s, municipal politics saw bitter skirmishes around this last point. For the Civic Party, led by Mayor Jean Drapeau with the active involvement of the businessman Pierre Desmarais, it was vital not to oppose a renovation project that had popular support; instead, an attempt would be made to redirect it, since some people felt that keeping low-income tenants in that location, subsidized by aid from the provincial and federal governments, represented a segregationist policy that prevented the French-Canadian population in the eastern parts of the city from increasing the value of their property and urban environment. Suspicion weighed heavily on what appeared to be an alliance between the populist government of Maurice Duplessis, which subsidized the project to the tune of a million dollars, and the English-speaking faction of the Municipal Council, who were suspected of protecting property values in neighbourhoods to the west by opposing speculative competition from the east.[78]

The Drapeau team had in reserve an alternative project that it hoped to be able to impose, in which the federal government had played a role. This was a "Cité des ondes"[79] – a "Radio City" – that would combine the studios and administrative offices of the CBC and Radio-Canada in one high-rise building. Excluded from the project was any social housing, which Drapeau hoped to export far to the north, in a "Family City" with "garden city" touches to be built on land along Metropolitan Boulevard owned by the Grand Séminaire. After obstructing the Dozois plan while seeking to preserve the principle of renovation, the mayor and his Civic Party were defeated at the polls in October 1957 on the basis of this proposal (figs. 93 and 94).

From then on, the way was open for the Jeanne-Mance housing project as it exists today, which was an amended version of a more radical initial concept; the changes made to the original version are a revelation about the mode of action of CMHC as the centralized real estate arm of the federal government (see pages 120–124). These high-rise buildings, aligned with geographic north and mostly disassociated from the geometry of the surrounding streets, are strikingly similar to what was being mass-produced at the same time in a number of other industrialized

Figures 93 and 94
Jean Drapeau, *Cité-Famille* (1957). Ville de Montréal, Service de la mise en valeur du territoire et du patrimoine

80 "La cité future: La cité radieuse au centre de Montréal,"
La Patrie, 18 July 1954.

countries, particularly in France, notably in the working-class neighbourhoods in the eastern and southern parts of Paris. The newspaper *La Patrie* made no mistake in calling them "The Radiant City,"[80] in reference to Le Corbusier's famous project. What was different about the Montreal project was that popular pressure led to substantial amendment of the original plan, which was modified by the architectural firm of Rother, Bland, Trudeau. From the original dozen 8-storey parallelepipeds, the central portion evolved into a combination of low-rise housing on two levels and a few typical CMHC high-rise buildings – one with 14 storeys and four with 12 storeys. They were built by the architectural firm of Greenspoon, Freedlander, Dunne and the architect Jacques Morin. This alternative took into account local resistance to high-rise housing and doubts about the relevance of such dwellings in a city consisting essentially of row houses.

Force versus Countervailing Force

Were Montrealers receptive to such swift change? For the French-speaking elite, this transformation of the physical environment was in keeping with the development of an urban culture whose social values were rapidly changing, moving to the beat of the Quiet Revolution (fig. 95). The case of the Quebec pavilion for Expo 67 was completely typical of this cultural development (see pages 56–61). It was observable first in the content of the pavilion, which devoted a large amount of its space to industry and the urban environment, the end result of Man's mastery of Nature. But it was the architecture of the pavilion, chosen through a competition open to architects in the province, that most accurately reflected Quebec's image of itself: a rectangular parallelepiped of reflective glass, built with the modernist techniques of the International Style, whose individuality resulted from its slightly sloping façades. Designed by the architects Papineau,

Figure 95
Sketch of Place Bonaventure float for Saint-Jean-Baptiste parade, 1968. Société Saint-Jean-Baptiste. Photograph: Studio Fernand Laparé. Centre de Montréal des Archives nationales du Québec

81 Marie-Josée Therrien and France Vanlaethem, "Modern Architecture in Canada, 1940-1967," in *Back From Utopia: The Challenge of the Modern Movement*, ed. Hubert-Jan Henket and Hilde Heynen (Rotterdam: 010 Publishers, 2002).

Gérin-Lajoie, Le Blanc, and Luc Durand, it was symbolic of a society that, in 1967, considered itself to be newborn on the international scene. General de Gaulle's harangue on 24 July 1967, when he stood on the balcony of Montreal's City Hall and shouted out his faith in a free Quebec, was part of this rebirth.

Montreal as World-Class City

Architectural evidence of the new Montreal was noticeable almost everywhere in the city. In contrast to the prosperous period of growth at the turn of the century, it was no longer exclusively large American architectural firms that were competing with local architects for prestigious commissions, but professionals with a wide variety of backgrounds, some of whom settled in Montreal.[81] Among them, the very talented Peter Dickinson from Britain, based in Toronto and Montreal, who designed the Canadian Imperial Bank of Commerce tower (fig. 96), was in

Figure 96
Canadian Imperial Bank of Commerce Building under construction, 19 June 1961. Peter Dickinson and Associates, architects. Photograph: Hayward Studios Ltd. Library and Archives Canada, Ottawa, PA-77115

Figure 97
Place de la Concorde, perspective detail, 22 April 1964. Alvar Aalto, architect. Diazotype, 56 x 95 cm. Canadian Centre for Architecture, Montréal, Fonds Mayerovitch and Bernstein

competition with the Chinese-born American architect I.M. Pei over Place Ville-Marie, and with the large and world-renowned architectural firm of Skidmore, Owings, and Merrill over the CIL Building. Canadian architects such as Victor Prus (originally from Poland), Daniel van Ginkel (from the Netherlands), and André Blouin (from France) were also very active.

Van Ginkel, a member of CIAM and Team X, used Montreal as a springboard for a career that took him to such varied locations as New York City and Newfoundland. André Blouin, whose plans were frequently published in the journal *L'Architecture d'aujourd'hui*, was very active in Montreal. Blouin had organized an exhibition on Le Corbusier shown in December 1959 in Redpath Hall on the campus of McGill University; his relation to Le Corbusier is evident in his own work. In addition to these architects, developers did not hesitate to call on the great names of modern architecture, like the American architect of German origin Mies van der Rohe for Westmount Square, the Italians Luigi Moretti and Pier Luigi Nervi for the Stock Exchange complex, and the Finnish architect Alvar Aalto, at one time considered for the Cité Concordia project (fig. 97). For Expo 67, the international architectural presence was augmented by names such as Frei Otto for the West German pavilion and Buckminster Fuller for that of the United States. The major Montreal firm involved was Affleck, Desbarats, Dimakopoulos,

82 Aubin, *City for Sale.*

83 Marcel Sévigny, *Trente ans de politique municipale* (Montreal: Ecosociété, 2001).

Lebensold, Michaud, and Sise (Place Bonaventure), under the leadership of Ray Affleck, which then took off to conquer Canada. Mention should also be made of unique talents such as the Château Champlain's architects, Roger D'Astous and Jean-Paul Pothier.

This opening up of Montreal to the world had a corollary that underlay it but was imperceptible to observers at the time, although it had an enormous effect on the new look of the city: the internationalization of the sources of capital invested in real estate development in the metropolitan area, which could come from anywhere in the world and whose suppliers were largely indifferent to the architecture or urban form of its eventual physical manifestation.[82] This was only one of the inherent paradoxes of French-Canadian society: the members of its elite were fascinated by the transformation taking place before their very eyes, and were actively involved in it for the first time in history, but they continued to regard this transformation as something in the hands of the English-speaking minority, while that minority was itself experiencing intense competition for control of capital in areas it had historically considered its own.

Countervailing Forces

The fascinating Sixties. The brutal Sixties. The dizzying construction site of a metropolitan area in full transformation mode, in which expressway trenches, metro tunnels, and gravel quarries were being dynamited, was the first supplier of explosives to the FLQ (Front de libération du Québec). Viewed after the fact, the bombs set off by the different terrorist cells might appear to have been following a design for some kind of situational project to call attention to the major sources of capital in the city (strikebound factories, mailboxes in neighbourhoods that housed the capitalist elite, etc.) and to those assigned to protect them (military barracks). But in light of the new economic geography in which Montreal was enmeshed, this struggle seems to have been a rear-guard action.

Simultaneously with demolition, a countervailing force was emerging in the neighbourhoods affected by urban renewal, less ideologically oriented and readier to work with the powers that be (figs. 98 and 99).[83] The first studies involving consultation with the local population were conducted early in the decade,

Figure 98
On fait le tracé de la future autoroute, n.d. Cartoon by Berthio. Pen and black ink on cardboard, 30.5 x 28.2 cm. Centre de Montréal des Archives nationales du Québec

Figure 99
Moi qui n'ai jamais pu me payer une auto . . . , 28 November 1966. Cartoon by Berthio. Pen and black ink and wash on cardboard, 30.5 x 28 cm. Centre de Montréal des Archives nationales du Québec

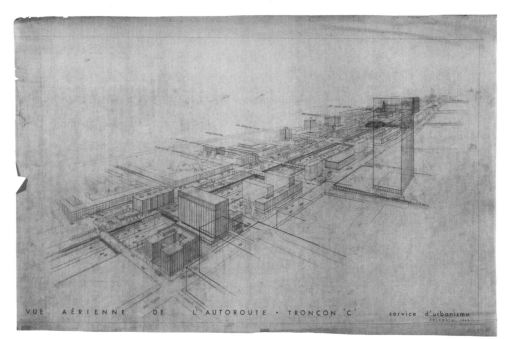

Figure 100
Îlots Saint-Martin, photograph of presentation model, 1968. Ouellet, Reeves, Alain, architects. Canadian Centre for Architecture, Montréal, Fonds Jean Ouellet

Figure 101
Dwellings expropriated for the construction of the east-west expressway, May 1971. Photograph: Brian Merrett. Collection Brian Merrett

Figure 102
East-west expressway, aerial perspective of section C, Place d'Armes area, 1963. City Planning Department, City of Montreal. Sepia diazotype with fibre-tip pen applied to verso, 67.2 x 100.3 cm. Ville de Montréal, Service de la mise en valeur du territoire et du patrimoine

84 Michel Blondin, *Le projet St-Henri: Description et analyse d'un projet centré sur la participation des citoyens* (Montreal: Conseil des oeuvres de Montréal, 1965).

85 On the evolution of this policy, see the very detailed account by Guy R. Legault in *La ville qu'on a bâtie* (Montreal: Liber, 2002).

86 Montreal Council of Social Agencies, *Rapport de la Commission d'audiences publiques populaires sur l'autoroute est-ouest à Montréal* (Montreal, 1971), and the episode on cars, *L'automobile*, in the documentary series *Urbanose*, directed by Michel Régnier (NFB, 1972).

as part of the renovation of Little Burgundy, a working-class neighbourhood just south of the planned route of the east-west expressway.[84] The consultations led to a revitalized neighbourhood that was relatively in keeping with Montreal's urban form and that also took into account the social and health concerns of the era (fig. 100).[85] The destruction caused by the building of the expressway outweighed the positive gains from the renovation projects, and considerable social pressure was required to counter it and prevent the disapearance of hundreds of dwellings near the Champlain Bridge (figs. 101 and 102).[86] Paradoxically, the top prize for eradicating working-class housing was won hands down by the Societé du renouvellement de l'est de Montréal, for its (never realized) Unest project, an east-end workers' university, which would have been

87 The Société du renouvellement de l'est de Montréal was made up of French-speaking businessmen and developers who pressured the various levels of government to develop the eastern part of the city so that it could compete with the business centre in the western part. The real estate development initiated by the Société included Place Frontenac (500 units, subsidized by CMHC) and Résidence Dupuis (212 units).

even more destructive than the razing of the "Faubourg à la mélasse" to make room for the CBC and Radio-Canada: the verdant campus was supposed to extend from Lafontaine Park all the way to Saint-Urbain Street between Pine Avenue and Rachel (figs. 103 and 104).[87]

Private speculative renovation of the more extreme kind moderated only gradually as Montrealers developed an interest in the city that was disappearing before their very eyes, and whose form – a product of its history – was finally being recognized as the heritage of a specific culture. This recognition was the driving force behind the exhibition (and accompanying publication) *Montreal: Plus or Minus?* conceived by the architect Melvin Charney for the Montreal Museum of Fine Arts. André Major wrote in his poem "Au coeur de la ville": "Mais toi quand tu n'as rien à faire / tu vas au bord de l'eau / le long des quais / et tu te demandes si Montréal a du coeur / même si tu vis au coeur de la ville" (But when

Figure 103
Site proposal for the Maison de Radio-Canada, perspective sketch, c. 1959–1960. André Blouin, architect, for the Centre commercial de Montréal Inc. Photostat, 27.5 x 48.5 cm. Ville de Montréal, Gestion de documents et archives

Figure 104
Preliminary scheme for a university in the eastern part of Montreal. La société du renouvellement de l'est de Montréal, *L'UNEST: La rénovation de l'est de Montréal par la création d'une université ouvrière* (September 1966). Canadian Centre for Architecture, Montreal, Fonds Mayerovitch and Bernstein

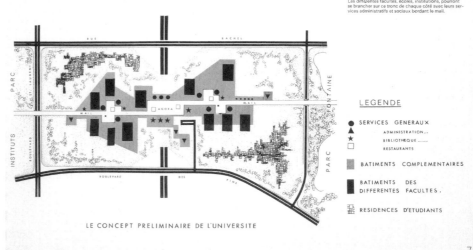

Figure 105
Demolition of the Van Horne house, 1973. Photograph:
Allan R. Leishman. Library and Archives Canada, Ottawa,
PA-159640

Figure 106
**Cité Concordia, presentation panel, 1962. Mayerovitch and
Bernstein, architects.** Gouache on photograph, on wood
support, 63.5 x 92 cm. Canadian Centre for Architecture,
Montréal, Fonds Mayerovitch and Bernstein

88 In Melvin Charney, *Montreal: Plus or Minus?* (Montreal:
    Montreal Museum of Fine Arts, 1972), 24.
89 Martin Drouin, "Les campagnes de sauvegarde de la
    maison Van Horne et du couvent des Soeurs grises ou
    les questionnements d'une identité urbaine (Montréal,
    1973–1976)," *Journal of the Society for the Study of
    Architecture in Canada* 26, no. 3–4 (2001): 25–36.

you've nothing better to do / you walk along the water's edge / along the docks
/ and you wonder whether Montreal has a heart / even though you live in the
heart of the city)."[88]

    The dual episode of the Van Horne house and the Grey Nuns' convent,
the one disappearing under the picks of the demolition team and the other rescued from the greed of developers, was a turning point (fig. 105).[89] Another event,
no less symbolic, was the struggle surrounding the Milton-Park project, so named
because of the two streets crossing it. This real estate development project provided for the destruction of housing located east of the McGill University campus,

90 This episode was noticed abroad; see Manuel Castells, *Luttes urbaines et pouvoir politique* (Paris: François Maspero, 1975).

91 From the texts by Alison and Peter Smithson that accompanied the chart "Urban Reidentification" at CIAM 9 (1953). Alison Smithson, *The Emergence of Team X out of CIAM : Documents* (London, 1982), quoted by Eric Mumford in *The CIAM Discourse on Urbanism, 1928–1960* (Cambridge, Mass.: MIT Press, 2000), 234–235.

92 La Haye and Ouellet, "'Place Desjardins': Thématique et concept," typewritten report (1971), 8.

93 Peter Blake, "Downtown in 3-D," *The Architectural Forum* 125, no. 2 (September 1966), 31–48.

and residents opposed it, sometimes violently (fig. 106). The low-key renovation that ended the confrontations, halfway between the extensive demolition desired by the developers and the preservation of the status quo demanded by local associations, demonstrated the limits of citizen action when faced with the power of free enterprise.[90] It should be noted, however, that in scarcely more than a decade, CMHC moved from brutal renovation, as in the Jeanne-Mance housing project, to support for cooperative co-ownership and more moderate renovation in the Milton-Park neighbourhood.

What characterized the end of the period was not a succession of different rationales, by which destructive renovation was replaced by conservation, but rather the coexistence of two divergent socio-economic forces, the second of which took a little longer to emerge as a credible alternative. And even today, the two principles are engaged in a struggle over the outcome of many projects.

CIAM's Ultimate Dream

The problem of reidentifying man with his environment (contents and container) cannot be achieved by using hierarchical forms of house-groupings, streets, squares, greens, etc., as the social reality they presented no longer exists. In the complex of association that is a community, social cohesion can only be achieved if ease of movement is possible and this provides us with only second law, [sic] that height (density) should increase as the total population increases, and vice versa. In a large city with high buildings, in order to keep ease of movement, we propose a multilevel city with residential "streets-in-the-air." These are linked together in a multilevel continuous complex, connected where necessary to work and to those ground elements that are necessary at each level of association. Our hierarchy of associations is woven into a modulated continuum representing the true complexity of human association . . . We are of the opinion that such a hierarchy of human associations should replace the functional hierarchy of the "Charte d'Athènes."[91]

While critical of some of the collateral effects of urban renewal, particularly on the social fabric of working-class neighbourhoods, Montrealers remained enthusiastic even in the face of the upheaval they witnessed and experienced in the 1960s. For Jean-Claude La Haye, the urban planner responsible for Complexe Desjardins (which brought the period to a close), "implementation of this project was supposed to commemorate and be the crowning achievement of a decisive stage in the socio-economic development of the French-Canadian collectivity."[92] But the reasons for this enthusiasm were not merely local. They also sprang from the fact that the dynamic was part of a movement shared by the majority of Western societies. And the attention that critics of architecture and urban planning brought to bear on the major transformations in the city centre were proportionate to their expectations for the era, which Montreal was seemingly supposed to embody.

This infatuation can be seen in Peter Blake's long article in *The Architectural Forum* in which he noted the "happy combination of expert foresight, private initiative, and luck" by which "Montreal is about to become the first twentieth-century city in North America" (see pages 180–185).[93] Blake's reference to the city's "multilevel core" would have fitted neatly into the great debate that had raged within the ranks of CIAM ever since their 1951 meeting in Hoddesdon,

94 Ibid.

95 Reyner Banham, *The New Brutalism* (London: Architectural Press, 1966).

96 Reyner Banham, "Megacity Montreal," in *Megastructure: Urban Futures of the Recent Past* (London: Thames and Hudson, 1976), 105–130.

97 From the cover of *Life* magazine, 28 April 1967; see the article by Tom Prideaux, "Architecture's Leap into the Future," 32–41.

98 Warren Chalk, "Hardware of a New World," *The Architectural Forum* 125, no. 3 (October 1966): 47–50.

99 Moshe Safdie, *Beyond Habitat*, ed. John Kettle (Montreal: Tundra, 1970).

100 Reyner Banham, *Age of the Masters: A Personal View of Modern Architecture* (New York: Harper and Row, 1975), 144–146.

England, which was devoted to that very topic. The attributes of Montreal that he mentioned were an echo of emblematic projects like the 1958 plans by Alison and Peter Smithson to rebuild the centre of Berlin: "What sets this core apart is not so much the towers as their spreading roots in a multilevel network of shops, transportation systems, and pedestrian promenades."[94]

Two years later, it was again in Montreal that the British architecture critic and historian Reyner Banham explored the matter, continuing his account of the discovery of "another kind of architecture" that he had first commented on in 1966 in his work on the new Brutalism.[95] Habitat 67, the theme pavilions, Place Bonaventure: the numerous megastructures developed on the Expo 67 site and in the city itself provided him with the occasion; he even wondered whether Montreal itself had not become a "megacity."[96]

The City and Its Double

In his account, Banham did not distinguish between the two sites – Expo 67 and the city centre – out of which the buildings, infrastructure, and megastructures emerged. They did not, however, share the same history. Expo 67, for its part, created a sort of pragmatic utopia consisting of fragments of leading-edge architectural and urban planning ideas, in line with those that had preceded them. On the other hand, the complex negotiations between the turn-of-the-century city and such mastodons as Place Ville-Marie and Place Bonaventure took on a veritable dynamic of "reidentification."

The lukewarm reception accorded to Expo 67 by architecture critics contrasted with the majority of accounts by news reporters. *Life* magazine's writers and photographers were dazzled by the spectacle – "Tomorrow Soars In at the Fair"[97] – while in the pages of *L'Architecture d'aujourd'hui* Sibyl Moholy-Nagy saw it as nothing but a collection of hats (an allusion to the ubiquitous polyhedra). It is true that Expo 67 sealed the fate of more than one dream. The huge difficulties and expenses involved in assembling the theme complex "Man the Explorer" led to complaints that such a megastructure was simply unrealistic, despite Warren Chalk's spirited defence of it.[98] The problem was similar in the case of the industrialization of the housing units so dear to Moshe Safdie, which he himself criticized afterwards in *Beyond Habitat*.[99] And when Banham returned to the subject of Habitat 67 several years later, he finally rejected it, which was unexpected in light of his favourable assessment in the 1960s.[100]

But the real innovation lay elsewhere, in fact; it was not formal but rather technical and systemic. It lay in the culmination of the frenzy that had set technicians and directors from every country (and particularly from Canada – see pages 70–73) to imagining and creating audiovisual productions that pushed back the boundaries of what could be done with cinematography. The results they achieved were beyond comparison with normally available technology, whether they took the form of Labyrinth's five synchronized screens or the Czechoslovak pavilion's interactive projection with multiple-choice scenarios.

Jacques Folch-Ribas felt that at Expo 67, the concept of complementary means of transportation, combined in a way that took into account the speed

101 Jacques Folch-Ribas, "Urbanisme et architecture à l'exposition internationale," *Vie des Arts*, no. 48 (Fall 1967): 16–17.

102 See, for example, Martin Meyerson and Edward C. Banfield, *Boston: The Job Ahead* (Cambridge, Mass.: Harvard University Press, 1966).

103 Donald Canty, "Philadelphia's Giant Shopping Machine," *The Architectural Forum* 125, no. 4 (November 1966), 38–43.

104 Zvi Hecker, "Proposition pour un nouveau centre à Montréal," *L'Architecture d'aujourd'hui*, no. 158 (October–November 1971), xxvii–xxx.

105 Michel Lincourt and Harry Parnass, "Métro éducation Montréal," *L'Architecture d'aujourd'hui*, no. 153 (January 1971), 54–59.

106 Jean-Guy Pilon, "Présentation," *Liberté*, no. 28 [vol. 5, no. 4] (July–August 1963), 275.

of each, had finally been implemented.[101] Expo-Express, the mini-rail, the cable car, the vaporetto, the hovercraft, and the little electric train that made local stops represented the whole panoply of transport that had been the subject of theorizing throughout the 1960s and were generally regarded as prototypical of the future of urban mobility.[102] However, the isolation of the site kept the larger-scale deployment of such mixed transport in check, and it never did spread to the rest of the city. The Expo-Express could not leave the port area to reach Place Bonaventure or the parking lot on the Radio-Canada site, as originally envisaged by the urban planners; no vaporetto braved the river's currents; the cable car carried its passengers inexorably back to where they started. Only the metro linked the site to the urban network. Isolated in the middle of the Saint Lawrence River, all this was merely a picturesque demonstration.

In the real city across the river, the megastructures may not have been innovative in form, but they were innovative in their planned use, social practices, and image. The combinations of means and speeds of transportation were less picturesque but highly efficient: expressways, boulevards, and streets; trains, metros, buses, and underground shopping centres; and intermodal facilities that a city like Philadelphia could only dream of at the time.[103]

The carry-over from the laboratory that was Expo 67 to the real city itself took place only in a "virtual" sense, through the efforts of a handful of dedicated visionaries who used Montreal to exemplify their avant-garde ideas and exploited its international status to launch these ideas into the wider world (see pages 160–163). They included Peter Cook, of the British group Archigram, with his "Montreal Tower," and Zvi Hecker, a German-born Israeli who, while teaching at Laval University in Quebec City, developed an interest in the Montreal site and exhibited a three-dimensional model of the downtown that has much in common with the spatial experiments of Yona Friedman in Paris and Kenzo Tange in Tokyo.[104] In their own way, Michel Lincourt and Harry Parnass shared and manifested the concerns of the architects of the Free University of Berlin, Candilis, Josic, and Woods, of Team X, in imagining education as the driving force behind urban organization.[105] A similar amalgam of pragmatism and theory could be discerned in an astonishing design by the City Planning Department, in which the future of the city was maintained in an improbable tension between reality and fiction: the sides of the Bonaventure Expressway were to be invaded by a sprawling megastructure from which the twin towers of the Stock Exchange would emerge (fig. 107).

Since Montrealers already identified strongly with their city, the process of defining a new identity was something they approached with both curiosity and alarm. Jean-Guy Pilon expressed this on behalf of his editorial team in the preface to an issue of the magazine *Liberté* devoted to Montreal: "I can affirm that in return, we are all very attached to Montreal, that this city is ours. If it does not always respond to us with the same tenderness we lavish on it, it has its own reasons, and we are reticent about asking what they are. Very strong ties keep us in its arms, ties or passions whose strength and intensity we have all experienced to some degree at one time or another."[106] A similar message was conveyed by

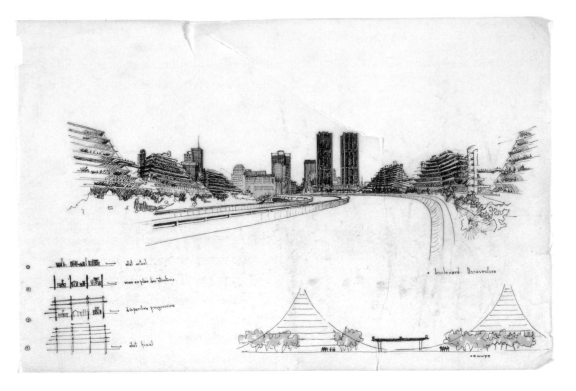

Figure 107
**Bonaventure Expressway, perspective and sections,
c. 1965. City Planning Department, City of Montreal.**
Black and green ink and graphite on tracing paper,
30.5 x 45.5 cm. Ville de Montréal, Service de la mise en
valeur du territoire et du patrimoine

107 Pierre Gravel, *À perte de temps* (Toronto: Anansi;
     Montreal, Parti pris, 1969), 26.
108 Their studies on traffic, the siting of Expo 67, and the
     airport are all used as opportunities to suggest general
     analyses and specific solutions. Similarly, as early as
     1961–1963, the large-scale study on the revitalization
     of Old Montreal defined the factors in an equation
     that has never been resolved (Montreal's City Planning
     Department still has the maquette that was created
     at the time). Canadian Centre for Architecture,
     Montréal, Fonds van Ginkel, 27-A17.

novelists such as Mordecai Richler (quoted in the epigraph to this essay) and
an equally unsettled Pierre Gravel: "To tell the truth, the city didn't exist. In its
place, a big, huge, monstrous thing that had never been given a name sprawled
around a mountain and ended by dwindling into suburbs: east, west, north, a few
scattered slums . . . In the centre, glass and girders. An artificial heart. Here and
there, banks, offices, headquarters, insurance companies, wide sidewalks, and a
bus line. That was all. Under those conditions, it was hard to talk about it as a city.
And in fact, people didn't talk about it: they lived in it."[107]

Criticism and History

A few years later, even before the 1976 Olympic Games fiasco, it was obvious that
Montrealers were in for a rude awakening. The large-scale plans for a metropolis
with 5 million inhabitants were not merely at a standstill; they had left the city
centre devastated, as the empty lots that had been cleared to make room for
profitable real estate development no longer found any takers. During the 1970s,
oceans of parking lots; today, polluting highway systems with a past sullied by
destruction: the urban planning of the glorious decades following World War II
surely merits public censure. And yet it was remarkable in a number of ways.

In terms of social and urban history, a case could be made that this
period was the one in which plans for society coincided with the embodiment
of such ambitions in real space, on the scale of a metropolis that would become
their heart. It takes only a small step to apply this thesis to architecture and
urban planning as well. Of crucial relevance to this interpretation are the studies carried out by Daniel van Ginkel and his wife, Blanche Lemco, who in their
work for the City Planning Department introduced some of the findings from the
ongoing discussion they had participated in as members of Team X.[108] Along with

109 Jean-Claude Marsan, *Montréal en évolution: Historique du développement de l'architecture et de l'environnement urbain montréalais* (Montreal: Fides, 1974).

110 Jean-Claude Marsan, "L'aménagement du Vieux-Port de Montréal: Les avatars de l'urbanisme promoteur," in *L'aménagement urbain: Promesses et défis*, ed. Annick Germain (Quebec City: Institut québécois de recherche sur la culture, 1991), 27–60.

111 Y. Buissière and Y. Dallaire, "Tendances socio-démographiques et demande de transport dans quatre régions métropolitaines canadiennes: Eléments de prospective," in *Plan Canada*, May 1994, 9–16.

112 M.A. Goldberg and J. Mercer, *The Myth of the North American City: Continentalism Challenged* (Vancouver: University of British Columbia Press, 1986).

113 Annick Germain and Damaris Rose, *Montréal: The Quest for a Metropolis* (Toronto: Wiley, 2000), 73.

the technical services project, guided by the urban planner Hans Blumenfeld, they provided Montreal with the terms of its metropolitan equation: extension, densification, and reidentification. This structure was in striking contrast to that of so many cities of the Western world whose downtowns were drained of their vitality by the renovation policies of the time. What happened to Montreal was quite special.

If we are to understand why this was so, we must not confuse history with criticism. In its day, Jean-Claude Marsan's *Montréal en évolution*[109] opened up unexplored paths toward an understanding of Montreal's urban dynamics, in the same vein as the "civic surveys" favoured by the followers of Patrick Geddes. Since then, scholarly studies have come thick and fast, and we would be well advised to move beyond the type of erudite criticism Marsan sometimes used in characterizing the most recent period of Montreal's transformation. A close-up view is always a partial one; moreover, it may compromise the rigour and fair-mindedness with which the 1960s should be approached. We need to step back a pace if we are to construct a sound critique, supported by the historical reality, which can help us get past the unsatisfactory situations of our own day. For example, the star-shaped city noted by Marsan[110] and the relative compactness that characterized the urban area when Buissière and Dallaire[111] or Goldberg and Mercer[112] compared it with American cities were by no means the result of chance. We must look beyond the *a priori* judgment that the positive side of contemporary Montreal "owes not so much to careful planning as to 'planning by not planning.'"[113] Such a step is an essential precondition for initiating a constructive debate that can draw lessons from past experiences and, provided they have been accurately described, transcend them.

Structure
and Society

Places and
Players

Perceptions

Expo 67

Urban Ills

The ills afflicting Montreal – traffic congestion, overcrowding, overpopulation, unsuitable and run-down housing – had been identified for several decades. The City Planning Department, created in 1941, initially focused on upgrading the road system and creating new parks. As the 1944 master plan indicates, the other major priority at the time was zoning, which assigns different types of uses to different parts of a city.

However, the concern that weighed more and more heavily on people's minds was housing. The federal government gradually intervened in this area, which had traditionally been left to the initiative of private enterprise. In 1945, the Central Mortgage and Housing Corporation (CMHC) was created to administer the National Housing Act of 1938, which enabled the federal minister of finance to grant reduced-rate loans to provincial and municipal governments or their agencies so that low-income families could be assisted in obtaining decent subsidized housing. A 1944 amendment to the Act authorized the central government to subsidize the demolition of slums, provided they were replaced with low-rental housing, and so city planners were now confronted with the housing issue. At the time, Montreal was considered to be the Canadian city with the most dire housing needs; according to the City Planning Department's Housing Committee, there was a shortage of 50,000 dwelling units in 1943. Pressured by groups of concerned citizens and by various government agencies, the municipality initiated a major study of housing conditions.

Figure 108
**Back of 1589 de Bullion Street,
June 1959.** Library and Archives
Canada, Ottawa, PA-119727

Figure 109
Slum House, from the National Film Board series *Urbanose*, directed by Michel Régnier. **Yukari Ochiai, artist.** Woodcut on paper, 1971. Collection Yukari Ochiai

Figure 110
Visit to the Dozois sector, May 1957, where the Jeanne-Mance housing project would later be built. Library and Archives Canada, Ottawa, PA-123794

Figure 111
The Automobile, from the
National Film Board series
Urbanose, directed by Michel
Régnier. Yukari Ochiai, artist.
Woodcut on paper, 1971.
Collection Yukari Ochiai

Figure 112
Advisory Committee on Slum
Clearance and Low-Rental
Housing, City of Montreal,
*Proposed Redevelopment of a
Blighted Residential Area and
Construction of Low Rental
Housing* (1954). Canadian Centre
for Architecture, Montréal

The 13 areas studied were among those in which housing and industry overlapped to an excessive degree (see page 80). The area selected for the project was the Jeanne-Mance site, where some of the most shocking photographs of working-class poverty were taken. In that neighbourhood of prostitution, physical and moral decay went hand in hand. Unfit housing and needy people seemed to be inextricably linked. Although the issue was never dealt with directly during the discussions held at the time, eradication of one ill was presumably considered an opportunity to eliminate the other.

There were those who felt that in light of modern trends in urban planning the downtown area should be reserved for commercial, administrative, and cultural uses, and should exclude housing, especially for the working class. In this view, the demolition of unfit housing was an opportunity not to build new housing, but to develop a part of the city that was falling behind when compared with areas to the west. As a result, a policy that would concentrate on the section between Bleury and Saint-Urbain would later be adopted (see pages 174–179).

Figure 113
Jeanne-Mance housing project, view after construction, July 1960. Rother, Bland, Trudeau, planning consultants; Greenspoon, Freedlander, Dunne, with Jacques Morin, architects. Library and Archives Canada, Ottawa, PA-113320

**Structure
and Society**

Places and
Players

Perceptions

Expo 67

Standardization
and Models

In the years following World War II, successive federal governments, prompted by the results of the interventionist policy required for the war effort, used Keynesian planning to reduce regional disparities and standardize the country's infrastructures and facilities (Craig Brown, ed., *The Illustrated History of Canada* [Toronto: Lester and Orpen Dennys, 1987], 469–543). This planning was based on certain technologies that left their mark on the national territory, particularly in the area of housing and transportation.

The financial assistance for the expansion of Trans-Canada Air Lines reflected the Department of Transport's

growing involvement in the development and maintenance of the airports, with all the standardization required for security and for compliance with international civil aviation norms (T.M. McGrath, *History of Canadian Airports* [Toronto: Lugus, 1992], 18–21). The other focus of development – a symbol of Canadian unity like the railway in the previous century – was the Trans-Canada Highway, for which federal aid to the provinces and municipalities was increased, in view of the growing number of Canadians who were acquiring and driving motor vehicles. Here, too, the standardization of bridges, tunnels, overpasses, and

lane configurations was essential to ensure safety. At the same time, careful consideration also had to be given to regional planning throughout Canada, since the highway would become an expressway as it approached the cities it was to run through, like the Queensway in Ottawa (even though the 1950 master plan for that city anticipated that it would remain outside the green belt).

In line with the growth in state planning power, CMHC submitted a brief to the Royal Commission on Canada's Economic Prospects in which it unequivocally asserted that "the provision of adequate shelter can be regarded as an essential prerequisite in releasing the full productive powers of the people. Housing is required in the right places and at the right price in order to bring the labour force into action where and when it is needed" (*Housing and Urban Growth in Canada* [Ottawa: CMHC, 1956], 5). This view sometimes resulted in CMHC's direct involvement in the production of housing, such as the renewal projects in Vancouver (McLean Park and Skeena Street), Montreal (the first version of the Jeanne-Mance housing project), and Halifax (Mulgrave Park), where the chief services architect, Ian MacLennan, designed a single standard-rise building. The other approach, which certainly took precedence, was to promote standard single-family dwellings. These dwellings were central to a system that aimed to encourage both the development of small suburban communities and the transition in the homebuilding industry from craft-based methods to mass production – an obsession that explained, in part, the success of Moshe Safdie's Habitat 67 project.

As Canada's centennial celebrations drew near, the federal government turned its attention to cultural projects, subsidizing the construction of museums and concert halls, the completion of which was managed locally.

ROUTE TRANSCANADIENNE SUR L'ÎLE DE MONTRÉAL
Autoroute "EST-OUEST"

VOIES EN CHARPENTE DE L'ÉCHANGEUR TURCOT À LA RUE GUY

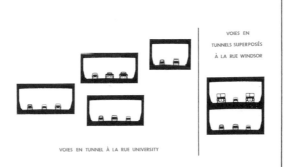

VOIES EN TUNNELS SUPERPOSÉS À LA RUE WINDSOR

VOIES EN TUNNEL À LA RUE UNIVERSITY

Propriétaire : Gouvernement du Québec	
1) Section Échangeur Turcot — Rue Fullum	
Ingénieurs-conseils :	
Lalonde, Valois, Lamarre, Valois & Associés	
TRONÇONS	
QIR 50	Échangeur Turcot (travaux complétés)
	Entrepreneur général : Janin Construction Ltée
QIR 51	Échangeur University (travaux complétés)
	Entrepreneur général : Entreprise conjointe : Atlas, Dufresne, Pitt
QIR 52	Mur de soutènement (travaux complétés)
	Entrepreneur général : Simard-Beaudry Inc.
QIR 53	Échangeur Turcot à la rue Greene (travaux en cours)
	Entrepreneur général : Janin Construction Ltée
QIR 54	Rue Greene à la rue Fulford (travaux en cours)
	Entrepreneur général : Françon Limitée
QIR 55	Rue Fulford à la rue de la Montagne (travaux en cours)
	Entrepreneur général : Miron Ltée
QIR 56	Rue de la Montagne à la rue University (travaux en cours)
	Entrepreneur général : Desourdy Construction Ltée
QIR 57	Finition et éclairage des tunnels (étude complétée — réalisation au cours de 1972)
QIR 58	Rue University à la rue Bleury (travaux en cours)
	Entrepreneur général : Janin Construction Ltée
QIR 60	Rue Bleury à la rue Sanguinet (travaux en cours)
	Entrepreneur général : Entreprise conjointe : Les Mir, Duranceau, Desourdy
QIR 61	Rue Sanguinet à la rue Fullum (projet à l'étude)
2) Section Rue Fullum — Pont tunnel L.-H. Lafontaine	
Ingénieurs-conseils : Desjardins, Sauriol & Associés	
TRONÇONS	
QIR 62	Rue Fullum à la rue Moreau (projet à l'étude)
QIR 63	Rue Moreau à la rue Viau (projet à l'étude)
QIR 59	Rue Viau au pont tunnel L.-H. Lafontaine (projet à l'étude)

VOIES EN CHARPENTE DE LA RUE FULLUM À LA RUE MOREAU

RUE LOCALE   RUE NOTRE-DAME

VOIES A NIVEAU DE LA RUE MOREAU A LA RUE VIAU

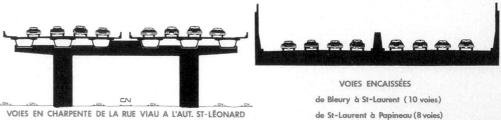

VOIES EN CHARPENTE DE LA RUE VIAU A L'AUT. ST-LÉONARD

VOIES ENCAISSÉES
de Bleury à St-Laurent (10 voies)
de St-Laurent à Papineau (8 voies)

Figure 115
Trans-Canada Highway, typical transverse sections, 1963. Lalonde, Valois, Lamarre, Valois, and Associates, engineers; Quebec Department of Roads and Public Works. *L'Ingénieur*, November 1971, 61. Bibliothèque des sciences de l'Université du Québec à Montréal

Figure 116
Central Mortgage and Housing Corporation, *Principes pour le groupement de petites maisons* **(1954).** Published in English as *Principles of Small House Grouping.* Canadian Centre for Architecture, Montréal

Figure 117
"Design 141." Central Mortgage and Housing Corporation, *House Designs* **(1974), 18.** Canadian Centre for Architecture, Montréal

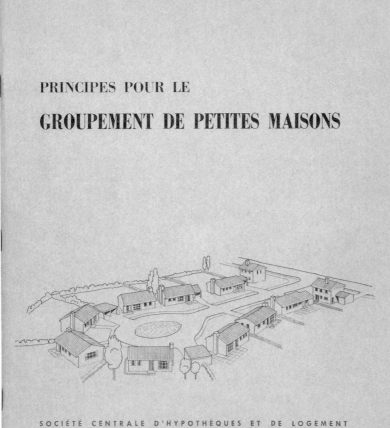

PRINCIPES POUR LE

GROUPEMENT DE PETITES MAISONS

SOCIÉTÉ CENTRALE D'HYPOTHÈQUES ET DE LOGEMENT

OTTAWA—CANADA

18

DESIGN / MODÈLE 141 Architect/Architecte: R. T. AFFLECK, Montréal, Qué.

The living room of this brick-veneer bungalow, overlooking the back garden for privacy, extends into an all-purpose area that can be closed off to become a study or guest room. The openness of the living room, dining room and kitchen give a feeling of space. Large closets are located throughout the house and the placing of windows allows for cross ventilation. There is ample clear space in the basement which could be made into a playroom. The same house with a frame exterior is available as Design 142.

Area/Aire: 1,049 □′

Le vivoir de ce bungalow en brique sur bois donne sur le jardin arrière pour plus d'intimité et se prolonge dans une aire polyvalente qui peut être isolée et ainsi servir de cabinet de travail ou de chambre d'amis. Les plans ouverts du vivoir, de la salle à manger et de la cuisine augmentent l'impression de spaciosité. Les garde-robes sont spacieuses et les fenêtres situées pour permettre la ventilation transversale. Le sous-sol, très dégagé, pourrait être aménagé en salle de jeu. La même maison, mais à pans de bois, fait l'objet du modèle 142.

BACK /ARRIÈRE

Figure 118
Perspective of two buildings.
Central Mortage and Housing
Corporation. Advisory Com-
mittee on Slum Clearance and
Low-Rental Housing, *Proposed
Redevelopment of a Blighted
Residential Area and Construc-
tion of Low-Rental Housing*,
1954, p. 18-D, plan no 9C, Cana-
dian Centre for Architecture,
Montréal

Figure 119
Mulgrave Park, Halifax, staircase
elevation and end elevation.
Ian MacLennan, chief architect,
Central Mortgage and Housing
Corporation. *Journal of the
Royal Architectural Institute
of Canada* (January 1959): 21.
Canadian Centre for Architec-
ture, Montréal

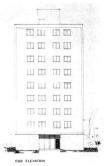

STAIRCASE ELEVATION

END ELEVATION

Figure 120
McLean Park project,
Vancouver, view of first stage.
Ian MacLennan, chief architect,
Central Mortgage and Housing
Corporation. *Journal of the
Royal Architectural Institute
of Canada* (August 1960): 330.
Canadian Centre for Architec-
ture, Montréal

Structure
and Society

**Places and
Players**

Perceptions

Expo 67

The Champlain Bridge,
Candiac, and Nuns' Island

The Champlain Bridge marked the beginning of a new relationship between Montreal and its outlying areas. It spurred the growth that followed (and, to a certain degree, had anticipated) the construction of the major highway networks extending to the outermost limits of Quebec, as well as down to the United States and eastward to the Atlantic provinces. Beginning in 1961, the Champlain Bridge facilitated the development of Nuns' Island and many municipalities on the South Shore, including Candiac, an extreme example of suburbanization. Nuns' Island and Candiac were both urbanized at the same time by private companies that planned to assume sole responsibility for their development.

Candiac

In 1953 and 1954, a group of businessmen, seeking to take advantage of the plan for the Saint Lawrence Seaway to bypass the Lachine Rapids, started buying up agricultural lands with waterway access rights in order to develop them into an industrial site. But their scheme turned out to be incompatible with the requirements of inland waterway and sea transportation, so the group decided to change the project into a residential development. The population goal for the new community, based on a study by the Toronto planning firm of Armstrong, Kingston, and Hanson, was approximately 60,000. Given the large scope of the project, the group set up the Candiac Development Corporation and, in order to acquire sufficient land, the Corporation sought capital from investors, including some very powerful ones (Bernard Vachon, "La création de Candiac en banlieue de Montréal," *Revue de géographie de Montréal* 27, no. 1 [1973]: 29–39).

In 1957, the municipality was incorporated. During the 1960s, the community's size increased at an average rate of 100 houses per year (with a low of 38 in 1961, and a high of 172 in 1968). The standard homes, designed by architects like André Blouin and Max Roth, compared favourably with those promoted by CMHC, and the master plan truly reflected the schemes that CMHC had developed. The only difference was that Candiac had hardly any of the public amenities that are a normal part of urban living. Still, the project attracted the attention of the housing development community: it was voted suburb of the year by the Montreal Home Builders' Association in both 1964 and 1968 (Henry Aubin, *City for Sale* [Montreal: Éditions l'Étincelle; Toronto: J. Lorimer, 1977], 332–337).

Figure 121
Champlain Bridge under construction, 18 September 1960.
Photograph: Hans Van der Aa.
Library and Archives Canada,
Ottawa, PA-119836

Figure 122
Candiac Development Corporation, *Candiac: The Modern Town Designed for Happy Living,* **n.d.** Canadian Centre for Architecture, Montréal, Fonds André Blouin

Figure 123
"Plan of Candiac." Candiac Development Corporation, *Ideal Industrial Sites in Candiac,* **n.d.** Canadian Centre for Architecture, Montréal, Fonds André Blouin

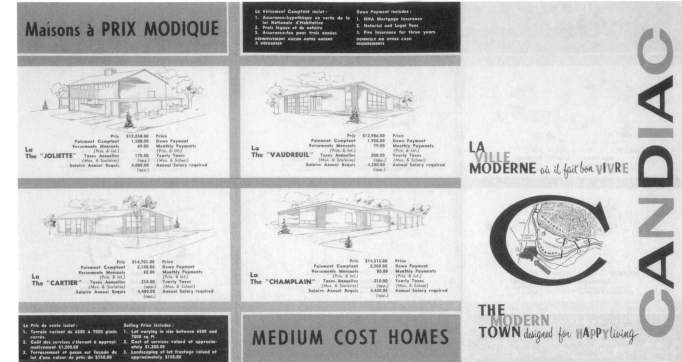

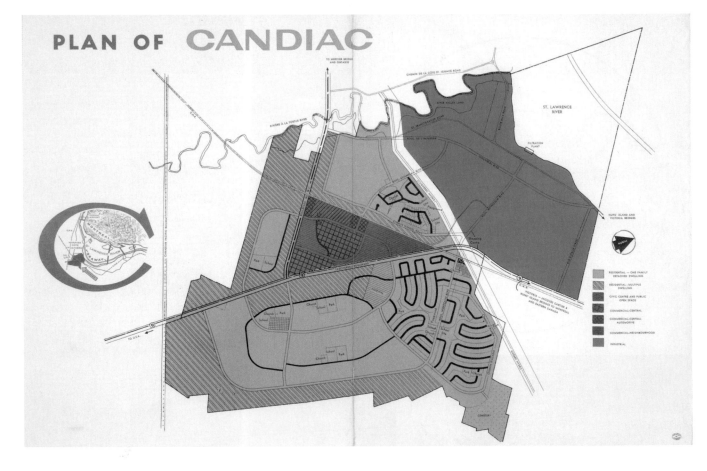

La RICHELIEU · The RICHELIEU

The ST. LAURENT · La ST-LAURENT

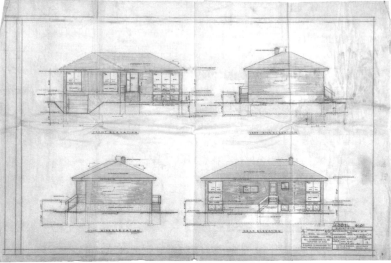

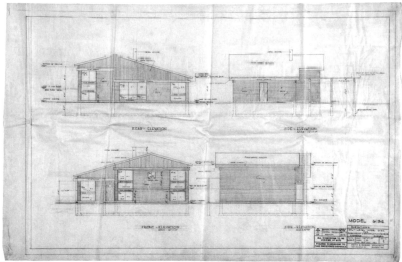

Figures 124 and 125
"The Richelieu" and "The St. Laurent." Candiac Development Corporation, *Candiac: The Modern Town Designed for Happy Living*, n.d. Canadian Centre for Architecture, Montréal, Fonds André Blouin

Figures 126 and 127
Bungalow model no. 6101 and split-level model no. 6132, for the Paramount Construction Company, elevations, 31 July 1961. Max Roth, architect. Graphite on paper, each 61 x 92 cm. Canadian Centre for Architecture, Montréal, Fonds Max Roth

Figure 128
**Aerial view of Nuns' Island,
n.d.** Canadian Centre for
Architecture, Montréal, Fonds
Philip Bobrow

Nuns' Island

The Nuns' Island project was developed during the same period, but was residential in nature from the outset – a logical decision, considering its location on the river, a stone's throw from downtown Montreal. In 1955, the Quebec Home and Mortgage Corporation, which was created to ensure the development of the project, declared that Saint Paul's Island (its former name) would contain the "most marvellous" residential estate in North America (Anne Cormier, "L'Île-des-Soeurs, le plus merveilleux domaine résidentiel en Amérique du Nord," *ARQ: Architecture/Québec*, February 1993, 18–19; *The Architectural Forum* 125, no. 5 [1966]: 19; "Île-des-Soeurs," *Architecture, bâtiment, construction* 22 [January 1967]: 20–23; "Nuns' Island, Montreal," *The Canadian Architect* 15, no. 6 [June 1970]: 32–39).

The first drawings were prepared by the Montreal architect Harold Ship, before the Canadian subsidiary of the Chicago-based developer Metropolitan Structures assumed responsibility for the project in 1965. The German-born architect Mies van der Rohe, who had long collaborated with the developer, took part in the studies and their implementation. For him, this project was an opportunity to further his urban planning and architectural thinking in the field of housing – thinking that was already embodied in the Lafayette Park project (Detroit, 1955–1963) and Highfield House project (Baltimore, 1963–1965).

The master plan was prepared by a multidisciplinary team set up by the American firm of Johnson, Johnson, and Roy. Mies van der Rohe was responsible for the design of the high-rise buildings and the Montrealer Philip Bobrow for that of the medium-height dwellings. The American Stanley Tigerman, who was also acquainted with the developer, produced studies for the row houses based on four standard plans of similar design, which could be combined by computer into 700 different layouts of four to eight units.

Careful attention was paid to the overall cluster plan, which resembled upscale experiments combining different types of space, as in the Radburn project in New Jersey, more than the cul-de-sac subdivisions promoted in CMHC publications.

The Nuns' Island project seemed to deliver on its promises. Phase I was quickly occupied, and Phase II offered an opportunity to make some changes, including the addition of balconies to Mies's buildings (which gave them an uncharacteristic look, for anyone familiar with his work). This was also the point at which Bobrow left the project, dismayed at what he considered to be a lowering of quality.

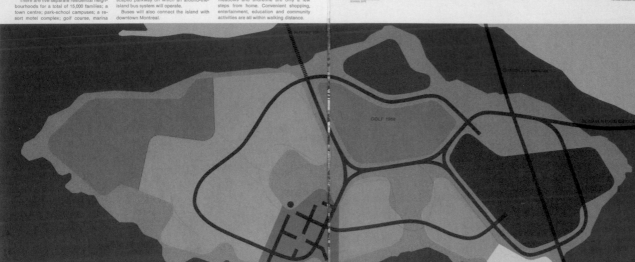

A place for living, for work and play, and everything in its place

Nuns' Island is being developed over a 15-year period under a comprehensive zoning plan.

There are five separate residential neighbourhoods for a total of 15,000 families; a town centre; park-school campuses; a resort motel complex; golf course, marina

and recreational facilities; and areas for institutional and commercial development.

The different areas are linked by a landscaped parkway on which an around-the-island bus system will operate.

Buses will also connect the island with downtown Montreal.

Utmost care has been taken to preserve the island's natural beauty. Nuns' Island is a city of open spaces where woodlands, meadows and shoreline are only a few steps from home. Convenient shopping, entertainment, education and community activities are all within walking distance.

Figure 129
Plan of Nuns' Island. Metropolitan Structures of Canada, promotional brochure. Canadian Centre for Architecture, Montréal, Fonds Philip Bobrow

Figure 130
Nuns' Island, master design plan, n.d., Philip Bobrow, architect. Photograph from a promotional album. Canadian Centre for Architecture, Montréal, Fonds Philip Bobrow

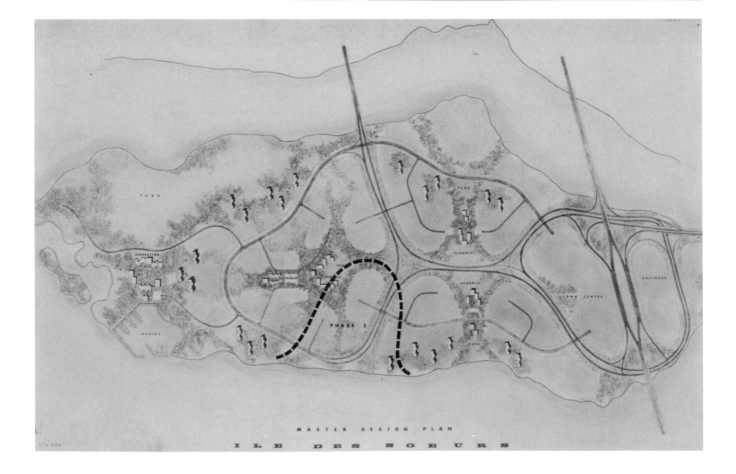

MASTER DESIGN PLAN

ILE DES SOEURS

Structure
and Society

**Places and
Players**

Perceptions

Expo 67

Metropolitan Boulevard

Figure 135
**Aerial view of Metropolitan
Boulevard from above Saint-
Michel Boulevard, looking east,
30 June 1966.** Photograph:
Armour Landry. Centre de
Montréal des Archives natio-
nales du Québec

Decided upon in the 1950s, Metropolitan Boulevard was the northern equivalent of the new east-west thoroughfare created when Dorchester Street was widened during the same period. Like Dorchester, which served the growing tertiary centre in downtown Montreal and, at the same time, increased the value of the land cleared through the demolition of houses, its role was two-fold: to serve a fast-growing industrial sector and to open up the far reaches of the island to development.

It belonged to an intermediate generation of public works: it was not really a boulevard, but was not yet an urban expressway. Although partly elevated and partly below grade, its earliest-built section was integrated into the system of city blocks, and was flanked by a service road at ground level to ensure continuity with the network of streets it traversed. The service road became home to a number of new industrial buildings, including the head office of the National Film Board, inaugurated in September 1956. The Metropolitan's interchanges with other roads and highways, such as the link to the Laurentian Autoroute at the L'Acadie traffic circle, were at grade. The Metropolitan is different from an expressway like the Queensway in Ottawa, which bisects city streets, creating numerous dead ends. Subsequent additions brought it up to the category of an expressway, particularly when the interconnections with Décarie and Montée Saint-Léonard were built.

This generation of projects was as ephemeral as the one that produced the Rockland Shopping Centre, which for nearly two decades was linked in people's minds with the Laurentian Autoroute's entry point into the city. Designed by Victor Prus, Rockland was an open, user-friendly, and high-quality version of the California shopping mall, which would be rendered obsolete in a matter of years by large, enclosed, air-conditioned bastions of consumerism, like Galeries d'Anjou, set down beside their own expressway exits.

For many years, the Metropolitan constituted a sort of virtual border between the brick residential development to the south and the isolated industrial and office buildings and single-family dwellings to the north. The main roads that intersected it then generally opened onto a world that was similar and yet often different in scale. Beyond the Metropolitan, as Hugh Hood wrote, "Pie-IX was just a ribbon development a few years ago, but now there is beginning to be a bit of a spread eastwards towards Ville de Saint-Léonard. There are Dairy Queens, closed for winter, on our right, and used-car lots, small restaurants and raw new shopping centers all the way to Rivière des Prairies" (*Around the Mountain: Scenes from Montreul Life* [Toronto: Peter Martin Associates, 1967], 5).

Figure 136
National Film Board Building, perspective, 1 November 1952. Ross, Patterson, Townsend, and Fish, architects. Photostat, 25.2 x 49 cm. Canadian Centre for Architecture, Montréal, Fonds Ross and Macdonald

Figure 137
Place d'Anjou, aerial perspective. Fairview Corporation, brochure, *Place d'Anjou* (c. 1974). Canadian Centre for Architecture, Montréal

Figure 138
Place Crémazie, aerial perspective. Hyman M. Tolchinsky, architect. Three-Star Construction Company, brochure, *Place Crémazie* (c. 1962). Canadian Centre for Architecture, Montréal

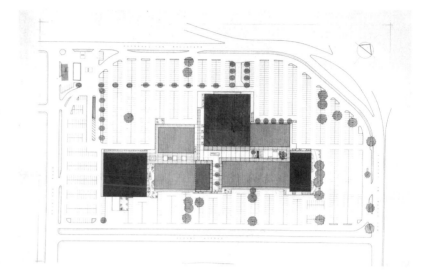

Figure 139
Rockland Shopping Centre, perspective, c. 1958. Victor Prus, architect. Photostat with self-adhesive plastic film, 33 x 49.5 cm. Collection Victor Prus

Figure 140
Rockland Shopping Centre, massing plan, c. 1958. Victor Prus, architect. Photostat, 40 x 58 cm. Collection Victor Prus

Figure 141
Rockland Shopping Centre, perspective, c. 1958. Victor Prus, architect. Photostat with self-adhesive plastic film collage, 33 x 49.5 cm. Collection Victor Prus

Figure 142
Rockland Shopping Centre, c. 1958. Victor Prus, architect. Collection Victor Prus

Structure
and Society

**Places and
Players**

Perceptions

Expo 67

The East-West Expressway

A cursory glance at the master plan for Montreal published in 1944 immediately reveals the extent to which it was influenced by trends prevailing in the first half of the century, notably in the use of green belts and ring roads to control urban development. In this scheme, the extreme confusion of the segments crowded between the river and the mountain was still far from being solved, and that was precisely where the pressure of rapidly increasing automobile traffic was most acutely felt.

The "magic" solution that was next proposed for Montreal, as in Paris and Boston, was a new type of highway, an expressway, which would "float" above the city, practically independent of it. That, at least, is what was suggested by the cover of the 1948 City Planning Department report, *An East-West Expressway*, which shows an oblique aerial photograph of Montreal with a broken line tracing the path of the expressway. Ten years later, the engineers Lalonde and Valois continued these efforts in a similar vein: the broken line was now replaced by a drawing of the expressway neatly superimposed over the city. The studies subsequently prepared by the Planning Department, which provided "the view from the road" (to quote the title of Kevin Lynch's book), offered a more descriptive picture of the proposed structure.

As with Décarie Boulevard, it was the strategic position of the east-west expressway in the national highway network that facilitated its commissioning, albeit somewhat late in comparison with the efforts made to prepare Montreal for Expo 67. But it was certainly the series of projects completed at that time that made it desirable, since it was the missing link in the main east-west route through the city centre.

The Ville-Marie Expressway, when it was finally built, caused much more devastation than these illustrations reveal. To its detractors in the early 1970s, it represented all of the most appalling aspects of top-down, voluntarist planning: collusion between the different levels of government in a project to destroy a working-class neighbourhood, devised in the name of economic development, justified by vague, technocratic arguments, subsidized by public funds, and serving – indirectly and unavowedly – the growth of private capital (see Montreal Council of Social Agencies, *Rapport de la Commission d'audiences publiques populaires sur l'autoroute est-ouest à Montréal* [Montreal, 1971]).

Figure 143
Port of Montreal and downtown core, 1958. Photograph: Armour Landry. Centre de Montréal des Archives nationales du Québec

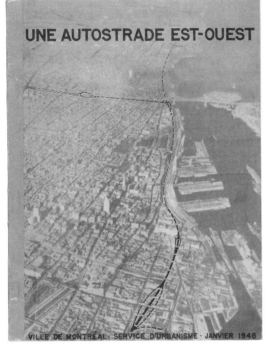

UNE AUTOSTRADE EST-OUEST

VILLE DE MONTRÉAL · SERVICE D'URBANISME · JANVIER 1948

Figure 144
City Planning Department, City of Montreal, *Une autostrade est-ouest* (1948). Published in English as *An East-West Expressway*. Canadian Centre for Architecture, Montréal

Figure 145
Study for layout of east-west expressway. Lalonde and Valois, engineers, *Autostrade est-ouest, cité de Montréal* (1959), 39. Canadian Centre for Architecture, Montréal

Figure 146
Trans-Canada Highway, photograph of presentation model of east-west expressway section, 6 April 1964. City Planning Department, City of Montreal. Ville de Montréal, Service de la mise en valeur du territoire et du patrimoine

Figure 147
Impact study of the Trans-Canada Highway in southwest Montreal. Lalonde and Valois, engineers, *Autostrade est-ouest, cité de Montréal* (1959), plan no. 8. Canadian Centre for Architecture, Montréal

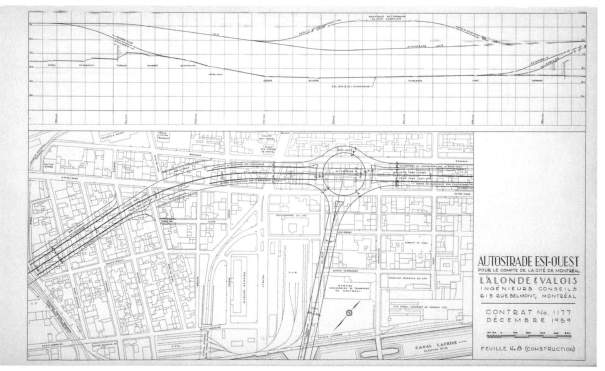

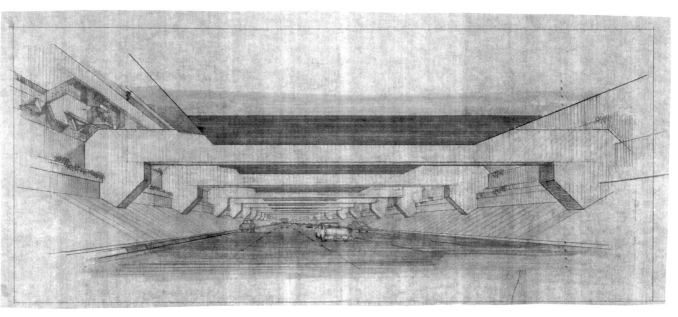

Figure 150
East-west expressway, study of section C, tunnel under the business district, 1963. City Planning Department, City of Montreal. Coloured pencil on diazotype, 29.5 x 66 cm. Ville de Montréal, Service de la mise en valeur du territoire et du patrimoine

Figure 151
East-west expressway, study of section D, tunnel in the east-central area, 1963. City Planning Department, City of Montreal. Sepia diazotype with fibre-tip pen applied to verso, 15.8 x 41 cm. Ville de Montréal, Service de la mise en valeur du territoire et du patrimoine

Figure 152
East-west expressway, perspective study of eastern section, 1963. City Planning Department, City of Montreal. Sepia diazotype with fibre-tip pen applied to verso, 30.5 x 46 cm. Ville de Montréal, Service de la mise en valeur du territoire et du patrimoine

Structure
and Society
Places and
Players
Perceptions

Expo 67

Territorial Expansion and
Urban Laboratory

Preparations for Expo 67 spurred the commencement of work on a series of infrastructure projects that had been studied by municipal departments for several decades. The occasion also provided an opportunity to think about the city's future development and the urbanization of new areas. The sites that were being considered for Expo in the fall of 1962 included parcels of land to be made viable and neighbourhoods that were due for renewal, in Pointe Saint-Charles, Maisonneuve, Saint-Léonard and Anjou, Lasalle, and Mercier. It was only later that the island site eventually chosen even became a contender. The decision came as a great disappointment to the young designers working with Daniel van Ginkel, the architect who had been hired as a planning consultant by the Canadian Corporation for the 1967 World Exhibition and who was strongly in favour of locating Expo in Pointe Saint-Charles. It also proved a disappointment to the architectural firm of Bédard, Charbonneau, and Langlois, who had prepared a study of the river site at their own expense but would never be given proper credit for originating the idea.

In the fall of 1963, the Corporation retained the services of Eugène Beaudouin, a French architect. Beaudouin had prepared the superb lighting studies for the 1937 world's fair in Paris, working under Jacques Gréber, the former boss of Édouard Fiset, now Expo 67's chief architect. Beaudouin's drawings, which even integrated the studies by Blouin and Prus for the "Confederation Promenade" (see pages 97 and 172), illustrated most of the options subsequently developed by Fiset and his team in the short time they had to complete their mandate.

The master plan corresponded to the main guidelines set out by a committee of intellectuals who met at Montebello, including figures as diverse as the actor Jean-Louis Roux, the neurosurgeon Wilder Penfield, the poet

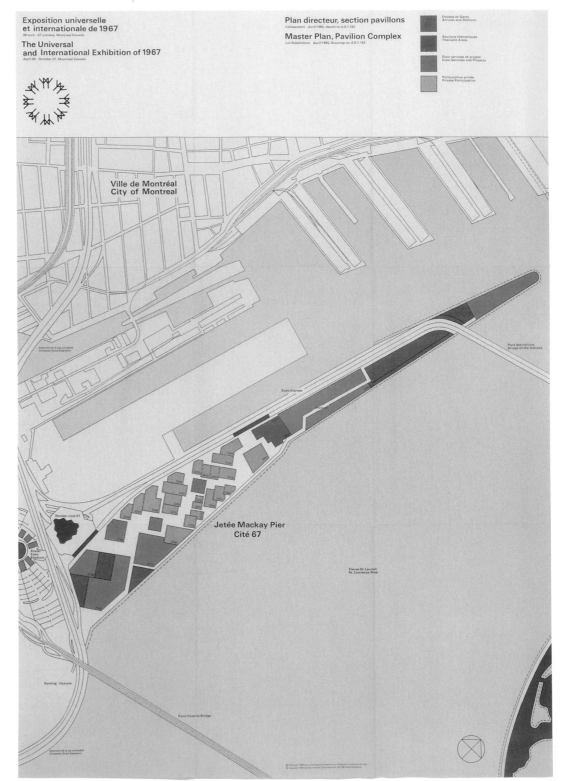

Figures 153 and 154
"Master Plan, Pavilion Complex,"
drawings 162 and 163, April
1965. Canadian Corporation
for the 1967 World Exhibition.
Reproduction prints, each
84 x 58.5 cm. Ville de Montréal,
Gestion de documents et
archives

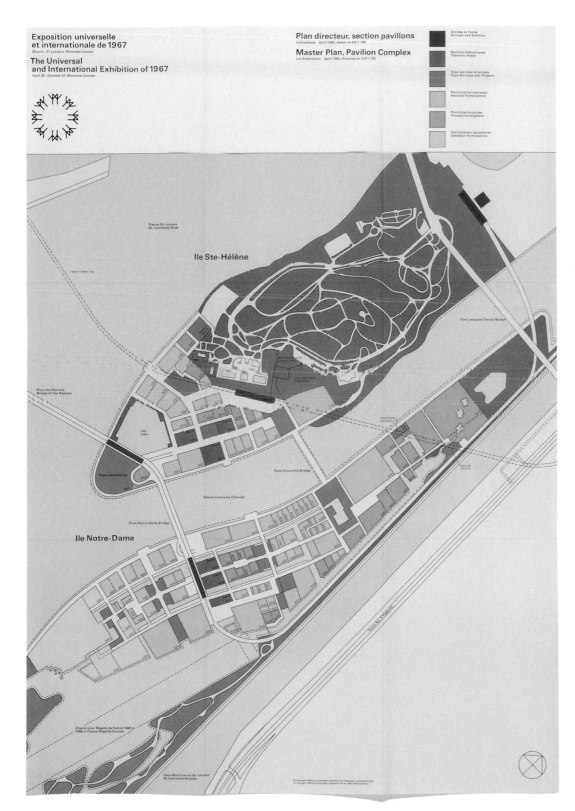

and law professor F.R. Scott, and the architect Ray Affleck. It was this committee that chose the overall theme of "Man and His World," a humanistic expression that was at once very specific and very broad. What it signified, as Roux explained, was "Man as opposed to corporations," and "Man as opposed to nations." The sub-themes, which were in keeping with the spirit of the January 1963 recommendations of the Province of Quebec Association of Architects, flowed naturally from it: "Man the Explorer," "Man the Creator," "Man the Producer," "Man in the Community," and so forth.

Through its detailed zoning of the site, the master plan also met the requirements of a complex program that combined shows, areas for relaxation, amusement rides, and concessions, with thematic exhibits and performances characteristic of the countries represented. Special attention was paid to the flow of visitor traffic, handled by a transportation network that was inspired by the latest multimodal theories.

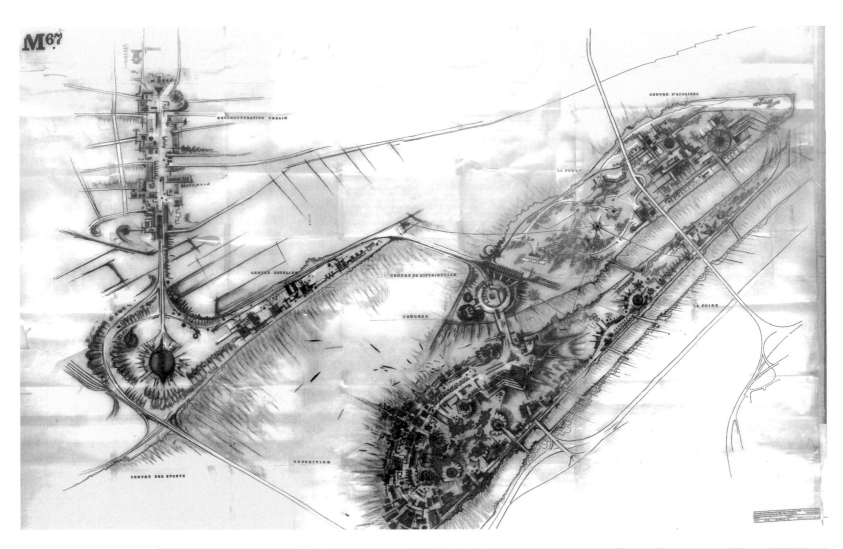

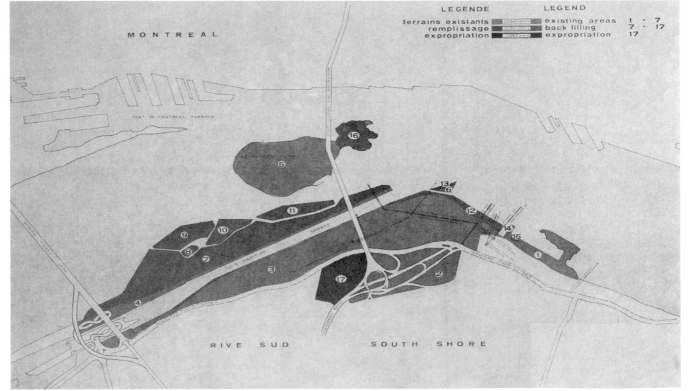

Figure 155
Sketch proposal for Expo 67 master plan, November 1963. Eugène Beaudouin, architect and planner. Reproduction from microfilm. Library and Archives Canada, Ottawa, RG 71M, acc. 85603/4

Figure 156
Site proposal for Expo 67, 1962. Bédard, Charbonneau, Langlois, architects. Reproduction print, 51 x 102.5 cm. Collection Bruno Bédard

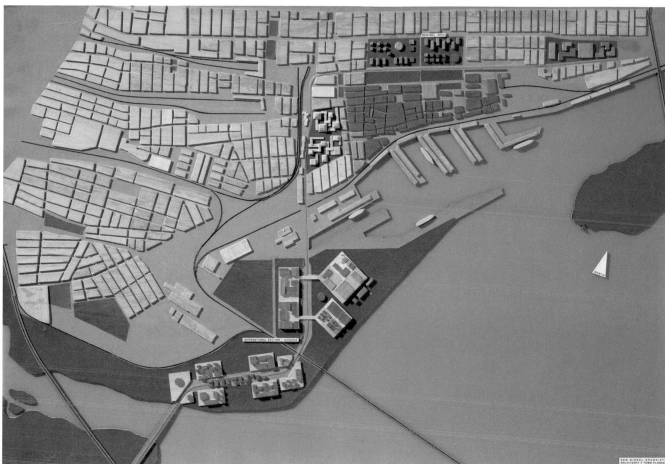

"Man and the City," presentation model for the Canadian Corporation for the 1967 World Exhibition, 1962. Van Ginkel Associates, architects and planners. Paper, cardboard, balsa wood, and tape on plexiglass mounted on plywood, 84 x 125 cm. Canadian Centre for Architecture, Montréal, Fonds van Ginkel. In addition to the site proposed for the world's fair, the model shows the results of the van Ginkels' various studies for the central section of Montreal: a slab-based housing development on McGill Street; Old Montreal; renovation of the La Gauchetière and Hôtel-de-Ville sector; the area around the Maison de Radio-Canada.

Figure 158
Locations studied for the site of Expo 67. Map adapted from "Existing Street Network on the Island of Montreal, 1960," in Lalonde, Girouard, and Letendre, engineers, *Plan directeur: Routes à caractère métropolitain* (1961), plan no. 14. Ville de Montréal, Service de la mise en valeur du territoire et du patrimoine

A: The islands
B: Pointe Saint-Charles
C: LaSalle
D: Maisonneuve
E: Mercier
F: Saint-Léonard and Anjou

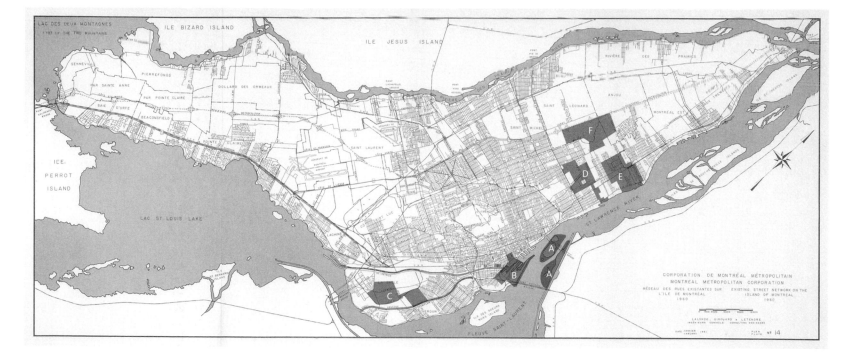

Figure 159
Mini-rail, Expo 67. Photograph: Joseph Messana. Canadian Centre for Architecture, Montréal

Figure 160
Expo-Express station, Expo 67. Photograph: Joseph Messana. Canadian Centre for Architecture, Montréal

Figure 161
Vaporetto, Expo 67. Photograph: Joseph Messana. Canadian Centre for Architecture, Montréal

Figure 162
Postcard of the Sky Ride cable cars at La Ronde, Expo 67. Photograph: Benjamin News Company, Montreal. Canadian Centre for Architecture, Montréal

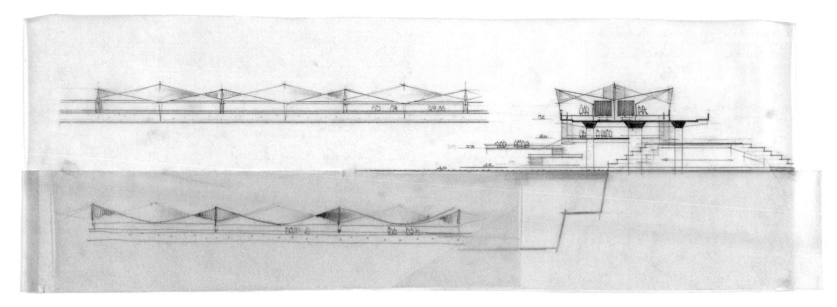

Figure 163
Expo-Express station, elevations and section, n.d. André Blouin, architect. Graphite on tracing paper, 27.5 x 76 cm. Canadian Centre for Architecture, Montréal, Fonds André Blouin

Figure 164
Cable car system for La Ronde, elevations, July 1965. D'Astous and Pothier, architects. Graphite and pen and black ink on graph paper, 81 x 108 cm. Canadian Centre for Architecture, Montréal, Fonds Roger D'Astous

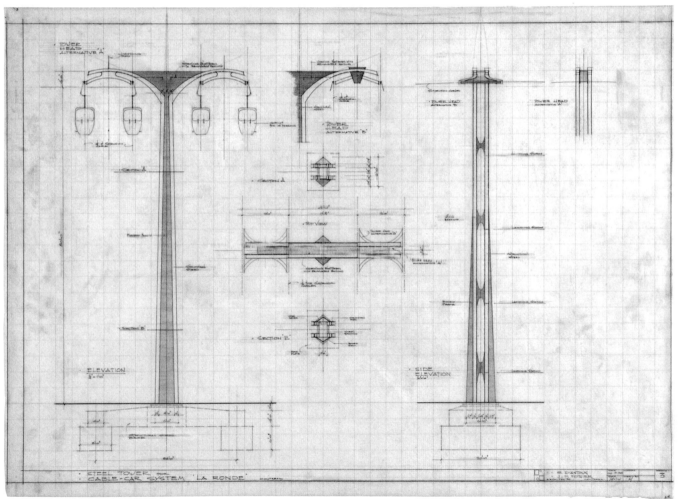

Learning from Montreal

On 17 February 2004, André Lortie invited Jean-Louis Cohen and Michael Sorkin to join him in a discussion of their various recollections and analyses of how Montreal in the 1960s was perceived from abroad. The following is an edited version of their conversation.

Decline and Renaissance

Michael Sorkin: The interesting thing about Montreal in the 1960s, if you compare it to certain other cities – Buffalo, for example – that went through similar economic highs and lows, is the way in which its transformation was handled, and the composite of actions that were undertaken to realize this attempt to convert, at a stroke, the old economy into a new service economy, with the national banks and so on. The astonishing thing is that every single standard-issue piece of mid-century modernist strategizing happened here. And the Montreal experience was a harbinger of later developments, in which every city was trying to use sports facilities as a pump primer, or trying to get a world's fair as a pump-primer, or trying to build a subway as a pump-primer, or trying to lay in a cultural infrastructure as a pump primer. It all happened in a very brief span of years. But in the end, it seems that the attempt failed, as Toronto would capture the influx of head offices from Montreal, while Vancouver would attract the capital investment from Asia.

Jean-Louis Cohen: Indeed, Montreal was almost the perfect example of a rail-based economy that was being challenged by the development of air and road alternatives as well as by improvements in water transportation; in short, it makes for an interesting postscript to Le Corbusier's *Four Routes*. But Montreal's relationship with Toronto, for instance, was not a zero-sum game in which Toronto would absorb the energy Montreal was losing. Also, Canada as a whole was experiencing development in that decade. Major natural resources were being exploited, an agricultural boom was taking place, and new types of development based on information technology were appearing, at least insofar as I am able to judge from my vantage points south of the border and across the ocean. Much of the surplus went to Toronto, but not necessarily as a clear and absolute transfer from Montreal, as far as I understand it. At the same time, the railway link became less important, since the car- and truck-based economy

Figure 165
Life, **28 April 1967.** Canadian Centre for Architecture, Montréal

Figure 166
***Paris Match*, 20 May 1967.** Photograph: Paris Match / Tony Saulnier. Canadian Centre for Architecture, Montréal, Fonds André Blouin. *Paris Match* is currently the largest news magazine in France and fifth largest in the world.

had emerged. It is exciting to try and capture the phenomenon of Montreal in the 1960s, a time when the two types of infrastructures still coexisted, with the former dwindling as the latter was emerging.

MS: I think we all continue to be astonished by the optimism and the all-at-onceness that marked the decade. The simultaneous production of a world's fair, a subway, and a new downtown represents both the highwater mark of a certain strain of post-war planning and a bit of a miracle. Afterwards, there was a reaction against this kind of "by command" urban development, rendering it impossible.

JLC: There seemed to be a wholeness, or rather a sort of climactic convergence – much as in classical theatre we have a unity of place, of time, and of action. It was a moment in which the city exploded and, at the same time, invited the best experts on the planet, bought the best, and aspired to become one of the best. The celebrated combination of underground infrastructure and roads shaped the new Montreal, but one should not overlook the complex ways in which the metropolitan highway network and the subway were interwoven. A dense metropolitan landscape was being shaped, and concurrently, a suburban landscape was emerging, and the city's surface became a battleground. An unprecedented process of expansion met the new forms of identification of a great North American city. I think the phenomenon was quite unique.

André Lortie: What you are describing here is the process by which Montreal shifted from a national metropolis to a regional metropolis. Simultaneously, Montreal was emerging on the international scene as a very autonomous and singular city.

The Elites and the Collection

MS: The mayor, Jean Drapeau, obviously played a part in this, motivating it in some way. He certainly had a vision of architecture and of the consequences of design.

JLC: This raises the question of the elites, which is a fundamental one. Alongside the technological experts, the political elites of the city and of the province were attracted to the architectural elite. The objective was to assemble a collection of urban pieces, urban facilities, according to a pattern of collecting similar to the one seen in museums of contemporary art when they purchase signature works.

MS: The collecting model, I think, is very important – what is a world's fair if not a competitive collection? There was communication and connection between the collecting style of Expo and the collecting style of the big architectural infrastructure being imposed on the city: each modelled and confirmed the taste of the other.

JLC: I agree, but Expo and the city were not only homologous but also, at the same time, opposite to each other, because a world's fair is a projection of the desires of the participating nations. No Canadian would have been invited to conceive the

monstrous French pavilion designed by Jean Faugeron. He built it because he was backed by a powerful lobby located thousands of miles away in Paris. In this respect, the city remains a rather subconscious process of the collecting of teams, projects, and figures, shaped by forces native to the Montreal culture. What do you think?

Influences

AL: That's possible. However, one must not forget that many architects or urban planners then working in Montreal were foreign-born. I think of André Blouin, for instance, who was from France, and who submitted his projects to the magazine *L'Architecture d'aujourd'hui* for a long period. Also Victor Prus, who came to Montreal from Poland after 1945. Then there were the van Ginkels. Blanche Lemco van Ginkel was from Canada, but Daniel was from the Netherlands. The Israeli-born architect Moshe Safdie is another example.

MS: It is funny to think about this agglomeration of "star" architects from what is distinctly the second tier. One might ask what kinds of autonomous centres of local architectural culture flourished back then? McGill was a pretty good school at that point, wasn't it? Was anything else happening on the local scene?

AL: Yes, McGill University was strong at the time. In fact, McGill was where the Le Corbusier exhibition took place in 1959, in Redpath Hall. It was organized by André Blouin, who was then living in Montreal.

MS: That makes for an interesting lineage, doesn't it?

JLC: To me, this reveals a pattern of subordination, of what I would say was a certain degree of submission by the city to professional or ideological hegemonies

Figure 168
André Blouin at the opening of the *Le Corbusier* exhibition, Redpath Hall, McGill University, 10 December 1959. Canadian Centre for Architecture, Montréal, Fonds André Blouin

based in New York, Philadelphia, or Paris. But what remains to be measured is the actual input of professionals migrating from the outside world. I refer not only to architects such as I.M. Pei or others who retained a sort of colonizing posture, accompanying a strong injection of external capital. Another line of inquiry is into how the collective desire was shaped, even if it seems sometimes to be implicit. What kind of city did Montreal want to be? And to what stereotypes did it subscribe? Civilized, like Paris? Efficient, like New York or Chicago? Different from what Montreal had been before – or, more than that, even a counter-image to it?

MS: That's a good question. The francophile inflection, the idea of a North American Paris, was very pronounced – it reflected a notion of French civility that, to put it mildly, was not current in the United States. I remember how much publicity there was at the time about the fact that the metro in Montreal was on rubber tires, like the recently constructed lines in Paris. It was considered superior to other subways both because it ran so quietly and because of its "Frenchness." But I love those rubber tires. The idea of appropriating automobile technology as a mass transit modality is fabulous. It's an implicit rebuke to the transit monoculture south of the border.

JLC: So being the "Paris d'Amérique" at this point meant bringing in the rubber-tire metro, because you couldn't bring in the boulevards. In terms of the process described by Freud in his *Interpretation of Dreams*, the desire of being another city is both displaced and condensed in this technology. But the way that Montreal addressed the question of climate control is also revealing, because you can't dissociate it from underground city-living. Other types of cities have created an inverted system, as in Houston, for instance, where the issue is surviving humid heat. Also, there is the notion that Montreal is among the northernmost outposts of Western civilization, one of the ones closest (in the popular imagination) to the polar regions, even if its actual geographic

Figure 169
Plans of the pedestrian concourse under Rockefeller Center, New York, and the underground pedestrian network in Montreal. Peter Blake, "Vincent Ponte: A New Kind of Urban Designer," *Art in America* 57, no. 5 (September–October 1969): 64. Archives of Pei, Cobb, Freed, and Partners, Architects

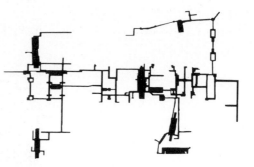

latitude is much more southern than Scandinavia's, for example. Anyway, there is something striking about the heroism in dealing with the climate and the intelligence in using sophisticated devices to this effect.

MS: Phenomena like the tunnels in Montreal and Houston or the skyways in Minneapolis are not simply about climate control, they're about social control and class suppression. Their history goes back to the Paris arcades or the Corridoio Vasariano. But it is noteworthy that this grafted subterranean infrastructure should appear in a city with such a strong envy of Paris. The idea of the displacement of the boulevard to below grade is fundamentally weird. It's understandable only on the basis of the Rockefeller Center model, which was, even then, holy urbanistic writ. Rockefeller Center also represents a return to the paradigm of the ensemble, and to the idea – however paradoxical – of enlightened development, the privatized paradise.

JLC: The discussion is now leading to the issue of shopping, but you should not forget that underground facilities and sunken transportation networks had already been planned in the United States before 1914.

Architectural Landmarks

MS: William Zeckendorf, the developer of Place Ville-Marie, was a hugely important character in Montreal in those days, as an avatar of responsible modernity and enlightened private-sector activity.

JLC: The most interesting aspect is the basic infrastructure system that was built; it was an original feat for that period. As to the buildings themselves, they were closer to a collection of stereotypes than to an original production of a new generation of experimental objects.

AL: But shouldn't we make a distinction between the architectural look of these huge buildings and the way that the programs they house were handled? For instance, Place Bonaventure, with its train station underneath, its two levels of boutiques and the four- or five-storey-high showroom hidden in its core, topped by a hotel containing a rooftop garden, is quite astonishing in the way it handled the program. At the same time, its architectural appearance wavers between a concession to the Brutalist style and a metaphorical reference to cities of the desert.

Figure 170
**Place Ville-Marie and Dorchester Boulevard, looking west,
19 August 1964.** Photograph: Henri Rémillard. Centre de
Montréal des Archives nationales du Québec

JLC: And then there is a kind of utopia of public space in all these schemes, relating and integrating extremely diverse public facilities. A connective fabric of public space corresponding to the transportation infrastructure connects a series of shopping centres, some of which emerge above ground. Such an attempt is very brave, and second only to the so-called *subnades* in Tokyo – a neologism for "subterranean promenades." Maintenance and appropriation problems of overextended public spaces are now well known, but the initial enterprise remains brave and resolute.

MS: This idea of a kind of adjacent, captive utopia as a goad to the reorganization of public spaces in the "real" city is remarkable. Expo 67 – pedestrian paradise, architectural zoo, pleasure garden – constantly informs what's happening across the river in Montreal. Such a parallel can also be suggested in regard to the transit system. The exhilaration of motion is one of the historic agendas of fairs and amusement parks. Disneyland is, among other things, a prototype for a mass-transit-enabled pedestrian realm. By transmuting commuting to a "ride," mass transit is de-politicized and transferred to the world of pleasure. The transit system at Expo was in dialogue with the new Montreal transit system, just as the two collections of architecture mutually affirmed their separate importance.

JLC: "Learning from Montreal" (to paraphrase Venturi and Scott Brown's *Learning from Las Vegas*) – what did people learn from what they saw? I suspect that the initial experience was quite meagre. The European or North American celebration of Montreal as an experimental place happened at a later time. You had a contemporary critique by Peter Blake, and then there was Reyner Banham, who was searching for a conclusive focus for his *Megastructure* book and found Montreal, where he knew François Dallegret. At some point, judging from the vibes my generation picked up from Montreal in the early 1970s, the aura stuck to the Expo buildings and, above all, to Habitat. But that rather loose image would very soon be obscured by the more futuristic image of Osaka. And the Canadian fair seemed tame in comparison to the Japanese one. So interest focused on the underground networks, which contributed to the stereotyping of Montreal as a crazy city buried under vast icy expanses.

MS: And I believe that was the last point at which many of us thought that all those buildings were actually good architecture. I, for one – in the fullness of my undergraduate taste – certainly bought into the idea that Montreal was putting up really good buildings, in large numbers. I have in mind the Château Champlain Hotel, with its curvy windows.

Figure 171
Peter Desbarats, *The Outside-In City: Place Bonaventure* (1968). Canadian Centre for Architecture, Montréal

Figure 172
Place Ville-Marie, interior view showing the commercial shops, 1962. I.M. Pei and Associates, architects; Henry N. Cobb, architect-in-charge. Photograph: George Cserna. Archives of Pei, Cobb, Freed, and Partners, Architects

Figure 173
Habitat 67, October 1967. Moshe Safdie, architect;
David, Barott, Boulva, associate architects. Photograph:
Jeremy Taylor. Collection Jeremy Taylor

JLC: Frankly, I don't remember having had mental images of these buildings at the time. The images were about public spaces, about the networks of public spaces. The buildings were less important, and were not noticeable, perhaps because, from a European perspective, they were rather devoid of glamour.

MS: I think, from an American perspective, we considered them to be buildings of a quality that was superior to what we were seeing at home. Definitely. Even if hindsight suggests otherwise, those three or four buildings – the mixed-use merchandise mart with a hotel on top, the Château Champlain Hotel, Place Ville-Marie – seemed to be something singular at that point. And there was, of course, Habitat. Somehow, in light of the existence of Habitat, I inferred that everything else was more interesting than it actually was, part of a family of innovation.

JLC: Habitat truly has had a very important role in promoting the architecture of residential megastructures – nicknamed, in French, "proliferating" architecture – as it confirmed that ideas in the air, if I may put it that way, could really be built. It had a major impact. Safdie's scheme gave instant credibility to ten years of experimentation in accumulative pyramidal shapes, and led directly to real schemes in the "villes nouvelles" of the 1970s.

MS: But also, since we were in the waning days of the functionalist religion, the fact that a form such as Habitat could be produced out of what appeared to be a completely rational set of arguments probably kept the discourse alive for another ten years. This is a cyclical fantasy, the dream of the factory-built environment. It keeps coming back, and its appeal – as a surrogate for real social policy – is great.

JLC: The intriguing thing is to look into what images we were identifying Montreal with at that time. They were images of Habitat's building site – a crane and 3-D blocks floating in the air. This was perhaps the most powerful image. And other than that we also had images from an underground that had nothing to do with artistic subversion. If you compare Quebec to the United States in those days, what is striking is the expansion of the public sphere, of public regulation, and in fact the rather controlled play of private development. A different kind of negotiation was taking place between private profit-making and public rule-making in Quebec, and it showed the Americans an example of a more reasoned and socially responsive way of developing a metropolis.

Political Issues

AL: So Montreal in the 1960s was the locus of important structural forces such as major international real estate investments and federal planning policies mostly concerned with infrastructures like highways or airports. The shape of the

Figure 174
"Canadian Pacific Railways, Windsor-Lagauchetiere Site, Montreal, P.Q., Hotel Development, Preliminary Study," perspective at entrance, September 1963. D'Astous and Pothier, architects. Photostat, 64.5 x 45.5 cm. Canadian Centre for Architecture, Montréal, Fonds Roger D'Astous

Figure 175
Report in support of creation of the Thiers housing block concerted development zone, Nancy, June 1971. Binoux and Folliasson, architects. Collection André Lortie

city and suburb was rapidly changing under the pressure of these forces, with highways crossing the landscape and new corporate images rising in the core. And Montrealers were watching all this – in amazement, during the first years, and then, as time went by, with growing worry about the disappearance of their traditional houses and neighbourhoods.

JLC: And they started reacting.

AL: They started reacting at the very end of the 1960s, and then even more in the 1970s.

MS: It fits a kind of classic revolutionary paradigm – the half-life of enthusiasm before the terror arrives. I wonder how this spasm of improvements produced the desire for separatism. This kind of exposure to a sense of possibility and a sense of the singularity of the city surely helped make possible the thought of going it alone.

JLC: That is indeed a very good analysis. At some point, it brought back a certain narcissism to a city that always had a sort of inferiority complex in relation to Paris, in relation to London, in relation to New York, and now perhaps in relation to Toronto. In a city that always perceived itself as competing with stronger, more established models, this was an important narcissistic moment.

MS: That's right. Definitely a declaration of autonomy and independence, and a bid to become "world class."

JLC: I would add to what Michael has said that this surge of narcissism perhaps strengthened the urge to independence. Having Montreal as a world-class metropolis, as a *Weltstadt*, Quebec could become a nation standing on its own.

AL: The Quebec pavilion at Expo 67 fits exactly into this state of mind: a purely late-modernist glass box with slightly sloping façades revealing the maturity of Quebec society. But even as these changes were taking place in the heart of Montreal, some people – maybe even the same people – would be thinking, why push for independence if we can achieve all this within the present system?

JLC: So it works both ways, in the end.

AL: Yes. It's a paradox. In Quebec, it often ends with this type of paradox. Maybe that's why, in general, it's the status quo that is the final outcome.

International Architectural Influences and References

Figure 176
Midtown development, Civic Forum, Philadelphia (1956–1957), perspective. Louis Kahn, architect and planner. Heinz Ronner and Sharad Jhaveri, *Louis I. Kahn: Complete Work, 1935–1974* (1987), 35. Canadian Centre for Architecture, Montréal

Figure 177
Berlin-Hauptstadt competition design, axonometric of the city centre, 1957. Peter Sigmonde, Alison and Peter Smithson, architects and planners. Reyner Banham, *The New Brutalism: Ethic or Aesthetic* (1966), 84. Canadian Centre for Architecture, Montréal

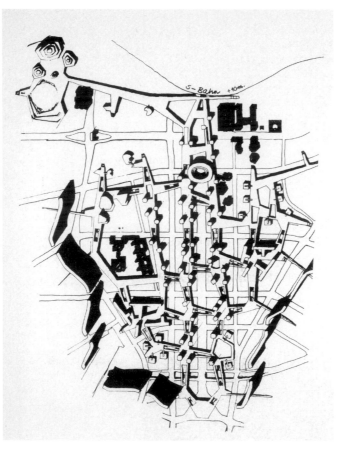

After World War II, the utopias designed by the most engagé architects, following ideas originally explored by the Modern Movement during the interwar years, reflected radical changes in scale. Fuelled by the promises of industry and technology, systems expanded and became specialized, evolving into megastructures, while living and working spaces tended to be based on prefabrication and standardization. Unlike Le Corbusier's city of 3 million inhabitants, these utopias (or, to be more precise, manifestos) were situated in very real places – Paris, New York, Tokyo – which made them even more striking. These were projects that did not all involve the same reasoning or deal with the same issues, but it is interesting that Montreal became an internationally known locus of experimentation for such a great variety of them.

For Alison and Peter Smithson, the accepted option of separating traffic flows was less important in the reconstruction of downtown Berlin than the commitment to set down the roots of a powerful "reidentification," in line with the ideas of Team X. This was a process that seemed to be underway in Montreal in the 1960s, one that attracted the attention of the international community and that was somewhat reminiscent of the razing of historic Philadelphia proposed by Louis Kahn in the 1950s.

Buckminster Fuller's idea of covering part of Manhattan with a geodesic dome (an example of his interest in emerging environmental concerns) was in sharp contrast to the megastructural cities designed by Tange, Friedman, and Cook. The latter were more obviously relatable to the Montreal projects by Safdie (Tange) and Hecker (Friedman), whereas the "metro education" project by Lincourt and Parnass was in keeping with the statement by Shadrach Woods, co-author of the plan for the Free University of Berlin, that "schools represent the future of cities" and that "education, then, is urbanism" (Shadrach Woods, "The Education Bazaar," *Harvard Educational Review* 39, no. 4 [1969]: 119).

Figure 178
Perspective sketch for city suspended above the Seine near the Pont de Tolbiac. Yona Friedman, architect. Noël Boutet de Monvel, *Les demains de Paris* **(1964).** Photograph: P. Joly and Vera Chardot. Collection André Lortie

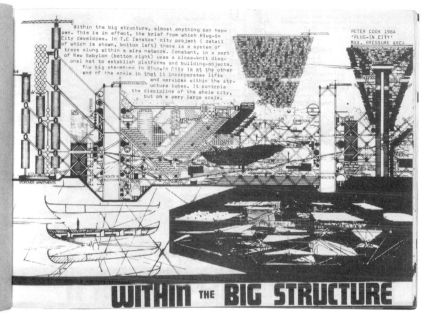

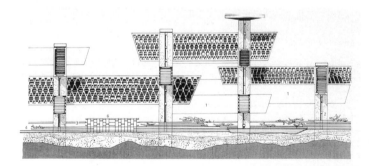

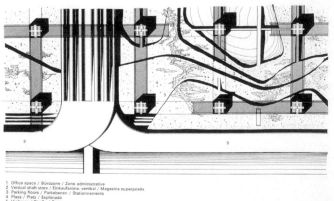

Figure 179
"Within the Big Structure." Archigram, architects. *Archigram,* **no. 5 (Autumn 1966), "Metropolis" issue.** Canadian Centre for Architecture, Montréal

Figure 181
Plan for Tokyo, section and plan, 1960. Kenzo Tange, architect. Udo Kultermann, ed., *Kenzo Tange: 1946–1969, Architecture and Urban Design* **(1970), 133.** Canadian Centre for Architecture, Montréal

Figure 180
Save Our Cities, **from the series "Save Our Planet," 1971. R. Buckminster Fuller, architect.** Serigraph, 63.3 x 70 cm. Montreal Museum of Fine Arts, donation of the Olivetti Corporation. Photo: Montreal Museum of Fine Arts, Christine Guest

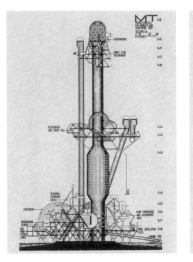

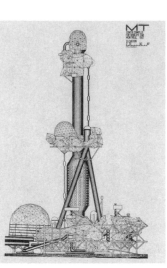

The clip-together aesthetic of the Archigram group came nearest to realization in this project for an entertainment tower, devised by Peter Cook and modeled by Dennis Crompton (left) for the Montreal World's Fair of 1967. The components are to be clipped together and include a number of Buckminster Fuller geodesic domes and a standard prefabricated 800-foot TV tower core projected by an English construction company for export to various parts of the world.

Right: Plan at the level of the auditoria and the main concourse area.

19

Figure 182
Montreal Tower, Expo 67, elevations and plan. Peter Cook, architect. *Design Quarterly*, no. 63 (1965): 19. Canadian Centre for Architecture, Montréal

Figure 183
Cité des Îles, with view of Nuns' Island and Expo islands, photograph of model, c. 1967–1968. Moshe Safdie, architect. Specific Collection, Rare Books and Special Collections Division, McGill University Libraries, Montreal

Figure 184
Tri-dimensional city above Montreal, model. Zvi Hecker, architect. "Proposition pour un nouveau centre à Montréal," *L'architecture d'aujourdhui*, no. 158 (October–November 1971): xxviii. Collection André Lortie

In asserting, along with Reyner Banham, that "a home is not a house," François Dallegret distanced himself from advocates of suburban communities who were proclaiming that "a house is not a home," and at the same time provided architectural criticism with a new slogan (Reyner Banham, "A Home Is Not a House," with drawings by François Dallegret, *Art in America* 53, no. 2 [April 1965]: 70–79; Marc H. Choko, Jean-Pierre Collin, and Annick Germain, "Le logement et les enjeux de la transformation de l'espace urbain: Montréal, 1940–1960," *Revue d'histoire urbaine* 15, no. 3 [February 1987]: 245). In keeping with the capsules and spray-plastic houses of the Archigram group, his vision was in complete opposition to the destruction of the old city, which another Montrealer, Harry Mayerovitch, wanted to replace with "overstreet" developments (as described in his book *Overstreet*) – a local version of the "housing over the highway" proposed by Paul Rudolph for New York's contentious and never-built Lower Manhattan Expressway.

In the end, Montreal became the testing ground for a different dream, that of prefabricated housing, for which Habitat 67 was meant to serve as a model. Its competition was Y67, a kind of phalanstery made of precast concrete panels in the manner of the French Camus system, which was supposed to dominate the river banks.

Figure 185
Un-house: Transportable Standard-of-Living Package / The Environment-Bubble, drawing no. 5 of 6 by François Dallegret for the article by Reyner Banham, "A Home Is Not a House," *Art in America* 53, no. 2 (April 1965). India ink

in facsimile on translucent film and gelatin on transparent acetate, 76.5 x 76.6 cm. Collection François Dallegret

Figure 186
Diagram plan showing multifunctional development. Michel Lincourt and Harry Parnass, "Métro éducation Montréal," *L'Architecture d'aujourdhui*, no. 153 (January 1971): 58. Collection André Lortie

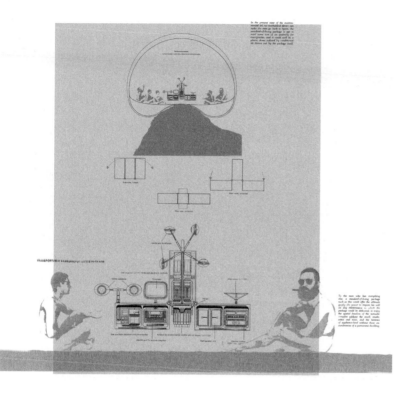

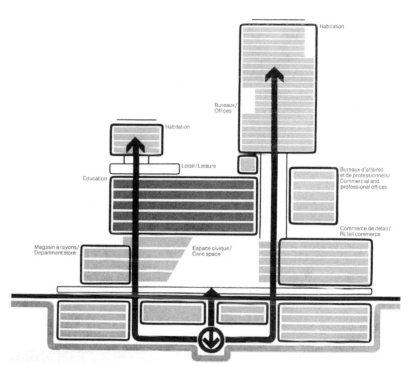

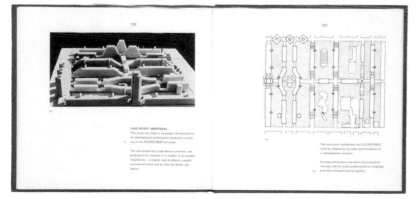

Figure 187
"Case Study Montreal," model and plan. Harry Mayerovitch, *Overstreet: An Urban Street Development System* (1973), 102–103. Canadian Centre for Architecture, Montréal

Figure 188
Y67 project, perspective sketches, 1964. Jean Duret, architect; Papineau, Gérin-Lajoie, Le Blanc, architects; Luc Durand, associate architect. Fibre-tip pen, graphite, and self-adhesive plastic film on tracing paper, 28 x 21.5 cm. Canadian Centre for Architecture, Montréal

Structure
and Society

**Places and
Players**

Perceptions

Expo 67

The Effects of the Metro

In 1965, the City of Montreal published a small brochure titled *2,000,000 People in Your Own Basement*, detailing the building rights it was offering over specific metro sites it had acquired as the land needed for construction of the underground system was expropriated. This offer was the outcome of a long, slow process.

In Quebec, property owners also own the land beneath the surface of their lots, whereas the public domain is theoretically inalienable. A specific law had to be passed so that the City of Montreal could tunnel between two streets rather than directly beneath them, using the ground under private parcels of land, consequently allowing the metro to connect with the buildings overhead and serve either or both of the roads parallel to its system (such as in the case of Sainte-Catherine and de Maisonneuve). The City is thus permitted to tunnel under private property at a minimum depth of 10 metres; a connection to the metro can be built at the expense of the private property owner, who is then responsible for its maintenance. Under certain circumstances, the municipal charter does authorize the occupancy of the land beneath the public domain.

This situation enabled the municipality to obtain private capital to finance the development of a multi-line system under buildings and streets. The partnerships took various forms, depending on whether the City directly granted the right to build over the metro, as in the case of the building erected by the developer David Bloom, or whether it negotiated with the owners of land located close to the metro, such as around the Atwater station, between the old Forum and Alexis Nihon Plaza. The Bonaventure station was a somewhat borderline application of this principle, as it is far from everything but connected to the most powerful tertiary and commercial centres.

The urban designer Vincent Ponte provided the germ of this idea for the system. Ponte was part of I.M. Pei's team set up by the developer of Place Ville-Marie, William Zeckendorf; he adamantly defended the concept of an underground shopping centre running all the way to Central Station. Events proved him right when the metro extended the effects of this initial link, and he became

the theorist of a system that gradually infiltrated and enlivened the downtown core (Peter Blake, "Vincent Ponte: A New Kind of Urban Designer," *Art in America* 57, no. 5 [September–October 1969]: 62–67).

Judging from the intensity of urban as well as suburban growth that ultimately took place, it is reasonable to conclude that the development of the metro system, and of the real estate linked to it in the business, shopping, and entertainment district, influenced land values outside the city core: the promise of an uninterrupted transit connection from the core to outlying areas would explain, for example, the rapid development that occurred around the Longueuil metro station.

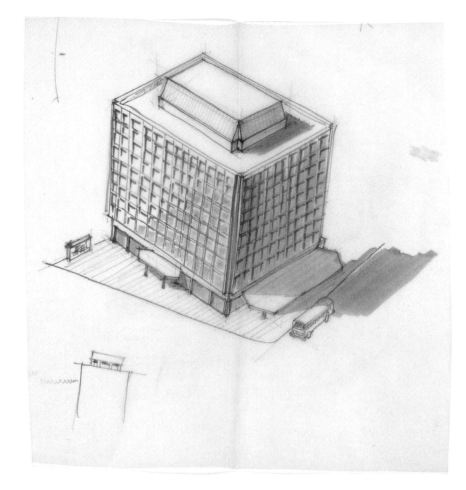

Figure 189
Perspective sketch of the Bloom Building, 1965. Mayerovitch, Bernstein, architects. Charcoal and graphite on tracing paper, 34.5 x 32.5 cm. Canadian Centre for Architecture, Montréal, Fonds Mayerovitch and Bernstein

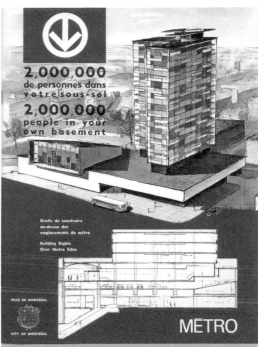

Figure 190
Project for buildings above the Guy metro station, perspective, 1962. City Planning Department, City of Montreal. Ville de Montréal, Gestion de documents et archives

Figure 191
Guy metro station, photograph of perspective of platform level, 1962. City Planning Department, City of Montreal. Ville de Montréal, Gestion de documents et archives

Figure 192
City of Montréal, 2,000,000 *People in Your Own Basement* (1965). Ville de Montréal, Gestion de documents et archives

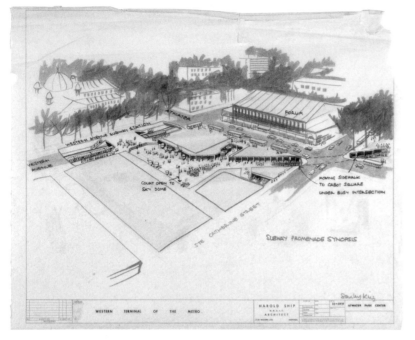

Figure 193
"Subway Promenade Synopsis," Alexis Nihon Plaza, circulation study, c. 1964. Harold Ship, architect; Stanley King, draftsman. Pen and black ink, fibre-tip pen, and graphite on translucent paper, 71 x 86.5 cm. Canadian Centre for Architecture, Montréal, Fonds Harold Ship

Figure 194
Port-de-Mer complex, Longueuil, photograph of perspective, 1966. Jean Grondin, architect. Seen in a still image from television footage. Archives Radio-Canada

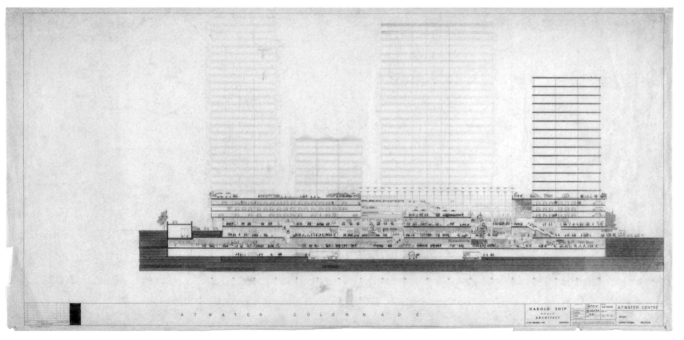

Figure 195
Alexis Nihon Plaza, longitudinal section, 25 July 1964. Harold Ship, architect; Stanley King, draftsman. Pen and black ink, fibre-tip pen, and graphite on translucent paper, 71 x 147 cm. Canadian Centre for Architecture, Montréal, Fonds Harold Ship

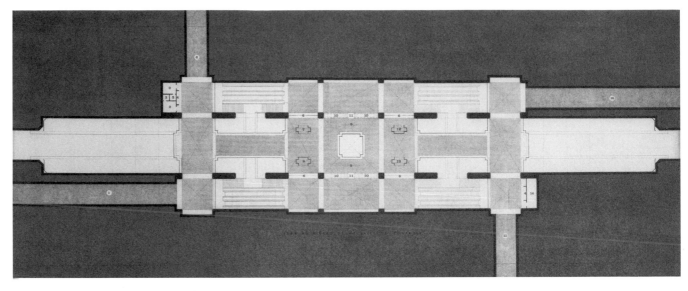

Figures 196 and 197
Bonaventure metro station, plan and longitudinal section, c. 1964. Victor Prus, architect. Photo negatives. Collection Victor Prus

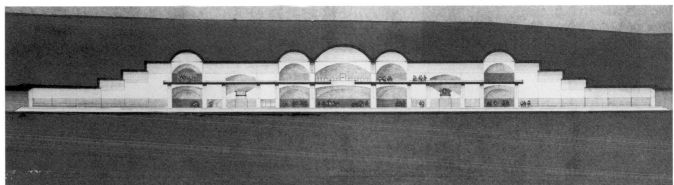

Figure 198
Aerial view of Montreal's downtown core with superimposed plan showing system of underground pedestrian passages. Vincent Ponte, architect and planner. Peter Blake, "Vincent Ponte: A New Kind of Urban Designer," *Art in America* 57, no. 5 (September–October 1969): 65. Archives of Pei, Cobb, Freed, and Partners, Architects

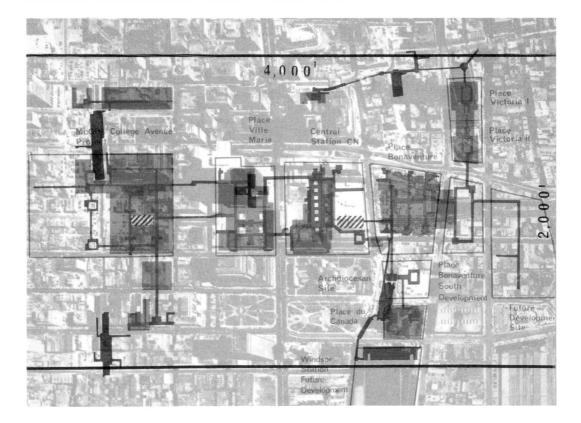

Structure
and Society

**Places and
Players**

Perceptions

Expo 67

North-South Axis in the West

Figure 199
**City Planning Department,
City of Montreal, land-use map,
1949, section 52-68.** Canadian
Centre for Architecture,
Montréal, courtesy Ville de
Montréal, Gestion de docu-
ments et archives

Figure 200
**Aerial view of downtown
Montreal, 1973.** Photograph:
Quebec Photographic Surveys.
Cartothèque de l'Université du
Québec à Montréal

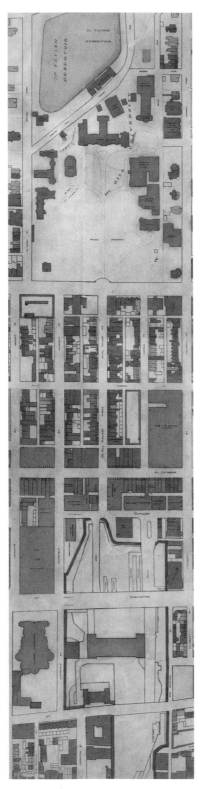

The Queen Elizabeth Hotel, inaugurated in 1958, was the
first step in a slow process of change, the form of which
was roughed out many times after the Canadian Northern
Railway Company dug a wide trench at that location in
the side of the mountain so that it could build the Mount
Royal underground railway line (see *Montreal Metropolis,
1880–1930*, ed. Isabelle Gournay and France Vanlaethem
[Montreal: Canadian Centre for Architecture, 1998]). In the
1960s, this gaping hole, these abandoned remains of the
Industrial Age's ruthless urbanization, became the site of
unprecedented development.

When the developer William Zeckendorf entered the
picture in 1956, the most recent study for this sector was
undoubtedly that commissioned from Jacques Gréber in
1946, which he submitted in the early 1950s. It included
the basic elements of what was to come: access ramps to
the east-west expressway, multilevel construction over the
railway line between Cathcart and Saint-Antoine, and the
widening of McGill College Avenue. But it was the daring
construction of Place Ville-Marie by Zeckendorf, at a time
when no one in Montreal would have gambled on a large-
scale office complex, that stimulated development not
only in this area, but in the downtown as a whole.

The complex is clever in design and elegant in architectural style. From Dorchester, it links a large "Cartesian"
tower, slender despite its cruciform plan, to a promenade
of shops accessible on the Cathcart side. The slightly sloping topography allowed the promenade to extend under
Dorchester to Central Station and its future satellites.

Much more austere, Place Bonaventure is a fortified
city that reveals nothing of the programming feat inside:
shop-lined promenade, exhibition hall, and offices, with
a hotel built above, featuring a rooftop garden, and the
Central Station railway line below, along with the delivery
ramps needed for the exhibition area.

Figure 201
Aerial view of downtown
Montreal, looking east, 25 April
1967. Photograph: Armour
Landry. Centre de Montréal des
Archives nationales du Québec

As a centennial project, Blouin and Prus proposed covering the railway line, further to the south, with an enormous slab extending out like a diving board over the mouth of the Lachine Canal, dominated by twin towers reminiscent of those in Brasília; however, the funds needed for this ambitious plan could not be raised. The "Centre Hochelaga," sketched by Daniel van Ginkel for the site where Place Bonaventure now stands, would never reach fruition either. It was a key part of his "Central Area Circulation Study," and would have taken advantage of the plateau topography to submerge the expressway and the metro and train lines under an artificial ground level.

The Place Ville-Marie and Place Bonaventure projects represented a surprising strategic reversal, opting for a view of the river and the industrial and working-class areas rather than of the mountain. Place Victoria (the Stock Exchange Tower) was part of this reversal. With its precast corner columns that gradually taper as they rise, it is a building of absolute elegance that seemed destined to be emulated but never was.

Figure 202
Study for alterations to the Central Station area in relation to the east-west expressway. Attributed to Jacques Gréber, urban planning consultant to the City of Montreal, c. 1953. Letterpress half-tone print, 48 x 25.5 cm. Canadian Centre for Architecture, Montréal, Fonds André Blouin

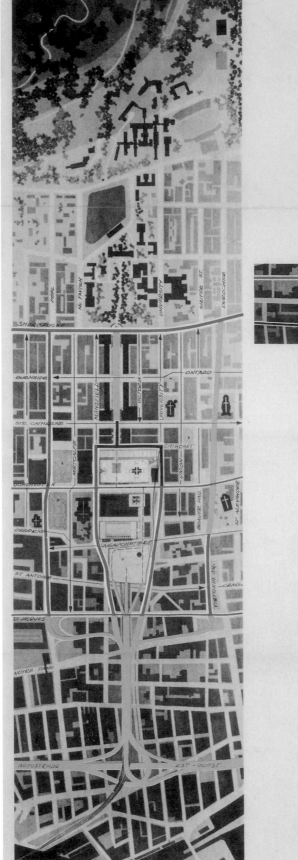

PLAN D'ENSEMBLE

RESEAU DES VOIES DISTRIBUTRICES PROJETEES POUR LE CENTRE DE LA VILLE ....

sections actuelles

améliorations projetées

améliorations soumises pour approbation: parties des rues University, Cathcart et McGill College.

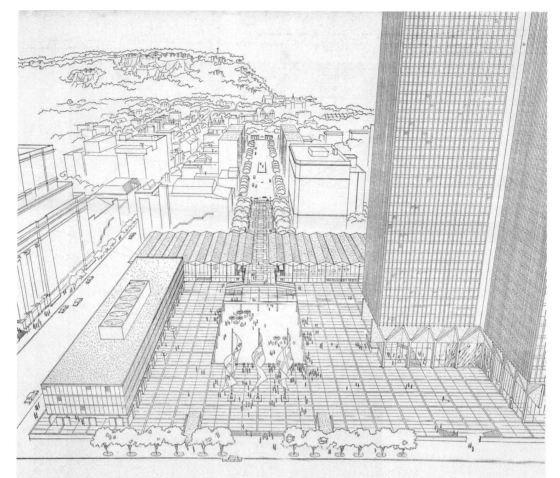

Figure 203
Place Ville-Marie, perspective sketch of preliminary scheme for north block, from photomontage of the site. I.M. Pei and Associates, architects. *Progressive Architecture* (February 1960): 128. Canadian Centre for Architecture, Montréal, Fonds André Blouin

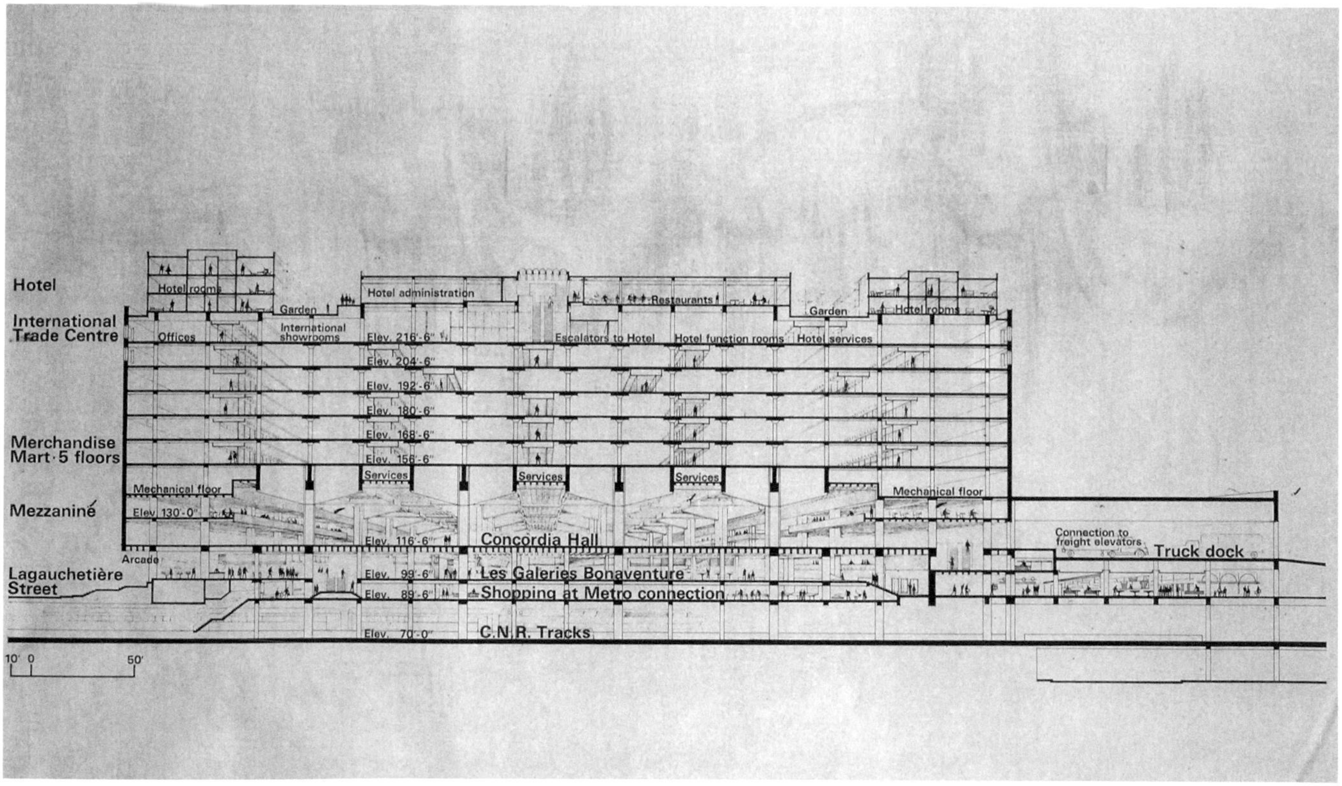

Figure 204
Place Bonaventure, north-south section looking east, 23 February 1966. Affleck, Desbarats, Dimakopoulos, Lebensold, Michaud, and Sise, architects. Sepia diazotype with graphite border, 89 x 115 cm Bibliothèque nationale du Québec

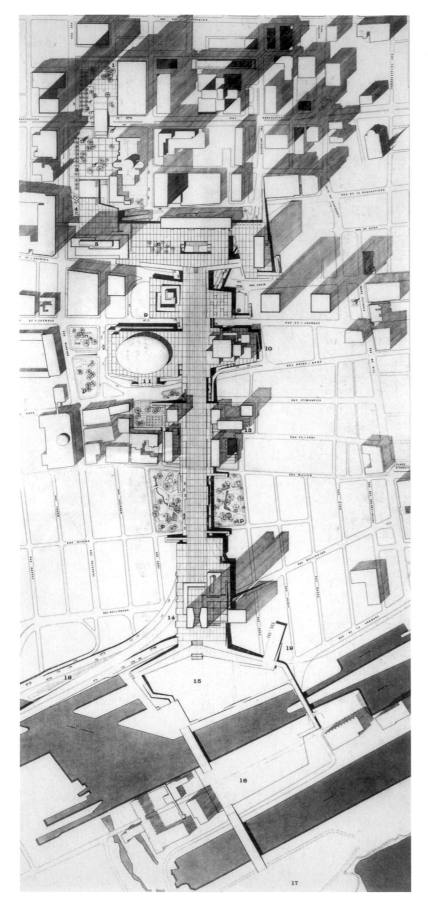

Figure 205
Plan for "Confederation Promenade," c. 1960–1961. André Blouin and Victor Prus, architects. Photostat, 15 x 35.2 cm. Canadian Centre for Architecture, Montréal, Fonds André Blouin

Figure 206
Canadian Pacific Railways Hotel Development, elevation study, September 1963. D'Astous and Pothier, architects. Photostat, 64.5 x 45.5 cm. Canadian Centre for Architecture, Montréal, Fonds Roger D'Astous

Figure 207
Place Victoria, model, 1965. Luigi Moretti, architect. Photograph: Arnott Rogers Batten Ltd. Ville de Montréal, Gestion de documents et archives

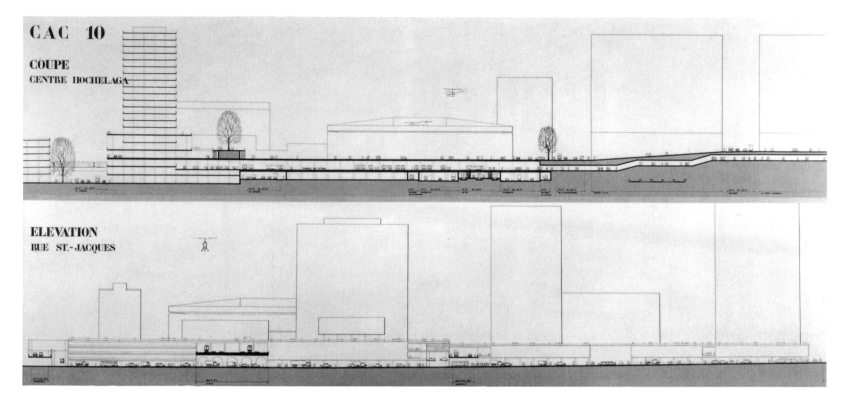

CAC 10

COUPE
CENTRE HOCHELAGA

ELEVATION
RUE ST.-JACQUES

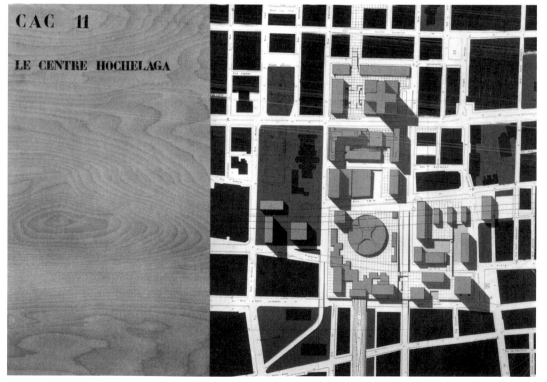

CAC 11

LE CENTRE HOCHELAGA

Figures 208 and 209
Centre Hochelaga, section, elevation, and massing plan, c. 1960–1961. Van Ginkel Associates, architects and planners. Canadian Centre for Architecture, Montréal, Fonds van Ginkel

Structure
and Society

**Places and
Players**

Perceptions

Expo 67

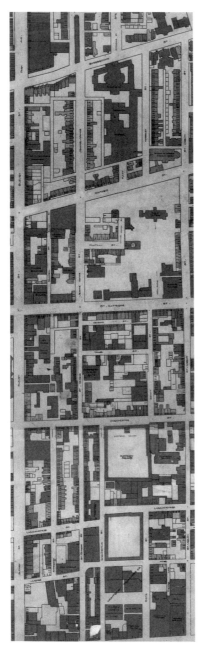

Figure 210
**City Planning Department, City
of Montreal, land-use map,
1949, section 56-68.** Canadian
Centre for Architecture,
Montreal, courtesy Ville de
Montréal, Gestion de docu-
ments et archives

Figure 211
**Aerial view of downtown
Montreal, 1973.** Photograph:
Quebec Photographic Surveys.
Cartothèque de l'Université du
Québec à Montréal

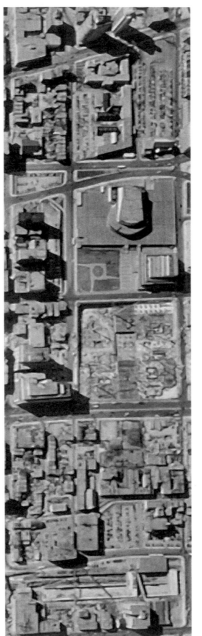

While the development of a tertiary axis in the west
depended primarily on an underlying growth dynamic,
that in the east – albeit well defined by illustrated urban
planning documents – was entirely the result of a political
and technocratic process targeting the area bounded by
Craig, Bleury, Sherbrooke, and Saint Lawrence for renewal
(*Proposed Development of a Blighted Residential Area and
Construction of Low Rental Housing*, City of Montreal, 1954).
The area was, in fact, gradually renewed, and several sectors were identified for potential redevelopment, including
Pointe Saint-Charles, Little Burgundy, and the eventual site
of the Jeanne-Mance housing project. Those sectors were
primarily residential, whereas the one between Bleury and
Saint Lawrence was designated for cultural institutions,
stores, and businesses – an orientation that Mayor Jean
Drapeau had advocated for the Jeanne-Mance housing
project site (Cité des Ondes). This area would become the
locus of French-Canadian pride and prestige.

The first project to be completed along this axis
was Place des Arts, the result of a study assigned to the
French-born American designer Raymond Loewy, who
recommended the creation of a cultural and commercial
complex, with performance halls and streetfront shops.
The architectural firm responsible for the project – Affleck,
Desbarats, Dimakopoulos, Lebensold, Michaud, and Sise
– designed the main auditorium in the shape of a scallop
shell, a form characteristic of the Modern Movement. The
initial versions of the project were somewhat reminiscent
of Lincoln Center in New York.

Figure 212
Aerial view of Place des Arts
sector, 1968. Affleck, Desbarats,
Dimakopoulos, Lebensold,
Michaud, and Sise, architects.
Photograph: Armour Landry.
Centre de Montréal des
Archives nationales du Québec

Figure 213
Institut de technologie de Montréal, perspective sketch, c. 1966–1967. Jean Michaud, architect. Graphite on tracing paper, 52.8 x 34.8 cm. Canadian Centre for Architecture, Montréal, Fonds Jean Michaud

Figure 214
Institut de technologie de Montréal, master plan, August 1967. Jean Michaud, architect. Ink, graphite, and self-adhesive plastic film on translucent paper collage, with sepia diazotype, 78.5 x 70.5 cm. Canadian Centre for Architecture, Montréal, Fonds Jean Michaud

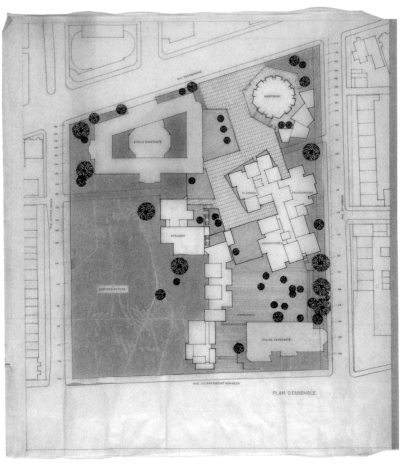

In the north, the Brutalist project by the architect Jean Michaud would not be built, and it would take many years before the Université du Québec à Montréal would erect a contemporary-style building. Things moved more quickly in the south, where ambitious studies were submitted one after another. The grandiose scheme proposed by André Blouin to mark the centennial of Confederation was followed by a project for the Caisses populaires Desjardins, led by the urban designer Jean-Claude La Haye. The series of high-rises proposed in the initial studies, which could have counterbalanced the skyscrapers to the west, were dropped in favour of a more sensible cluster of buildings, whose austerity was meant to be softened by a planned dome over the pedestrian intersection, consisting of an assemblage of hyperbolic paraboloids forming a saddle shape. With the construction of the neighbouring Hydro-Québec head office, designed by the architect Gaston Gagnier and completed in 1960, before the nationalization of electric power, Québec's new technocracy asserted itself.

Van Ginkel's project for the area bordering the east-west expressway must be understood in relation to the traffic studies he carried out for the City Planning Department; this project proposed the elimination of brick housing and the production of clusters of buildings in the form of Aztec pyramids.

Figure 215
Proposal for Place des Arts, photograph of perspective, c. 1958–1959. Affleck, Desbarats, Dimakopoulos, Lebensold, Michaud, and Sise, architects. Société de la Place des Arts de Montréal

Figure 216
Complexe Desjardins, photograph of presentation model, c. 1970. Office of La Haye and Ouellet, planners and architects. Canadian Centre for Architecture, Montréal, Fonds Jean Ouellet

Figure 217
Proposal for Maison de Radio-Canada, perspective, 31 October 1958. Canadian Broadcasting Corporation. Ville de Montréal, Gestion de documents et archives

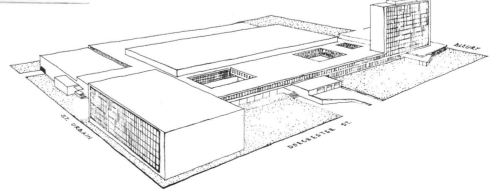

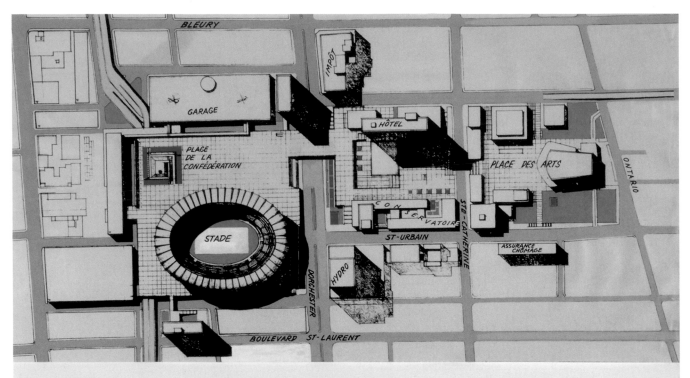

Figure 218
"Place de la Confédération,"
massing plan study, 1960.
André Blouin and Jean Gareau,
architects and planners. Ink
and gouache over reproduction
print mounted on heavy card,
76 x 102 cm. Canadian Centre
for Architecture, Montréal,
Fonds André Blouin

Figure 219
"Place de la Confédération,"
perspective, July 1960. André
Blouin and Jean Gareau, archi-
tects and planners. Canadian
Centre for Architecture,
Montréal, Fonds André Blouin

Figure 220
Hydro-Québec Building. Gaston
Gagnier, architect. Cover of
Entre-nous (February 1959).
Archives Hydro-Québec, Fonds
Commission hydroélectrique
de Québec 1944–1963

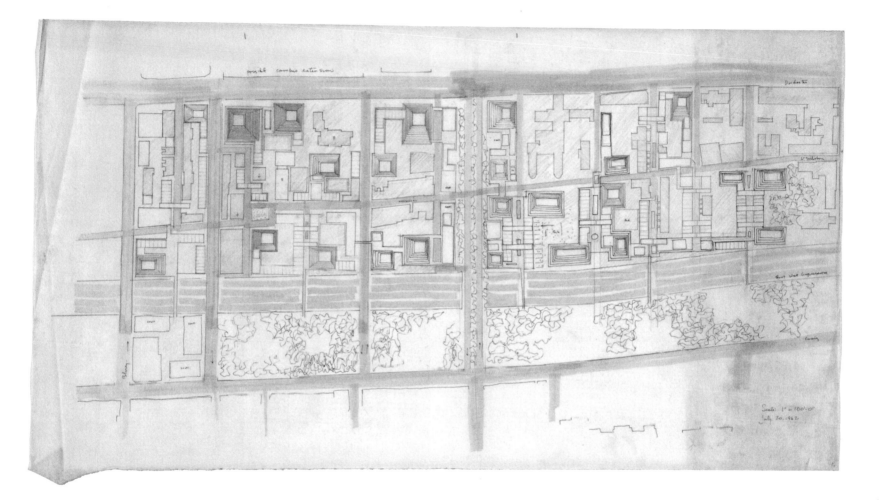

Figure 221
Proposed redevelopment plan for the area east of Bleury Street, July 1962. Van Ginkel Associates, architects and planners. Pen and black ink, graphite, fibre-tip pen, and coloured pencil on paper, 50.5 x 91.5 cm. Canadian Centre for Architecture, Montréal, Fonds van Ginkel

Structure
and Society

Places and
Players

Perceptions

Expo 67

Perceptions from Abroad

The radical changes taking place in downtown Montreal attracted the attention of architecture critics even before Expo 67, when all eyes were fixed on the Canadian metropolis. The cycle the city had entered at that time seemed to fulfil the promises of avant-garde thinkers both in terms of programs (separation of functions, large specialized buildings, specialization of infrastructures) and organization (concentration of economic and symbolic functions in the core, combination of means of transit). But it was also the very strong identity growing out of this change that elicited admiration, even if it was never stated outright. Montreal developed a singular character that was consistent with the objective of reidentification favoured by Team X.

The sampling of testimonials reproduced here clearly reflects an evolution in the way Montreal was perceived from abroad, from an architectural appreciation of a large-scale but isolated tertiary undertaking ("Le nouveau centre d'affaires de Montréal," *L'Architecture d'aujourd'hui*, June–July 1959, 82–83) to the perception of something that could constitute a system (Peter Blake, "Downtown in 3-D," *The Architectural Forum* 125, no.2 [September 1966], 31–48) and that was in line with ideas being debated at the time: the separation of traffic flows, the linking of transit modes operating at varying speeds and scales, control of the environment, and so forth (J.M. Richards, "Multi-Level City," *The Architectural Review*, no. 846 [August 1967]: 86–96).

Figure 222
Peter Blake, "Downtown
in 3-D," *The Architectural
Forum* 125, no. 2 (September
1966). Canadian Centre for
Architecture, Montréal

DOWNTOWN IN 3-D

Through a happy combination of expert fore-sight, private initiative, and luck, Montreal is about to become the first 20th century city in North America. Its Downtown, compressed between Mount Royal and the St. Lawrence, is seen here outlined in white, erupting skyward. But what sets this core apart is not so much the towers as their spreading roots in a multilevel network of shops, transportation systems, and pedestrian promenades.

Among those who assisted greatly in the preparation of this article was the architect Herbert C. Auerbach, who was I.M. Pei & Associates' on-site representative when the Place Ville Marie complex was built. Mr. Auerbach is now a project coordinator to urban redevelopment group the Concordia Estates. Full credits for design of the major Downtown projects are on page 106. The views expressed on these pages are, of course, those of the author.

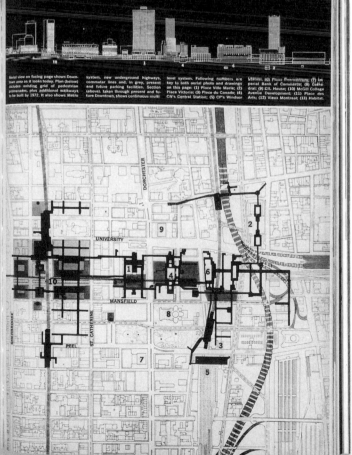

13

NOMINAL NORTH

TRUE NORTH

THE SHAPING OF A MULTI-LEVEL CORE

It wasn't really planned quite that way; indeed, hardly anyone really believed that it was going to happen—until the facts became impossible to ignore.

And even now, with tunnels for the new rubber-wheeled subway reaching into the very heart of Downtown; with underground expressways built to link Downtown to the Trans-Canada Highway; with more than 4 miles of shopping promenades either completed or about to be—and separated out from automobiles, parking, service trucks, subways, and commuter lines by a continuous, multilevel complex (facing page) much larger than anything of this sort ever built before—even now, few people in Montreal seem to realize that they are building the most advanced urban core of our time.

What is happening in this approximately 200-acre core of Montreal is that the vision of a multilevel metropolis is finally being realized. What is happening also is that "urban architecture" is being redefined: Downtown Montreal is no grandiose Potemkin Village; it is, instead, an urban organism—architecturally good, bad, or indifferent.

Downtown Montreal began to erupt about ten years ago, when William Zeckendorf's Place Ville Marie (PVM) started to take shape. To get PVM underway, Zeckendorf brought in a team under the leadership of Architects I.M. Pei and Henry N. Cobb, and Planner Vincent Ponte. There had been considerable spadework during the preceding 30 years (see pp. 36-37); but it was the construction of PVM which sparked the new Downtown, and it is the planning principles established by the PVM team that are shaping it.

To Ponte, Downtown Montreal is contained in a rectangle about 2,000 ft. wide and 4,000 ft. long (see aerial view at left). Ponte believes that a viable urban area rarely exceeds 200 to 250 acres—any such area can be traversed by pedestrians in 15 minutes or less, which is about the limit of comfortable pedestrianism in this automanic age.

Ponte and his associates are making Downtown pedestrianism more comfortable than it has ever been made in any North American city in this century. For the new Downtown Montreal is a network of climate-controlled promenades that will, by 1972, criss-cross and connect some 100 out of the 180 acres that make up the core.

This pedestrian network is fed by intercity buses, whose terminal is on the periphery of the core; by suburban trains that terminate on the fringes of the new Downtown, or traverse it at another level; and by the new Metro subway lines bracketing Downtown, which alone will bring some 500,000 people into the core on every single working day. The network is completely separated from the surface streets and the new highways, whose tentacles will reach underground into the very center of the core, ramp up to street level, and feed into Mansfield Street—a distribution spine siphoning traffic directly into parking garages with an ultimate capacity of 9,000 stalls.

On their way to and from work, and during lunch hours, those who use the network will circulate past and through more than a million square feet of stores, restaurants, movie theaters, book shops, and galleries. And, in doing so, they may help establish a new urban prototype: Downtown's answer to the suburban shopping center.

The other day, a secretary in a brokerage firm that had just moved into PVM from an older building was asked how she liked the new neighborhood. "It's just great," she said. "It's like a party all day long. You can get everywhere, see anyone, anytime, regardless of weather. There's nothing like it." There isn't—but it took a lot of doing.

Aerial view on facing page shows Downtown area as it looks today. Plan (below) includes existing grid of pedestrian promenades, plus additional walkways to be built by 1972. It also shows Metro system, new underground highways, commuter lines and, in grey, present and future parking facilities. Section (above), taken through present and future Downtown, shows continuous multilevel system. Following numbers are key to both aerial photo and drawings on this page: (1) Place Ville Marie; (2) Place Victoria; (3) Place du Canada; (4) CN's Central Station; (5) CP's Windsor Station; (6) Place Bonaventure; (7) Imperial Bank of Commerce; (8) Cathedral; (9) CIL House; (10) McGill College Avenue Development; (11) Place des Arts; (12) Vieux Montreal; (13) Habitat.

DORCHESTER

UNIVERSITY

9

2

10

1

4

6

MANSFIELD

8

3

PEEL

ST. CATHERINE

SHERBROOKE

7

5

The new core is the product of topography, tradition—and vision

Metropolitan Montreal (population 2.2 million) covers the island formed by the St. Lawrence and the Rivière des Prairies, spilling onto the opposite shore. But the essential Montreal is compressed between the mountain and the big river. This fact accounts in large measure for the exciting urban character of Montreal: the core has been prevented from leaking out into sprawl.

There are other facts that have contributed: the fact that its population is largely French-speaking, and traditionally urban oriented; the fact that Montreal is a great port; the fact that it is an important railroad hub, with both the Canadian National (CN) and the Canadian Pacific (CP) railroads converging in the city's core; the fact that it is a famous university town and thus a major intellectual and cultural center; and the fact that it has always had a considerable architectural tradition.

And there is one supremely important fact of topography that enabled Downtown's planners to develop their multiple decks: the fact that Downtown Montreal, from the McGill campus to the banks of the St. Lawrence, drops off between 150 and 200 feet in elevation. "All you need is a 15-foot change in elevation to put out of sight one entire system of services," Harry Cobb said recently.

Vincent Ponte immediately recognized the overriding importance of the third dimension

in Montreal's topographic potential. "Planners are beginning to go beyond the 2-D of paper plans," Ponte says. "In this city we are concentrating the core functions into a tight, totally interrelated unit, doubling and tripling the use of the same par-

cels of precious Downtown land by inserting several levels above and below ground."

One should probably know one or two additional facts of geography, history, and local tradition: first—a matter of clarification—"north" in Montreal is, in fact, almost west; second, St. Lawrence Boulevard (which runs "north-south") is considered the dividing line between French-speaking Montrealers (east) and English-speaking ones (west). This division determines some planning decisions that might make little sense otherwise.

So these were the preconditions for the new Downtown Montreal: a geographic fact; an urban tradition; a crossroads location; a cultural preoccupation and heritage; and a topographic advantage. Now all that was needed was the opportunity to plan on a big scale, and men with vision, and in the right places, to do the planning. Between 1956 and 1966—the period which Ponte calls the "ten golden years of Montreal's Downtown"—significant things began to happen:

First, the CN's president, Donald Gordon, decided that the time had come to develop the railroad's 22 acres of land (mostly air rights) around Central Station. As early as the 1920's, Sir Henry Thornton, a predecessor of Gordon, had commissioned plans for such a development, and these plans already contained the basic principle of a multilevel Downtown core.

Second, Gordon brought in

Bill Zeckendorf, who immediately recognized the potential of the CN property: its ideal location in terms of existing and possible future transportation facilities; and its location in the path of the shift in Montreal's center of gravity.

Third, Zeckendorf, in turn, brought in Pei, Cobb, and Ponte to design not only the 7-acre PVM site, but to prepare a master plan as well for the entire 22-acre CN property. (Actually, they went far beyond the confines of that site.)

Fourth, Zeckendorf's enormous gamble—to build 1.5 million square feet of rental office space in one great cruciform tower, at a time when Montreal's annual office space construction came to a mere 300,000 square feet—paid off when the late James Muir, president of the Royal Bank of Canada, moved from his old St. James Street headquarters into PVM.

And, **Fifth,** there was the significant contribution of the city of Montreal itself, and that of its mayor, Jean Drapeau. He had been re-elected in 1960 on a platform that promised construction of a long-discussed mass transit system—the "Metro" subway.

These were the most crucial events of Montreal's "ten golden years." Because Mayor Drapeau and others showed the vision to build the new Downtown core, Montreal succeeded in attracting next year's official World's Fair (EXPO 57). That coup was the final boost that the city needed.

37

PHASE ONE: PVM PAVES THE WAY

The aerial photograph at left was taken in the spring of 1963, a few months after the 7-acre PVM complex was dedicated.

To those who observed the dedication, the most significant aspect of PVM may have been the part that showed above ground level: the 48-story cruciform tower (right) placed off-center next to a 4-acre plaza. That tower contained 1.5 million square feet of rentable office space (five times the amount then being built annually in all of Montreal put together)—and it was an impressive sight indeed.

But more significant in terms of urban design were the four levels (totaling 1.2 million square feet) underneath the plaza—the part of PVM that did not meet the eye.

On those four levels (see section, opposite), Zeckendorf's team of architects and planners had created an organism consisting of promenades a half-mile in length, lit in part through sunken courts, and serving about 160,000 square feet of retail space. Below these promenades there were two levels of parking (capacity: 1,200 cars), and below it were

the CN's tracks and platforms. Trucks were brought into PVM through underground roadways, without interference at any level with parking or pedestrians.

PVM's network did not stop at the property line. It was tied into adjacent buildings so that, for example, pedestrians could move under cover from PVM to Central Station. All told, the initial construction created 1½ miles of promenades, and there were plans to tie PVM's subplaza organism to future buildings as well.

When Zeckendorf first proposed his great Downtown system

of promenades, "experts" predicted inevitable failure. The truth is that the retail space has been fully rented since PVM was opened, and the turnover in tenants has been zero.

What made the location of Place Ville Marie so attractive to Bill Zeckendorf? Some of the reasons are obvious: the CN's property was served by a system of commuter trains (including a railroad tunnel that bends due north from Central Station, and passes under Mount-Royal); the CP's Windsor Station was nearby, as was a major bus terminal;

St. Catherine Street, Montreal's principal shopping thoroughfare, with three big department stores, was a short block to the north; and there were good hotels nearby as well.

Moreover, there was a noticeable shift taking place in Montreal's center of commercial gravity: Vieux Montreal, now a historic district, had been the original core; the St. James Street area to the west had become the Wall Street of Montreal at the turn of the century; and by then the residential areas had moved up to the slopes of

39

Phase One (continued):
PVM began with
a hole in the ground

Mount Royal. Retailing followed its customers, and centered on St. Catherine Street. The final shift began as the office center, in the years between the first and second world wars, slowly moved towards Mount Royal. The PVM site stood squarely in the path of this movement.

At this point, Montreal's Mayor Drapeau initiated plans for the new Metro system which will open next month. The system—possibly the most modern in the world—will bracket the new Downtown area. And its tracks are located so far underground that each station includes a mezzanine level halfway between the tracks and the street. These mezzanines will become integral parts of the Downtown network of promenades; by the time the Metro opens, this public contribution to the Downtown organism will add another mile of connecting walkways.

When PVM was little more than a hole in the ground (opposite page), Bill Zeckendorf needed one—just one—really big tenant who would make the move from the St. James Street district into the emerging new core. That tenant was the Royal Bank of Canada, whose then president, the late James Muir, shared Zeckendorf's optimism.

Today PVM's tower bears the Royal Bank's name. And soon after Muir decided in 1958 to move into PVM, several others joined the exodus from St. James Street. The Canadian Imperial Bank of Commerce built its 43-story tower on Dominion Square; the 34-story CIL House went up diagonally across the street from PVM; and all around PVM, properties were being assembled and new office space was being planned on a scale that would have seemed inconceivable a few years earlier.

One significant detail emerged as these new structures went up; most of those that were tied into the PVM complex and other networks tended to rent very rapidly. Some of those that stood alone found it harder to attract tenants. The lesson was not lost upon the planners and developers of the new Downtown.

Opposite page: The bird's eye view at left was taken in 1954, showing the same blocks, part of which were to become PVM's site. The bottom photo was taken of the same area a few years ago. Just behind PVM, to the left, is CIL House; and rising at the photo's right edge is the CIBC tower. This page: From top to bottom, four levels of Montreal's downtown network. First comes the PVM plaza; then the promenade level, with escalators leading to commuter railways; then the mezzanine of one of the Metro stations a few blocks away; and finally the Metro tracks.

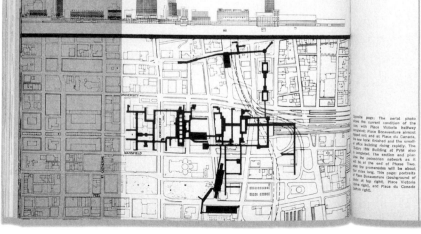

Opposite page: The aerial photo shows the current condition of the core, with Place Victoria halfway completed; Place Bonaventure almost topped out; and at Place du Canada, the new hotel finished and the smaller office building rising rapidly. The sleek IBM Building at PVM also is completed. The section and plan show the pedestrian network as it will be at the end of Phase Two, when the promenades will be about four miles long. This page: portraits of Place Bonaventure (background of photo at top right), Place Victoria (above right), and Place du Canada (bottom right).

PHASE TWO: THE CORE IN FULL SWING

Next to deciding to develop the CN's 22-acre downtown site, President Donald Gordon's most important decision may have been to insist that Zeckendorf produce a master plan for the entire area.

Even in its first phase (PVM), that master plan proved to be so convincing that Vincent Ponte was retained by Place Bonaventure and, more recently, by other major developers planning in the new Downtown. As a result, there has been a consistency and continuity in the fundamental approach unmatched in any other modern city.

Yet the architectural expression, above grade, could hardly be more diverse. Among the new buildings now going up (or recently completed) in the new Downtown are these:

Place Victoria—the sleek 47-story concrete and glass tower by Moretti and Nervi, housing the Stock Exchange. Its tapering corner columns have given Montreal's skyline a striking new silhouette (below). Hopefully, the

initial tower, with its six-story annex, will be duplicated, in mirror-image fashion; and the entire complex will then be tied into Place Bonaventure and the Metro.

Place Bonaventure—the "New Brutalist" 15-story, rough concrete structure (above right, behind Place Victoria, and page 45)

by ARCOP, which will contain 3.1 million square feet of space, including shopping galleries, exhibition halls, and a 400-room hotel on the roof. PB is being built over 5 acres of the CN's tracks, and will be completed next spring. It, too, is intimately tied to subsurface systems, including underground service roads for trucks. The owners are Concordia Estates, perhaps the brightest developers on the Montreal scene at present.

Place du Canada—a complex of two dissimilar buildings that share a common pedestal (below). The first to be completed, the

"raised-eyebrows" Hotel Chateau Champlain, is 38 stories high, contains 640 rooms, and was designed by D'Astous & Pothier. The second building, an elegant 28-story precast concrete office tower by John B. & John C. Parkin, is nearing completion. Under the paved plaza, in a five-story podium, are located a bank, shopping promenades, a movie theater, and other facilities. There is also underground parking on five levels; and the entire complex is tied, by means of a pedestrian bridge at plaza level, to Dominion Square to the north. The Canadian Pacific is the owner (or part owner) of the entire Place du Canada complex.

Other construction, on a smaller scale, is also under way in the area. Meanwhile, the new Downtown is receiving massive infusions of assistance from other sources as well. Specifically:

The Metro is rapidly nearing completion, and its mezzanine platforms will form an increasingly important part of the overall system of Downtown pedestrian promenades.

The Trans-Canada Highway System is being extended, rapidly, into the center of Downtown. Originally planned as an elevated expressway to run along Mon-

43

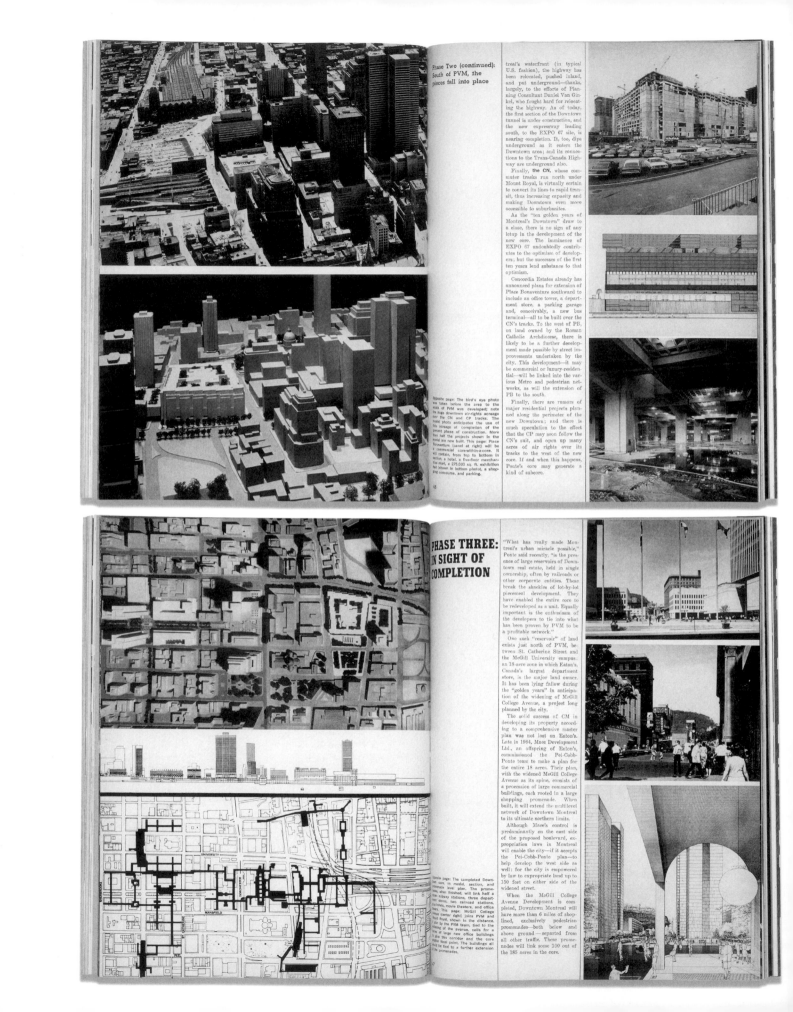

Phase Two (continued): South of PVM, the pieces fall into place

treal's waterfront (in typical U.S. fashion), the highway has been relocated, pushed inland, and put underground—thanks, largely, to the efforts of Planning Consultant Daniel Van Ginkel, who fought hard for relocating the highway. As of today, the first section of the Downtown tunnel is under construction, and the new expressway leading south, to the EXPO 67 site, is nearing completion. It, too, dips underground as it enters the Downtown area; and its connections to the Trans-Canada Highway are underground also.

Finally, **the CN**, whose commuter tracks run north under Mount Royal, is virtually certain to convert its lines to rapid transit, thus increasing capacity and making Downtown even more accessible to suburbanites.

As the "ten golden years of Montreal's Downtown" draw to a close, there is no sign of any letup in the development of the new core. The imminence of EXPO 67 undoubtedly contributes to the optimism of developers; but the successes of the first ten years lend substance to that optimism.

Concordia Estates already has announced plans for extension of Place Bonaventure southward to include an office tower, a department store, a parking garage and, conceivably, a new bus terminal—all to be built over the CN's tracks. To the west of PB, on land owned by the Roman Catholic Archdiocese, there is likely to be a further development made possible by street improvements undertaken by the city. This development—it may be commercial or luxury-residential—will be linked into the various Metro and pedestrian networks, as will the extension of PB to the south.

Finally, there are rumors of major residential projects planned along the perimeter of the new Downtown; and there is much speculation to the effect that the CP may soon follow the CN's suit, and open up many acres of air rights over its tracks to the west of the new core. If and when this happens, Ponte's core may generate a kind of subcore.

Opposite page: The bird's eye photo was taken before the area to the south of PVM was developed; note the huge downtown air-rights acreage over the CN and CP tracks. The model photo anticipates the use of this acreage at completion of the present phase of construction. More than half the projects shown in the model are now built. This page: Place Bonaventure (panel at right) will be a commercial core-within-a-core. It will contain, from top to bottom in section, a hotel, a five-floor merchandise mart, a 275,000 sq. ft. exhibition hall (shown in bottom photo), a shopping concourse, and parking.

PHASE THREE: IN SIGHT OF COMPLETION

"What has really made Montreal's urban miracle possible," Ponte said recently, "is the presence of large reservoirs of Downtown real estate, held in single ownership, often by railroads or other corporate entities. These break the shackles of lot-by-lot piecemeal development. They have enabled the entire core to be redeveloped as a unit. Equally important is the enthusiasm of the developers to tie into what has been proven by PVM to be a profitable network."

One such "reservoir" of land exists just north of PVM, between St. Catherine Street and the McGill University campus: an 18-acre zone in which Eaton's, Canada's largest department store, is the major land owner. It has been lying fallow during the "golden years" in anticipation of the widening of McGill College Avenue, a project long planned by the city.

The solid success of CM in developing its property according to a comprehensive master plan was not lost on Eaton's. Late in 1964, Mace Development Ltd., an offspring of Eaton's, commissioned the Pei-Cobb-Ponte team to make a plan for the entire 18 acres. Their plan, with the widened McGill College Avenue as its spine, consists of a procession of large commercial buildings, each rooted in a large shopping promenade. When built, it will extend the multilevel network of Downtown Montreal to its ultimate northern limits.

Although Mace's control is predominantly on the east side of the proposed boulevard, expropriation laws in Montreal will enable the city—if it accepts the Pei-Cobb-Ponte plan—to help develop the west side as well: for the city is empowered by law to expropriate land up to 150 feet on either side of the widened street.

When the McGill College Avenue Development is completed, Downtown Montreal will have more than 6 miles of shop-lined, exclusively pedestrian promenades—both below and above ground—separated from all other traffic. These promenades will link some 100 out of the 185 acres in the core.

Opposite page: The completed Downtown core in model, section, and intermediate level plan. The promenades, when finished, will link half a dozen subway stations, three department stores, two railroad stations, hotels, movie theaters, and office buildings. This page: McGill College Avenue (center right) joins PVM and Place Ville Marie, shown in the distance. The plan, by the PVM team, tied to the widening of the avenue, calls for a series of large new office buildings at this corridor and the core's other focal point. The buildings all would be tied to a further extension of the promenades.

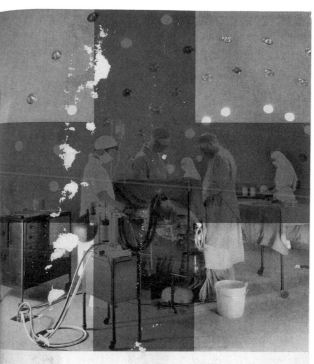

Phase Three (continued): A new kind of city and "a fresh excitement"

There are some unanswered questions about the new core of Montreal, and they may not be answered until the core has had a chance to function for some years. Among them are:

• Will there remain enough reasonably priced housing in or near the core to retain the present vitality of Downtown?

• Will the vastly improved system of mass transit and fast highways encourage flight into the suburbs?

• Can Montreal's beautiful waterfront be rescued from its present, largely industrial blight —and will the construction of EXPO 67 on the St. Lawrence hasten this process?

• Can Montreal absorb as much commercial space as is being projected at present?

• And will some of the other, smaller cores now growing up, without much planning, to the east and the west, detract from the new Downtown?

Those who give optimistic answers to these and similar questions base their optimism upon the special quality of Montreal and Montrealers. "When I was working in Toronto," the City Planning Department's Harry Lash recalled recently, "they argued for years about whether or not to install trash baskets in public places, and how to make them straight-sided so the city could sell advertising space on those baskets! Here, in Montreal, it is just assumed that a city should be a pleasant place; and so, one day, they just installed some very handsome baskets on all our street corners." Montreal is a town that likes itself.

In describing the achievement, now about two thirds complete,

of a multilevel core, Vincent Ponte has this to say:

"The conception itself is not new. Four hundred and eighty years ago, Leonardo da Vinci sketched a plan for putting wagons and walkers on different levels (bottom). The idea has been proposed time and time again, and sometimes tried out on a small scale.

"The best known example, New York's Rockefeller Center Concourse, winds through 17 acres, but its labyrinth of passageways scarcely invites people to linger. Montreal's, when it is finished, will link six subway stops, 9,000 parking spaces, five skyscrapers, three department stores, two railroad stations, four luxury hotels, eight theaters, 30 first-class restaurants, and scores of smart shops and markets in a meander of pleasant, skylighted malls, enlivened by greenery and fountains. It is more than a pedestrian thoroughfare; it is an environment that people may enjoy all day long.

"The new Downtown Montreal has given the city a fresh excitement and vitality."

It has done even more than that: It has demonstrated what the new cores of our cities could be like—if only those who planned their bits and pieces would learn to plan together, to produce urban organisms, rather than plan separately and produce only glossier versions of the mixture as before.

In North America, in short, Montreal may be the city to watch. If it turns out to be as good as it promises to be, most of our planners will have to go back to their drafting boards.

—Peter Blake

Above, plans of New York's Rockefeller Center Concourse (17 acres) and of the ultimate Montreal promenade system (100 acres) drawn at the same scale. Left, Downtown Montreal in transition: at left, the platform of Place du Canada; in the middle, Place Bonaventure; at right, the first tower of Place Victoria.

PHOTOGRAPHS: George Cserna, except pages 31-32, page 40 (bottom); Aerial Photos of New England pages 33-34, page 38 (top), page 40 (top), page 43 (top), page 44 (top), Lockwood Survey Corporation Limited.

48

architecture d'aujourd'hui

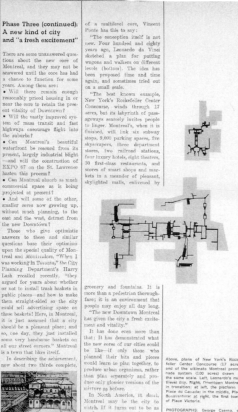

LE NOUVEAU CENTRE D'AFFAIRES DE MONTRÉAL · VILLE MARIE

L.-M. PEI ET ASSOCIÉS, ARCHITECTES URBANISTES · HENRY N. COBB, ARCHITECTE EN CHEF · VINCENT DE PASCUTO-PONTE, URBANISTE

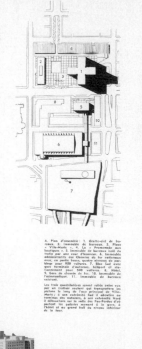

83

Figure 224
J.M. Richards, "Multi-Level City,"
The Architectural Review,
no. 846 (August 1967).
Photograph: Malcolm Lewis.
Canadian Centre for Architecture, Montréal

expo 67

THE ARCHITECTURE OF SUCCESSIVE INTERNATIONAL EXHIBITIONS IS PART OF THE HISTORY OF MODERN ARCHITECTURE ITSELF. THEY HAVE BEEN A LABORATORY FOR ARCHITECTURAL EXPERIMENT, A PROVING GROUND AND A SHOW-WINDOW IN WHICH IDEAS, STRUCTURES, STYLES AND PERSONALITIES HAVE FIRST BEEN PRESENTED TO THE WORLD. LANDMARKS IN ARCHITECTURAL HISTORY IDENTIFIED WITH SUCH EXHIBITIONS ARE TOO MANY TO BE LISTED. THEY INCLUDE THE EIFFEL TOWER AND COTTANCIN'S VAST MACHINE HALL (PARIS, 1889), THE ART NOUVEAU EXPERIMENTS OF VAN DE VELDE, SAARINEN AND OTHERS (PARIS, 1900), LE CORBUSIER'S ESPRIT NOUVEAU PAVILION (PARIS, 1925), MIES VAN DER ROHE'S PAVILION AT BARCELONA (1929), LARGE PARTS OF THE STOCKHOLM EXHIBITION OF 1930 (GUNNAR ASPLUND), IN WHICH MODERN ARCHITECTURE WAS DISPLAYED FOR THE FIRST TIME AS A COMPREHENSIBLE ENVIRONMENT RATHER THAN AS ISOLATED BUILDINGS, AALTO'S FINNISH PAVILIONS, REVEALING HIS VIRTUOSITY IN TIMBER (PARIS, 1937, AND NEW YORK, 1939), NERVI'S EXHIBITION HALL AT TURIN (1949), AND LE CORBUSIER'S PHILIPS' PAVILION AT BRUSSELS (1958). MONTREAL'S EXPO 67 IS THE FIRST CLASS-ONE INTERNATIONAL EXHIBITION SINCE BRUSSELS, AND ONCE AGAIN IT CONTAINS SEVERAL WORKS OF ARCHITECTURE THAT ARE LIKELY TO BE REMEMBERED AS PIONEERS OF THEIR KIND OR AS MARKING THE EMERGENCE INTO PUBLIC VIEW OF SOME NEW AESTHETIC CONCEPT OR STRUCTURAL IDEA. MORE IMPORTANT, FOR THE FIRST TIME IN SUCH A BIG EXHIBITION EXPO ILLUSTRATES DEVELOPING IDEAS ABOUT ENVIRONMENT, ABOUT WAYS OF USING SPACE AND ABOUT MOVEMENT WITHIN IT, REFLECTING THE PRESENT DAY EMPHASIS ON THE ENVIRONMENTAL ASPECTS OF ARCHITECTURE AND PLANNING. AMONG EARLIER EXHIBITIONS ONLY STOCKHOLM 1930, THE SOUTH BANK EXHIBITION AT THE 1951 FESTIVAL OF BRITAIN AND LAUSANNE 1964 MADE ANY ATTEMPT TO DO THE SAME.

IF THE SITE AND THE WAY IT IS LANDSCAPED AND LAID OUT, TOGETHER WITH OTHER ASPECTS OF ENVIRONMENTAL DESIGN, ARE MORE SIGNIFICANT AT EXPO 67 THAN ANYTHING ELSE, THERE ARE MANY OTHER THINGS WORTH OBSERVING: THE PICTURE THAT IT—LIKE OTHER EXHIBITIONS—GIVES OF CURRENT STANDARDS AND OBJECTIVES, THE NUMEROUS SOLUTIONS TO PLANNING AND STRUCTURAL PROBLEMS (WHICH ARE—OR SHOULD BE IN AN EXHIBITION—MADE ALL THE MORE CHALLENGING BY THE TEMPORARY NATURE OF THE BUILDINGS), THE WAY DETAILS OF ALL KINDS ARE HANDLED AND THE COMPETING EFFORTS OF VARIOUS COUNTRIES TO SHOW OFF THEIR ACHIEVEMENTS AND IDEAS, USING ARCHITECTURE AND THE TECHNIQUES OF DISPLAY AS A MEDIUM. A SURVEY OF WHAT IS BEST, AND A CRITICAL ASSESSMENT OF WHAT IS MOST CHARACTERISTIC, IS THEREFORE ALWAYS WORTH MAKING, AND

Opposite: distant panorama of the Expo grounds seen through the transparent walls of the US pavilion—a building which, in addition to showing off the potentialities of Buckminster Fuller's technique of dome construction, makes a real contribution to exhibition design in its interior. It has liberated itself from the fixed and familiar pattern of propaganda, industrial and product displays, and creates, in a far more relaxed way, a succession of images designed to build up atmosphere rather than offer information. As a totality, it is a work of art in its own right

87

'THE ARCHITECTURAL REVIEW' HAS A LONG TRADITION OF DEVOTING SPECIAL NUMBERS TO THESE MONSTER EXHIBITIONS WHEREVER THEY TAKE PLACE. THE PRESENT IS SUCH A NUMBER, THE CONTENTS OF WHICH ARE OF COURSE CHOSEN FOR THEIR ARCHITECTURAL AND RELATED INTEREST. THIS IS NOT A SURVEY OF THE EXHIBITION AS SUCH—AN EXHIBITION'S ORGANISERS AND THE PUBLIC THAT VISIT IT ARE LOOKING FOR MANY THINGS BESIDES ARCHITECTURAL ACHIEVEMENTS AND EXPERIMENTS; TO THEM ARCHITECTURE IS ONLY INCIDENTAL. THIS SURVEY IS SIMPLY WHAT ONE EDITOR OF 'THE REVIEW', EXPLORING THE EXHIBITION, CONSIDERED WORTH PUTTING ON RECORD IN THE CONTEXT OF 'THE REVIEW'. IT LOOKS TO SOME EXTENT BEYOND THE EXHIBITION, BEING INTRODUCED BY A GLANCE AT CURRENT DEVELOPMENTS IN MONTREAL ITSELF, WHOSE RELEVANCE TO EXPO—AND EXPO'S RELEVANCE TO THEM—ARE DISCUSSED IN THE ARTICLE THAT FOLLOWS.

EXPO 67: ORIGIN AND STATUS

According to the convention signed by 31 countries when the International Exhibitions Bureau met in Paris in November, 1928, the world is divided into three zones: European, American and other. No country is allowed to hold a Class-One exhibition more than once in fifteen years, countries in the same zone may not hold such exhibitions more than once in six years and, whatever the zone, such an exhibition may not be held more than once in two years.

The last Class-One exhibition (which is defined as one where the invited countries build their own pavilions) was that held in Brussels in 1958—the subsequent New York World Fair was of a more commercial kind organized outside the convention agreement. When the International Exhibitions Bureau met in 1960, to decide where the next Class-One exhibition should be, it had two applications before it: from Canada, who wanted to hold one in 1967 to commemorate the hundredth anniversary of Canadian Confederation, and from the Soviet Union, who wanted to hold one in the same year to commemorate the fiftieth anniversary of the Russian Revolution. The decision was put to the vote and the Soviet Union won. Two years later, however, the Russians decided not to go forward with their exhibition plans, Canada reapplied and in November, 1962, was granted the right to hold a Class-One exhibition in 1967.

Montreal (the seventh largest city on the North American continent and the second largest French-speaking city in the world) was chosen as the site, and the exhibition, described and illustrated on these pages, based on islands (partly man-made) in the St. Lawrence River opposite the city, is the outcome of this sequence of decisions. It is the main event of Canada's centenary year, but the centenary of Confederation is also being celebrated all over Canada by building and improvement schemes and events and entertainments of many kinds.

88

J M Richards

MULTI-LEVEL CITY

Towards a new environment in down-town Montreal

Montreal can justly claim—in this year of 1967—to have the most dynamically growing down-town area of any city in the world, and since the city is, because of Expo, on show for the summer, an examination of its newest developments—in the way of planning, building and transportation—can appropriately be included in this special issue.

There is indeed a direct link between these developments and Expo—or, rather, two links, ideological and organizational. The ideological link is that the significance of the new Montreal, with its separation of levels and its sheltered pedestrian network, is the contribution it makes to a controlled urban environment, while at Expo too the most interesting items are interesting because of the ideas about environment they bring forward: the Buckminster Fuller geodetic sphere, the Habitat housing, the indoor-outdoor tented structure of the German pavilion, the widespread use of public escalators, the experiments with monorail and other elevated transport systems and the overall landscape control.

The second link between long-term development in the city and the short-term phenomenon of Expo lies in the extent to which the impetus of Expo was responsible for bringing any number of ambitious schemes for improving Montreal to fruition at the same moment. Montreal's elaborate new highway system might have taken many more years to reach the stage it has if Expo had not set a short-term target, and the need to handle as smoothly as possible the crowds expected to flock to Montreal on account of Expo inspired the remarkable achievement of building the whole of the long-projected 16-mile underground railway system (officially called the Metro) in only three years. This system—Montreal's first subway—was opened to the public in October 1966. It extends under the St. Lawrence river to a station within the Expo grounds and terminates on the farther shore. Though some of the station architecture is a little on the flashy side, the standard of design achieved in the trains, escalators, direction-signs and booking-offices is first-rate.*

The only defect of the Metro system from a town-planning point of view is that the main interchange point has, for political reasons, been placed too far to the east for its own pattern to coincide with the present development pattern of the city, though the future direction of growth may of course rectify this.

The visitors to Expo will appreciate the up-to-date transportation system with which Montreal has now been equipped, but they will be there at the wrong time of year to value fully the benefits of Montreal's other major contribution to city planning: the extensive system of sheltered pedestrian streets which allows comfortable shopping, strolling and central area inter-communication even in the depth of the Canadian winter. In the extent and ramifications of this system Montreal has been a pioneer; no other city has anything like it. What began as an experiment has become a resounding success; so much so that the danger should be noted of its very success leading town planners to neglect the need to co-ordinate well designed surface circulation with the circulation spaces provided beneath the surface. It would be a tragedy if the eventual end-product of the imagination and enterprise shown in Montreal was the acceptance of a city-centre so anti-human as to drive its pedestrians underground.

As long as this is borne in mind, Montreal is a model that many other cities will do well to study. That it has achieved this pre-eminent position is to some extent due to business enterprise and foresight, but also, it must be said, to a series of fortunate accidents. The first of these was that a large area of down-town Montreal (amounting to 22 acres), hitherto not built on and in an ideal situation for development as a new business centre, was in the possession of one owner—the Canadian National Railways, whose president Donald Gordon saw the opportunities it presented. It was Gordon and his technical advisers who first conceived the idea of multi-level development and from whose initiative the sheltered pedestrian network—which is Montreal's contribution to urban design—may be said to have grown. It centred on the main-line railway station (Central Station) whose concourse was expanded into the vast multi-level development that now exists as a result of Gordon calling in Zeckendorf, the American property developer. Zeckendorf foresaw the role the area might play in the business future of Montreal, especially in relation to the tendency of the city's financial centre to shift westwards which was already taking place. Zeckendorf also had the initiative to ask his town-planner Vincent Ponte and his architect I. M. Pei, while laying out the 7-acre site he had decided initially to develop (now the Place Ville Marie), also to prepare a master-plan for the whole 22 acres.

On the strength of this, the owners of adjoining properties called in Vincent Ponte when their turn came to develop, with the result that the whole down-town area, though redeveloped in the ordinary North American way wholly by private enterprise, and in separately owned sites, has followed—if not a comprehensive plan (because each successive enterprise was a separately conceived development programme)—at least a consistent town-planning objective.

This consistency of aim was the second fortunate circumstance; the third was that this burst of activity coincided with the regime of a go-ahead mayor of Montreal, Jean Drapeau, whose election promises of 1960 included the construction of the underground railway system and who was chiefly responsible in getting Expo 67 for Montreal. The city government itself has thus played its part in Montreal's recent dynamic development in spite of the—to European eyes—strangely passive role of the city's planning authorities.

The centre of Montreal is a natural case for intensive vertical development since it cannot spread outwards, being compressed

* By way of contrast to the others, one of the Metro entrances (in Place Victoria) is adorned with one of Guimard's *Art Nouveau* iron arches from the Paris *métro*.

89

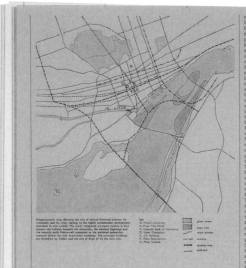

Diagrammatic map showing the site of central Montreal between its mountain and its river, leading to the highly concentrated development described in this article. The newly integrated transport system is also shown: the railway beneath the mountain, the elevated highways and the recently built Metro well connected to the sheltered pedestrian network below the new down-town buildings. The principal buildings are identified by letters and the site of Expo 67 by the dark tint.

key
A. McGill University
B. Place Ville Marie
C. Imperial Bank of Commerce
D. Hotel Champlain
E. CIL Building
F. Place Bonaventure
G. Place Victoria

green areas
major streets
subway
express way
railroad

between its river and its mountain. The other geographical fact that has determined the particular form the new central area development has taken is the slope of the ground, which drops between 150 ft. and 200 ft. This made practicable the multi-level underground element in the first building operation, and has been followed in successive schemes, endowing Montreal with four miles (eventually to be expanded to six) of sheltered pedestrian and shopping promenades interconnecting beneath the new down-town buildings. When all necessary connections have been made, on the completion of schemes now in progress, this pedestrian network and the buildings rising above them will have direct access from the Metro, from the low-level main-line railway station and from underground car-parks, including that below Place Ville Marie, which is entered from street level at the northern end of the plaza that is part of the building.

Although these successive building projects are the work of different developers employing different architects, each, as explained above, took the town-planning advice of Vincent Ponte. The first project, financed by Zeckendorf—which triggered off the whole enterprise—was Place Ville

Marie, now usually referred to simply as PVM. I. M. Pei was Zeckendorf's architect; the executive architect was his partner Henry Cobb. PVM is a 48-storey cruciform building, powerfully enough designed to serve visually, as it now has to, as the focal element in the whole down-town development. A large part of it is occupied by the Royal Bank of Canada—a fact of some importance because the decision of the bank to become the tenant of much of the building at the time construction was only just beginning was the first sign that Zeckendorf's initial enterprise was to be justified economically.

PVM's cruciform tower stands at one corner of a 4-acre plaza under which, at four different levels, are half a mile of shopping promenades—partly lit artificially and partly from a sunken court at each corner of the plaza—two levels of car-parking (capacity, 1,200 cars) and, below these, the Canadian National railway tracks and platforms. In addition to the car-parks (accessible, as already described, directly from street level) there is a system of underground service roads giving access to the basements of the PVM building.

These promenades, lined with shops, extend beyond the plaza in several directions, with connections to the basements of the

new Queen Elizabeth hotel and the Royal Bank's banking hall. Although the shops have for the most part no rear access (stock deliveries having to be made from the public promenades in the early morning or late at night) they have been highly successful commercially and all were occupied within a short time of the completion of the building. This was no doubt partly due to the comfortable shopping conditions they provide, especially in winter weather, but far more important is their integration into the transport system: a bus station as well as the Canadian National main-line station (bringing commuters from the northern suburbs via a tunnel under Mount Royal) being already incorporated in the building, the Metro being due soon to be connected to the building's network and the Canadian Pacific (Windsor) station being close by—so is St. Catherine Street, traditionally Montreal's main shopping street, though now losing its status and become, for much of its length, seedy and garish—thus pointing, incidentally, the contrast between the anarchic old and the coherent new. The only matter for regret is that the highly significant (from the social and urban design point of view) pedestrian network beneath PVM has not been made more evident in the building's external form and expression.

The newly created Metro with its own mezzanines has added another mile to the network of underground pedestrian ways, to connect with the lower levels of one of the main department stores and other adjoining buildings, and these will be extended and linked together, and presumably used for shopping purposes (some of these mezzanines, for example at the McGill station, are at present somewhat empty and forbidding) as new building schemes are completed.

Several of the most prominent of the completed buildings in the area are the direct result of the Royal Bank of Canada's decision, taken in 1958, to move into PVM, since several others—for instance the Imperial Bank of Commerce—decided also to move from the old financial quarter in the St. James's Street area into the new centre, and thus arose the cluster of new tall buildings that become the most striking feature of down-town Montreal. Not all of these new buildings are distinguished architecturally, but fortunately for the total effect some of the most prominent are also the best. The most beautiful of all, the Imperial Bank of Commerce, is a little way removed from PVM—south-west of it on the far side of Dominion Square, and therefore also on the far side of the Sun Life building, the classically embellished four-square building of the 1920s that for a long time dominated the centre of the city but is now completely hidden in the distant view. The Imperial Bank of Commerce is a slender glass-walled tower of outstanding elegance by the late Peter Dickinson, completed in 1962.

Also in Dominion Square, and unfortunately in a very prominent position, is another tower block nearly as high: Montreal's newest railway hotel, the Champlain, of

Some of the buildings that have contributed to the dynamic transformation of down-town Montreal: 1, the barely complete Place Bonaventure, left (architects, Affleck, Desbarats, Dimakopoulos, Lebensold and Sise), with Place Victoria (Moretti and Nervi) in the distance. 2, looking down Peel Street towards the Imperial Bank of Commerce (architect, Peter Dickinson), with the Hotel Champlain (architects, D'Astous and Pothier) at the far end. 3, air-view showing the cluster of tall buildings, the highest being the Place Ville Marie, left (architect, I. M. Pei), and the Imperial Bank of Commerce, right. It was taken (when Place Victoria, in the distance, was still building) from a point on the extreme left of the map on the facing page.

90

91

Place Ville Marie, the focal point of Montreal's new down-town development. 4, looking from the north towards the open side of the PVM plaza and the entrance to the car-park beneath it. 5, closer view of the car-park entrance and piazza. 6, on the piazza, looking across one of the sunken courts which light the shopping promenades towards the foot of the PVM building. 7, at piazza level—PVM building on left; CIL building (architects, Skidmore, Owings and Merrill) beyond. 8, steps up to the piazza from the west. 9 (facing page), Place Ville Marie from Dominion Square—the forty-year-old Sun Life building on the left; the Queen Elizabeth Hotel on the right. The associated Canadian architects of the PVM development were Affleck, Desbarats, Dimakopoulos, Lebensold and Sise.

92

93

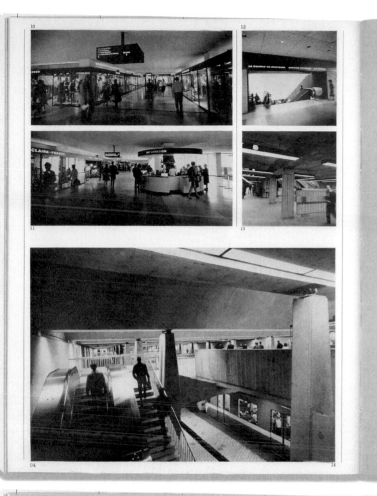

On the facing page, various levels of the sheltered pedestrian and transport network beneath the new central area of Montreal. 10 and 11, the shopping promenades below the Place Ville Marie piazza. 12, escalators leading down to the promenades from one of the main lobbies of the PVM building. 13 and 14, Metro stations, the latter taken at mezzanine level, where pedestrian galleries will eventually be lined with shops and will link up with the other shopping promenades. Escalators connect this mezzanine with the platform levels, bottom right.

vulgar and eccentric design quite out of keeping with the modern spirit in which the central area development as a whole has been conceived. The clients were the Canadian Pacific Railway and the architects D'Astous and Pothier. It has, however, the merit, in common with several of the other new buildings, of being a real tower—visible right down to the ground. It shares a small paved piazza with a new office building (by John C. Parkin) not yet complete, which piazza is connected to the raised green centre of the square by a footbridge.

North-east of this separate new development—back, that is, in the direction of PVM—is another new hotel, the Queen Elizabeth, undistinguished without and garish within. It faces, in fact, the PVM piazza, the third side of which is closed by the lower IBM building (like the PVM building designed by I. M. Pei), the fourth side, facing north-west, being open, with the entrance to the low-level garages beneath it. Adjoining the Queen Elizabeth Hotel is the rather dull new Canadian National Railways' building above the company's own Central Station and linked underground, as already described, to the bus station and the underground shopping promenades beneath the PVM piazza. Immediately to the north of the PVM development is another very elegantly designed glass-walled tower, the CIL building, by Skidmore, Owings and Merrill. Further to the south, and on the point of completion as these words are written,* is perhaps the most significant development of all: the square concrete-walled block, covering six acres, known as Place Bonaventure and designed by the Montreal firm of architects, Affleck, Desbarats, Dimakopoulos, Lebensold and Sise. This

*It is hoped to illustrate it in a later issue of the AR.

building lies south of PVM and the Central Station, over the railway tracks and also over the new trans-Canada highway—part of the recently completed main road system which passes below ground at this point. Further south still are other sites waiting to be developed, so Place Bonaventure is in a sense the hub of the whole of the rebuilt central Montreal as it will appear in a few years' time. It also provides an essential link with the rest because one of the Metro stations is in its basement and an underground passage will provide the connection between the Metro system and the pedestrian network beneath PVM. It is only to be regretted that the connection between the two is not stronger. The Place Bonaventure architects planned a bridge connection between their own main pedestrian level and the PVM and Canadian National developments, crossing the intervening street (Lagauchetière), but this was rejected by the city authorities. The pedestrian level of Bonaventure will provide sheltered shopping promenades similar in style to those underneath the PVM piazza, but in this instance above ground and therefore without the implication that traffic segregation can be achieved only by submerging the pedestrian. Nevertheless Place Bonaventure still, regrettably, relies on artificial light except for a rare glimpse of the outside world at the corners. There will be a slightly greater length of shopping promenade here than the half-mile of the PVM development. The remainder of the building is planned for multiple commercial use. On the level above the shopping promenade is a cavernous galleried hall for trade exhibitions, served (another example of skilful multi-level planning) by motor traffic by means of a long ramp rising alongside the railway lines. Above this

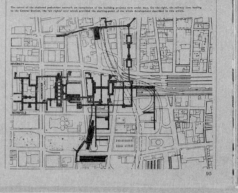

The extent of the sheltered pedestrian network on completion of the building projects now under way. On the right, the railway lines leading to the Central Station, the 'air-rights' over which provided the starting-point of the whole development described in this article.

---

are five floors of furniture trade showrooms, then a couple of floors of offices connected with the trade centre activities, and, occupying the two upper storeys, a hotel planned round a roof-garden. The building's deliberately weighty architectural character, obtained by boldly ribbed concrete inside and out, creates an interesting contrast to the glass-walled office towers nearby, though it arises of course principally from the use of the building which required uninterrupted wall-space inside on all the upper levels.

A little to the east of Place Bonaventure, across some acres still to be developed, and nearer the old financial centre of the city, is Place Victoria, a glass-walled 47-storey tower, designed by the Italians Luigi Moretti and Pier Luigi Nervi. This is a distinguished building with an unusual outline derived from its tapering corner columns (see AR, June 1966), and with a 6-storey block alongside. The tower contains, besides offices, a restaurant and the Montreal Stock Exchange, its own basement shopping promenade—in this case on two levels. Detailed design here does not quite compare with the admirably restrained and well thought-out detailing below PVM. The intention is, as a further stage of the Place Victoria development, to build a second tower and a second 6-storey block of the same design, and when these have been completed to link the below-ground shopping promenades that already exist in the first part to Place Bonaventure and the extension to the latter which is now under consideration. Through Place Bonaventure the Place Victoria development will therefore eventually be connected to the whole protected pedestrian network. Already Place Victoria has its own subway connection to the Metro.

By the foregoing series of accretions the dynamic new down-town area of Montreal has grown from nothing in a dozen years. There are plans for extending it in several other directions, especially north-westwards

from PVM, where McGill College Avenue now leads to the grounds of McGill University on the lower slopes of Mount Royal. This extension is chiefly being promoted by the department stores already established there. They have been sensible enough again to appoint Vincent Ponte as planner and the I. M. Pei-Cobb partnership as architects, but the final design that has resulted is something of a disappointment in that it creates a strong axis—in the form of a wide boulevard—along the present McGill College Avenue, culminating in symmetrically disposed tower blocks on either side. The present down-town development gets its dynamic character from the informal arrangement of its cluster of towers, and to change this, admittedly fortuitous but in practice effective, composition into an example of axial Beaux-Arts layout is likely to result in something duller as well as something out of keeping with the rest.

It is intended to continue the system of shopping promenades throughout this new development, and the extent of this central area pedestrian network will then (by about 1972) add up to six miles, connecting together about 100 of the 185 acres that the down-town area covers. It will be served by six Metro stations as well as the two main stations and give sheltered access to more hotels and theatres as well as to the whole down-town cluster of office towers.

Already this new conception of multi-level under-cover circulation, so eminently suited to the severe Canadian winter, has influenced developments in other Canadian cities; for example the vast new Dominion Bank building (by Mies van der Rohe) in down-town Toronto, due for completion this year, has extensive shopping promenades in its basement, and these will eventually link up with developments on adjoining sites, creating a pedestrian network similar to Montreal's though not so fortunately integrated with the city's transportation system.

from the city to expo

This airview shows the densely built up down-town area of Montreal (the subject of the preceding article). With the docks in front and in the foreground the roadbridge carrying the Expo Express railway across the St. Lawrence to the exhibition on its two islands, which are the subject of the remainder of this issue.

Structure
and Society
Places and
Players
Perceptions
Expo 67

Architectural Display and Megastructures

Expo 67 did not offer a portent of the city of the future; it was not even an exhibition of futuristic architecture. It was a testing ground for fragments of theories and for models of avant-garde thinking in both urban planning and architecture. In some cases, such as Habitat, with its dream of constructing housing out of precast concrete units, this experimentation came up against an inherent lack of realism, whereas other concepts, such as Frei Otto's taut structures for the West German pavilion, would be used again – at the 1972 Olympics in Munich and later at Expo 92 in Seville.

In addition to these grand displays, there were many national pavilions that sought a symbolic or formal register to express as convincingly as possible the spirit of a country or nation. It was that striving for uniqueness and self-affirmation that the organizers hoped to temper when they chose the theme of "Man and His World," which was meant to be explored in the various thematic pavilions. It was a noble idea, generously executed, but it was inevitably drowned out by the chorus of national delegations.

Many pavilions adopted an architectural language of recurring primary geometric forms, an approach that was well suited to the creation of structures that would be easy to build and equip (for example, Africa Place, and the Austrian, Cuban, and Venezuelan pavilions). Few pavilions lived up to all the requirements of a megastructure: synergy between structure and envelope, modularity and repetition of basic unit elements, prefabrication, mass production, and so on. Of those that managed to do so and are illustrated here, all except Habitat 67 encountered the same obstacle: they could not support traditional methods of fitting out or had difficulty doing it successfully.

Figure 225
Pavilion of the United States, Expo 67. R. Buckminster Fuller, Fuller and Sadao Inc. architects; Geometrics Inc., associate architects; Cambridge Seven Associates Inc., associate architects. Photograph: Joseph Messana. Canadian Centre for Architecture, Montréal

Figure 226
Pavilion of West Germany, Expo 67. Rolf Gutbrod and Frei Otto, architects. Photograph: Joseph Messana. Canadian Centre for Architecture, Montréal

Figure 227
Man the Explorer complex, Expo 67. Affleck, Desbarats, Dimakopoulos, Lebensold, Michaud, and Sise, architects. Photograph: Joseph Messana. Canadian Centre for Architecture, Montréal

Figure 228
Man in the Community pavilion, Expo 67, view out through the open roof. Erickson and Massey, architects. Photograph: Joseph Messana. Canadian Centre for Architecture, Montréal

Figure 229
Habitat 67. Moshe Safdie, architect; David, Barott, Boulva, associate architects. Photograph: Joseph Messana. Canadian Centre for Architecture, Montréal

Figure 230
**Pavilion of France, Expo 67.
Jean Fougeron, architect;
Blouin and Blouin, associate
architects.** Photograph: Joseph
Messana. Canadian Centre
for Architecture, Montréal

Figure 231
**Pavilion of Great Britain,
Expo 67. Sir Basil Spence,
architect; Bonnington and
Collins, associate architects;
Bland, LeMoyne, Edwards,
Shine, associate architects.**
Photograph: Joseph Messana.
Canadian Centre for Architecture, Montréal

While modernist formalism was totally appropriate for the feeling of maturity Quebec wished to convey, one can only wonder what Britain was trying to accomplish with its Brutalist monolith and deconstructed Union Jack (alluding, perhaps, to its dismantled empire?). Undoubtedly the strangest pavilion of all was that of France, which defied explanation. The universal symbolism of the Canadian pavilion aptly reflected the role Canada sought to fulfil after World War II. The boldly designed Soviet pavilion, positioned directly opposite America's geodesic dome, emphasized technological mastery. In contrast, the Japanese pavilion provided an understated interpretation of that country's architectural tradition.

Figure 232
Pavilion of the U.S.S.R., Expo 67. Mikhail Posokhin, architect. Photograph: Joseph Messana. Canadian Centre for Architecture, Montréal

Figure 234
Pavilion of Quebec, Expo 67. Papineau, Gérin-Lajoie, Le Blanc, architects; Luc Durand, associate architect. Photograph: Joseph Messana. Canadian Centre for Architecture, Montréal

Figure 233
Pavilion of Canada, Expo 67. Ashworth, Robbie, Vaughan, and Williams, architects; Schoeler and Barkham, associate architects; A. Matthew Stankiewicz, associate architect. Photograph: Joseph Messana. Canadian Centre for Architecture, Montréal

Figure 235
Pavilion of Iran, Expo 67.
A.A. Farmanfarmaian and
P. Moayed-Ahd, architects.
Photograph: Joseph Messana.
Canadian Centre for Architecture, Montréal

Figure 236
Pavilion of Thailand, Expo 67.
Chamlong Yordying, architect.
Photograph: Joseph Messana.
Canadian Centre for Architecture, Montréal

Among the many approaches adopted, those countries that decided to feature their traditional architecture – sometimes in a modernized version, sometimes not – undoubtedly made a wise choice, for traditional culture was one of the focuses of Expo. They aspired to a certain "authenticity," and it was for this that they would be appreciated (political circumstances permitting) by the globetrotting public of the late twentieth century.

Figure 237
Pavilion of Burma, Expo 67. Harry Aung, architect. Photograph: Joseph Messana. Canadian Centre for Architecture, Montréal

Figure 238
Pavilion of Japan, Expo 67. Yoshinobu Ashihara, architect. Photograph: Joseph Messana. Canadian Centre for Architecture, Montréal

Architects and Engineers
Active in Montreal in the 1960s

Abbreviations

AAPQ Association des architectes de la province de Québec
AIA American Institute of Architects
CUQ Corporation des urbanistes du Québec
FAIA Fellow, American Institute of Architects
FRAIC Fellow, Royal Architectural Institute of Canada
FRIBA Fellow, Royal Institute of British Architects
OAA Ontario Association of Architects
OAQ Ordre des architectes du Québec
RAIC Royal Architectural Institute of Canada
RCA Royal Canadian Academy
RIBA Royal Institute of British Architects

Affleck, Desbarats, Dimakopoulos, Lebensold, Michaud, and Sise

Architectural firm established in 1954 by Ray Affleck, Guy Desbarats, Dimitri Dimakopoulos, Fred Lebensold, Jean Michaud, and Hazen Sise in Montreal, for the competition to build the Queen Elizabeth Theatre in Vancouver. The firm became ARCOP Associates in 1970.

Raymond Tait Affleck

Penticton, British Columbia, 1922 – Montreal, 1989. B.Arch., McGill University, 1947. Worked at McDougall, Smith, and Fleming, and at Vincent Rother, Architects, 1953–1954; co-founded Affleck, Desbarats, Dimakopoulos, Lebensold, Michaud, and Sise, Montreal, 1954. AAPQ 1950, FRAIC, RCA, RAIC gold medal 1989.

ARCOP Associates

Acronym for Architects in Co-partnership, established in 1970. In 1985, ARCOP Associates started a sister firm, ARCOP Associates Pvt. Ltd., to handle architectural contracts abroad, mainly in India.

Claude Beaulieu

Sainte-Rose-de-Lima, Quebec, 1913 – Montreal, 2002. Diploma in architecture, École des beaux-arts de Montréal, 1935; studied at the École des beaux-arts, Paris, 1936–1940; diploma, Institut d'urbanisme, Paris, 1949. Professor of architecture, École des beaux-arts de Montréal, 1953–1964; private practice in Montreal from 1953; co-founder of the magazine *Vie des Arts*, 1956. AAPQ 1949, ARC.

John Bland

Lachine, Quebec, 1911 – Montreal, 2002. B.Arch., with honours, McGill University, 1933; diploma in urban planning, Architectural Association, London, 1937. Director of the School of Architecture, McGill University, 1941–1972; Macdonald chair of architecture, McGill University, 1953; professor emeritus from 1979; private practice in association with Vincent Rother, Charles Elliot Trudeau, Roy E. LeMoyne, Gordon Edwards, Michel Lacroix, and Anthony Shine, 1941–1979. AAPQ 1940, FRAIC 1954, RCA, AAPQ medal of excellence 1971, RAIC gold medal, Heritage Canada Gabrielle Léger medal 1994.

André Blouin

Born in Nantes, 1920. Diploma in architecture, École des beaux-arts, Paris, 1944. Worked in the studio of Auguste Perret, 1945; emigrated to Montreal in 1952; private practice from 1954: Blouin and Blouin (with his son Patrick), 1966–1975; Blouin, Blouin, and Associates (with Paul Faucher, Gilles Aubertin, and André Brodeur), 1975–1984; Blouin and Associates, 1984; Blouin, Faucher, Aubertin, Brodeur, and Gauthier from 1994. AAPQ 1954, FRAIC, RCA.

Philip Bobrow

Born in Montreal, 1936. B.Arch., McGill University, 1960; M.Arch., Yale University, 1961. Warshaw, Swartzman, and Bobrow, Montreal, 1963–1965; Philip D. Bobrow, Architects, Montreal, 1965–1970; Bobrow, Fieldman, Architects, Montreal, 1970–1985; Bobrow, Architects, Montreal, from 1985. AAPQ 1963, OAA 1963, AIA 1979, FRAIC.

Melvin Charney

Born in Montreal, 1935. B.Arch., McGill University, 1958; M.Arch., Yale University, 1959. Private practice, Montreal, from 1964; professor of architecture, University of Montreal, 1966–1995; Paul-Émile Borduas Prize, Quebec, 1996; represented Canada at the Venice Biennale in 2000. AAPQ 1963.

Morris Charney

Born in Montreal, 1939. B.Arch., McGill University, 1962; M.Arch., Harvard University, 1963. Private practice, Montreal, from 1972. AAPQ 1966.

Henry N. Cobb

Born in Boston, 1926. B.A., Harvard University, 1947, M.Arch., Harvard University, 1949. Worked at Webb and Knapp, 1950–1960; founded Pei, Cobb, Freed, and Partners, Architects, in 1979 (formerly I.M. Pei and Partners). FAIA, AIA New York chapter medal of honour 1982.

Roger D'Astous

Montreal, 1926 – Montreal, 1998. Diploma, École des beaux-arts de Montréal, 1952. Worked at Frank Lloyd Wright's studio, Taliesin, 1952–1953. Private practice, Montreal, from 1955; professor of architecture, École des beaux-arts de Montréal, 1962–1965; associate of Jean-Paul Pothier, 1965–1968; associate of Luc Durand, 1974–1983. AAPQ 1954, OAQ prize for excellence 1987.

Guy Desbarats

Montreal, 1925 – Sherbrooke, Quebec, 2003. B.Arch., McGill University, 1948. Worked at Abra, Balharrie, and Shore, Architects, Ottawa, at Fischer Laboratory, Chicago, and at the Polytechnic Institute of Virginia; co-founder of Affleck, Desbarats, Dimakopoulos, Lebensold, Michaud, and Sise, Montreal, 1954; professor of architecture, University of Montreal, 1964–1975. AAPQ 1949, FRAIC, RCA.

Peter Algood Rastall Dickinson

London, 1925 – Montreal, 1961. Diploma, Architectural Association, London, 1948. Designer at Wells Coates, London, 1947–1948, and H.T. Cadbury-Brown, London, 1948; emigrated to Canada in 1950; chief designer, Page and Steele, Toronto; senior partner, Page and Steele, 1958; founded Dickinson and Associates, Toronto, 1958. RIBA 1949, OAA 1952, AAPQ 1958.

Dimitri Dimakopoulos

Athens, 1929 – Montreal, 1995. Studied at the Experimental School, University of Athens, 1947; B.Arch., McGill University, 1955. Co-founded Affleck, Desbarats, Dimakopoulos, Lebensold, Michaud, and Sise, Montreal, 1954; professor of architecture, University of Montreal, from 1965; founded Dimakopoulos and Partners, 1969. AAPQ 1957, FRAIC, RCA.

Édouard Fiset

Rimouski, 1910 – Montreal, 1994. Diploma, École des beaux-arts, Quebec, 1932; diploma, École des beaux-arts, Paris, 1940. Official representative, Department of Reconstruction, France; assistant to Jacques Gréber, for the National Capital Commission, Ottawa; private practice from 1945: Fiset and Deschamps, Quebec City; Fiset, Deschamps, and Bartha, Westmount; and Fiset, Miller, Montreal. AAPQ 1945, FRAIC 1956, RCA, Companion of the Order of Canada 1967.

Richard Buckminster Fuller

Milton, Massachusetts, 1895 – Los Angeles, 1983. Studied engineering at Harvard University, 1913–1915. Founder and director of Dymaxion Corporation, Bridgeport, Connecticut, where he worked as chief engineer; founder and president of Geodesics Inc., New York, 1949–1983; president of Plydomes Inc., Des Moines, Iowa, 1957–1983; professor, Southern Illinois University, 1959–1983; senior partner, Fuller and Sadao, New York, 1979–1983; senior partner, Buckminster Fuller Associates, London, 1979–1983. AIA gold medal 1970, RIBA gold medal 1968, FRIBA.

Gaston Gagnier

1905(?) – 1982(?). Diploma, École des beaux-arts, Montreal, 1930. Private practice, Montreal and Geneva. AAPQ 1931.

Greenspoon, Freedlander, Dunne

Architectural firm established in Montreal by Henry Greenspoon (B.Arch., McGill University, 1933), who entered into partnership with Philip Freedlander and Joseph Dunne in 1949. The firm became Greenspoon, Freedlander, Plachta, Kryton in the late 1960s.

Jean-Claude La Haye
Kapuskasing, Ontario, 1923 – Montreal, 1999. Studied at the École polytechnique de Montréal; studied commerce at McGill University; Master of City Planning, Harvard University, 1953. Worked for the Quebec Department of Municipal Affairs from 1953; private practice, Montreal, from 1955; chairman of the Provincial Planning Commission, 1963–1968; founder and president of CUQ, 1963–1968; associate of Jean Ouellet, 1971–1985.

Lalonde, Girouard, and Letendre
Engineering firm established in Montreal in 1945 by J. Antonio Lalonde, Laurent Girouard, and Lucien Letendre, all from the École polytechnique de Montreal. In 1960, the firm became Lalonde, Girouard, Letendre, and Associates. It was acquired by Surveyer, Nenniger, Chênevert (SNC) in 1990.

Lalonde and Valois
Engineering firm established in Montreal in 1936 by engineers Jean-Paul Lalonde (graduate of École polytechnique de Montréal, 1926) and Roméo Valois (graduate of École polytechnique de Montréal, 1930, M.I.T., 1932). The firm operated under the name Lalonde, Valois, Lamarre, Valois, and Associates from 1963, then became Lavalin Inc. in 1977.

David Frederick Lebensold
Warsaw, 1917 – Toronto, 1985. Studied at Regent Street Polytechnic, London, 1931–1934, B.Arch. 1939. Worked at Connel, Ward, and Lucas, England, 1938–1939, and at Murray and Burrell, Galashiels, Scotland, 1939–1943; private practice, London, 1947; with Vincent Rother, Montreal, 1949; professor of architecture, McGill University, 1949–1955; co-founded Affleck, Desbarats, Dimakopoulos, Lebensold, Michaud, and Sise, Montreal, 1954; co-founded ARCOP, Montreal, 1970. RIBA 1941, AAPQ 1950.

Michel Lincourt
Born in Montreal, 1941. B.A., B.Arch., University of Montreal; studied at M.I.T.; M.Arch., Harvard University; Ph.D., Georgia Institute of Technology. Private practice in Quebec and abroad as an architect and planning consultant from 1963; professor, École nationale supérieure des arts et industries, Strasbourg, 1997–2000; strategic planning advisor, UNESCO, from 1995; political advisor on land use, urban planning, and architecture, City of Montreal, from 2001. AAPQ 1974, CUQ.

Harry Mayerovitch
Montreal, 1910 – Montreal, 2004. B.A., McGill University, 1928; B.Arch., McGill University, 1933; internships with Noffke, Morin and Sylvestre, Ottawa, Percy Nobbs, Montreal, and C.D. Goodman, Montreal. Private practice: Mayerovitch and Bernstein, Westmount. FRAIC, AAPQ 1936.

Jean Michaud
Montreal, 1919 – Montreal, 1995. Diploma in architecture, École des beaux-arts de Montréal, 1939–1941; B.Arch., McGill University, 1945; internship in Mexico, 1945–1946. Worked in Le Corbusier's studio, 1947–1948; private practice, 1949–1971; co-founded Affleck, Desbarats, Dimakopoulos, Lebensold, Michaud, and Sise, Montreal, 1954; left the firm in 1959; professor of architecture, Laval University, 1968–1989. AAPQ 1947.

Ludwig Mies van der Rohe
Aachen, Germany, 1886 – Chicago, 1969. Worked in Berlin with Bruno Paul, 1905–1908, and Peter Behrens, 1908–1912; head of the architecture section of the Novembergruppe, 1921–1925; chairman of the Deutscher Werkbund, 1926; director of the Bauhaus, Dessau, 1929–1933; private practice, Chicago, from 1938. RIBA gold medal 1959, FAIA 1960.

Luigi Moretti
Rome, 1907 – Capraia, 1973. Diploma in architecture, University of Rome, 1930; private practice from 1931; founded the Instituto Nazionale di Recerca e Operativa per l'Urbanistica, Rome, 1957; founded the magazine Spazio, 1956. FAIA 1964.

Pier Luigi Nervi
Sondrio, Italy, 1891 – Rome, 1979. Diploma in engineering, University of Bologna, 1913; engineer with the Società per Construzioni Cementizie, Bologna, 1913–1915 and 1918–1923; private practice from 1923: Nervi and Nebbiosi, 1923–1932; Nervi and Bartolia, 1932–1960; Studio Nervi (with his sons Antonio, Mario, and Vittorio), 1960–1979; professor of construction technologies and techniques, University of Rome, 1947–1961. RIBA gold medal 1960, AIA gold medal 1964.

Frei Otto
Born in Siegmar, Germany, 1925. Apprentice mason, Schadow-Schule, Berlin, 1931–1943; attended Berlin Technical University, 1948–1950; studied sociology and urban development at the University of Virginia. Private practice, West Germany, 1952–1957; founded the Institute for Lightweight Structures (IL) in Berlin, 1957; operated the Institute from Stuttgart, 1964–1990. FAIA 1968, FRIBA 1981.

Jean Ouellet
Rivière-du-Loup, Quebec, 1922 – Montreal, 2004. Diploma in architecture, École des beaux-arts de Montréal, 1952. Worked with urban planner Jean-Claude La Haye, Montreal, 1957; founded Ouellet and Reeves, Montreal, 1961; partner, La Haye and Ouellet, Montreal, 1971–1985. AAPQ 1954, FRAIC, CUQ, AAPQ president 1972.

Papineau, Gérin-Lajoie, Le Blanc
Architectural firm established in Montreal in 1958 by Louis-Joseph Papineau, Guy Gérin-Lajoie, and Michel Le Blanc, all graduates of McGill University's School of Architecture in the 1950s. In 1970, the firm became Papineau, Gérin-Lajoie, Le Blanc, Edwards, and then Papineau, Gérin-Lajoie, Le Blanc, Architects, 1974–1981.

Harry Parnass
Born in New York, 1935. B.Arch., Columbia University; M.Arch. and Master of Urban Design, Harvard University. Professor in the Faculté de l'aménagement, University of Montreal; professor emeritus, University of Montreal; founding president and honorary member of the Institut de design, Montreal.

Ieoh Ming Pei
Born in Canton, China, 1917. B.Arch., Massachussetts Institute of Technology, 1940; M.Arch., Harvard University, 1946. Worked at Stone and Webster, Architects, 1942–1945, and at Webb and Knapp, New York, 1948–1960; founded I.M. Pei and Partners, New York, 1955, which became Pei, Cobb, Freed, and Partners, Architects, in 1979. FAIA, RIBA, Pritzker Architecture Prize 1983.

Vincent de Pasciuto Ponte
Born in Boston, 1919. B.A., Harvard University, 1943; Master of Urban Planning, Harvard University, 1949; University of Rome, 1953–1954. Assistant urban transportation planner, City of New York, 1951–1952. Worked at Webb and Knapp, New York, 1956–1958, and at I.M. Pei and Partners, New York, 1959–1963; founded Vincent Ponte Planning Consultant, Montreal, 1964. Emigrated to Canada in 1967.

Victor Prus
Born in Minsk, Poland, 1917. Studied at the Technical University, Warsaw, 1935–1939; diploma in architecture, Liverpool, 1947; founded Prus and Scolly, Architects, London, 1950–1952; assistant to Buckminster Fuller, Princeton, 1953; associate at Vincent Rother, Montreal, 1952–1954; private practice, Montreal, 1954–1970; Victor Prus and Associates from 1970. AAPQ 1958, FRAIC 1968, FAIA 1977.

Max Wolfe Roth
Lachine, 1913 – Montreal, 2001. B.Arch., McGill University. Private practice, Montreal, from 1938. AAPQ 1938, RAIC 1962.

Moshe Safdie
Born in Haifa, 1938. B.Arch., with honours, McGill University, 1961. Worked at Van Ginkel Associates, Montreal, 1961–1962, and at Louis I. Kahn, Architects, Philadelphia, 1962–1963; founded Moshe Safdie and Associates, Jerusalem, 1970; opened Boston office in 1978, Toronto office in 1988. AAPQ 1964, Officer of the Order of Canada 1986, OAQ prize for excellence 1988, Governor General's Medal 1992, RAIC gold medal 1995, FAIA 1996.

Harold Ship
Born in Montreal, 1922. B.Arch., McGill University, 1951. Worked at Hutchison and Wood; partner, Wood, Blachford, and Ship; private practice, Montreal, 1958–1964; associate at Stanley King, 1964–1969; Ship, Krakow, Jenson, 1969–1972; Ship and Krakow from 1972. AAPQ 1953.

Hazen Edward Sise
Montreal, 1906 – Montreal, 1974. Studied architecture at McGill University, 1925–1927; B.Arch., Massachussetts Institute of Technology, 1929. Professor of architecture, McGill University, from the 1950s; co-founded Affleck, Desbarats, Dimakopoulos, Lebensold, Michaud, and Sise, Montreal, 1954. AAPQ 1931.

Skidmore, Owings, and Merrill (SOM)
Architectural firm originally established in Chicago in 1936 by Louis Skidmore and Nathaniel Owings, becoming Skidmore, Owings, and Merrill in 1939, after John Merrill's arrrival. The firm established offices in San Francisco in 1946, London in 1986, and Hong Kong in 1992.

Blanche Lemco van Ginkel
Born in London, 1923. B.Arch., McGill University, 1947; Master of Urban Planning, Harvard University, 1950. Worked in Le Corbusier's studio, 1948, and at Mayerovitch and Bernstein, Montreal, 1950; partner, Van Ginkel Associates, Montreal, from 1957; vice-president and founding member of the Corporation des urbanistes du Québec, 1963–1965; dean of the Faculty of Architecture, University of Toronto, 1977–1982, and professor until 1992. AAPQ 1952, FRAIC 1973, FAIA 1995, RCA.

Daniel van Ginkel
Born in Amsterdam, 1920. Studied architecture at the Elkerlyc Academy of Architecture and Applied Arts, Lage Vuurse, Netherlands, and sociology at the University of Utrecht. Founded Van Ginkel Associates: Montreal, 1957–1977, Winnipeg, 1966–1968, Toronto, from 1977. AAPQ 1952.

Bibliography

Social and Political Studies

150 ans de lutte: Histoire du mouvement ouvrier au Québec, 1825–1976. Montreal: CEQ-CSN, 1979.

Aquin, François. "Jean Lesage, un rassembleur démocrate." In *Jean Lesage et l'éveil d'une nation: Les débuts de la Révolution tranquille*, ed. Robert Comeau, 41–45. Montreal: Presses de l'Université du Québec, 1989.

Arès, Richard. "Le Rapport Parent: Approbations, réserves, et inquiétudes." *Relations*, no. 290 (February 1965): 35.

——. "Radio-Canada et le Canada français." *Relations* 21 (1961): 325–327.

Balthazar, Louis. "Aux sources de la Révolution tranquille: Continuité, rupture, nécessité." In *La Révolution tranquille 30 ans après, qu'en reste-t-il?*, ed. M.R. Lafond, 91–101. Hull: Éditions de Lorraine, 1992.

——. "Quebec and the Ideal of Federalism." In *Quebec Society: Critical Issues*, ed. Marcel Fournier, Michael Rosenberg, and Deena Whyte, 47. Scarborough: Prentice Hall, 1997.

Boily, Robert. "La transformation du Parti libéral du Québec sous Georges-Émile Lapalme (1950–1958)." In *Georges-Émile Lapalme*, ed. J.-F. Léonard, 222–237. Montreal: Presses de l'Université du Québec, 1988.

Bourdieu, Pierre, Luc Boltanski, and Monique de Saint-Martin. "Les stratégies de reconversion sociale." *Informations sur les sciences sociales* 12, no. 5 (1974): 61–113.

Breton, Albert. "The Economics of Nationalism." *Journal of Political Economy* 72, no. 4 (August 1964): 376–386.

Brown, Craig, ed. *The Illustrated History of Canada*. Toronto: Lester and Orpen Dennys Ltd., 1987.

Brunelle, Dorval. *La désillusion tranquille*. Montreal: Hurtubise HMH, 1978.

Cau, Ignace. *L'édition au Québec de 1960 à 1977*. Quebec City: Ministère des Affaires culturelles, 1981.

Coleman, William D. *The Independence Movement in Quebec*. Toronto: University of Toronto Press, 1984.

Comeau, Robert, ed. *Jean Lesage et l'éveil d'une nation: Les débuts de la Révolution tranquille*. Montreal: Presses de l'Université du Québec, 1989.

Couture, Francine. "Identités d'artiste." In *Déclics: Art et société, le Québec des années 1960 et 1970*, 50–90. Quebec City: Musée de la civilisation; Montreal: Musée d'art contemporain / Fides, 1999.

Couture, Francine, ed. *Les arts visuels au Québec dans les années 1960: La reconnaissance de la modernité*. Montreal: VLB, 1993.

——. *Les arts visuels au Québec dans les années 1960: L'éclatement du modernisme*. Montreal: VLB, 1997.

Daigle, Gérard, ed. *Le Québec en jeu*. Montreal: Presses de l'Université de Montréal, 1992.

Dandurand, Pierre, and Marcel Fournier. "Développement de l'enseignement supérieur, classes sociales et question nationale au Québec." *Sociologie et sociétés* 12, no. 2 (April 1980): 104–105.

Denis, Roch. *Luttes de classes et question nationale au Québec, 1948–1968*. Montreal: PSI; Paris: EID, 1979.

Desbarats, Peter. *The State of Quebec*. Toronto: McClelland and Stewart, 1965.

Dubé, Marcel. "Dix ans de television." *Cité libre* 13, no. 48 (June–July 1962): 24–25.

Dumont, Fernand. *Le sort de la culture*. Montreal: L'Hexagone, 1987.

Dumont, Fernand, ed. *La société québécoise après trente ans de changements*. Quebec City: Institut québécois de recherche sur la culture, 1990.

Fournier, Louis. *FLQ: The Anatomy of an Underground Movement*. Translated by Edward Baxter. Toronto: NC Press, 1984.

Fournier, Marcel. "Georges-Émile Lapalme: Culture et politique." In *Georges-Émile Lapalme*, ed. J.-F. Léonard, 81–83. Montreal: Presses de l'Université du Québec, 1988.

——. "La question nationale: Enjeux et impasses." In *La chance au coureur: Bilan de l'action du gouvernement du Parti québécois*, ed. J.-F. Léonard, 177–192. Montreal: Nouvelle Optique, 1978.

——. "L'artiste en jeune homme et jeune femme." In *Déclics: Art et société, le Québec des années 1960 et 1970*, 90–116. Quebec City: Musée de la civilisation; Montreal: Musée d'art contemporain / Fides, 1999.

——. *L'entrée dans la modernité: Science, culture et société au Québec*. Montreal: Les Éditions coopératives Albert Saint-Martin, 1986.

——. *Les générations d'artistes*. Quebec City: Institut québécois de recherche sur la culture, 1986.

——. "Portrait d'un groupe: Les écrivains." *Possibles* 10, no. 2 (Winter 1986): 129–149.

Gagnon, Alain G., ed. *Quebec: State and Society*. Toronto: Methuen, 1984.

Gervais, Paul. "Les diplômés en sciences sociales dans la fonction publique du Québec." Master's thesis, University of Montreal, 1970.

Guindon, Hubert. "Two Cultures: An Essay on Nationalism, Class, and Ethnic Tension." In *Contemporary Canada*, ed. Richard H. Leach, 33–59. Durham, N.C.: Duke University Press, 1967.

——. "Réexamen de l'évolution sociale au Québec." In *La société canadienne-française*, ed. Y. Martin and M. Rioux, 149–173. Montreal: HMH, 1971.

Harvey, Julien. "Les sources de la Révolution tranquille." In *La Révolution tranquille 30 ans après, qu'en reste-t-il?*, ed. M.R. Lafond, 81–90. Hull: Éditions de Lorraine, 1992.

Helman, Claire. *The Milton-Park Affair*. Montreal: Véhicule Press, 1986.

Jedwab, Jack. "La Révolution 'tranquille' des Anglo-Québécois." In *Traité de la culture*, ed. Denise Lemieux, 181–201. Quebec City: Institut québécois de recherche sur la culture, 2002.

Kwavnick, David. "The Roots of French-Canadian Discontent." *Canadian Journal of Economics and Political Science* 31, no. 4 (November 1965): 509–523.

Lafond, M.R., ed. *La Révolution tranquille 30 ans après, qu'en reste-t-il?* Hull: Éditions de Lorraine, 1992.

Lambert, Phyllis. "Land Tenure and Concepts of Architecture and the City: Milton-Park in Montreal." In *Power and Place: Canadian Urban Development in the North American Context*, ed. Gilbert A. Stelter and Alan F.J. Artibise, 133–150. Vancouver: University of British Columbia Press, 1986.

Lamontagne, Maurice. *Le fédéralisme canadien: Évolution et problèmes*. Quebec City: Presses de l'Université Laval, 1954.

Lamy, Suzanne and Laurent. *La renaissance des métiers d'art au Canada français*. Quebec City: Ministère des Affaires culturelles, 1967.

Landry, Réjean. "La Révolution tranquille." In *Le Québec en jeu*, ed. Gérard Daigle, 609–647. Montreal: Presses de l'Université de Montréal, 1992.

Lazure, Jacques. *La jeunesse en révolution*. Montreal: Presses de l'Université du Québec, 1971.

Leach, Richard H., ed. *Contemporary Canada*. Durham, N.C.: Duke University Press, 1967.

Lemieux, Denise, ed. *Traité de la culture*. Quebec City: Institut québécois de recherche sur la culture, 2002.

Léonard, Jean-François, ed. *Georges-Émile Lapalme*. Montreal: Presses de l'Université du Québec, 1988.

——, ed. *La chance au coureur: Bilan de l'action du gouvernement du Parti québécois*. Montreal: Nouvelle Optique, 1978.

Linteau, Paul-André. *Histoire de Montréal depuis la Confédération*. Montreal: Boréal, 1991.

Linteau, Paul-André, René Durocher, Jean-Claude Robert, and François Ricard. *Histoire du Québec contemporain: Le Québec depuis 1930*. Montreal: Boréal, 1986.

Lussier, Yvon. "La division du travail selon l'ethnie au Québec, 1931–1961." Master's thesis, University of Montreal, 1967.

Marshall, Dominique. *Aux origines sociales de l'État-providence*. Montreal: Presses de l'Université de Montréal, 1998.

Martin, Louis. "Les hommes derrière le pouvoir." *Le Magazine Maclean*, October 1964, 25.

McRoberts, Kenneth, and Dale Posgate. *Quebec: Social Change and Political Crisis*. Toronto: McClelland and Stewart, 1980.

Milner, Henry. *Politics in the New Quebec*. Toronto: McClelland and Stewart, 1978.

Newman, Peter C. "The U.S. and Us." *Maclean's*, 6 June 1964, 14.

Panitch, Leo. *The Canadian State: Political Economy and Political Power*. Toronto: University of Toronto Press, 1977.

Pelletier, Gérard. "Le retour de l'enfant prodigue." *La Presse*, 18 January 1964, 4.

Pépin, Marcel. "Commentaire." In *Georges-Émile Lapalme*, ed. J.-F. Léonard, 81–83. Montreal: Presses de l'Université du Québec, 1988.

Pontaut, Alain. "Les festivals sont fatigués." *Cité libre* 15, no. 69 (August–September 1964): 27.

Renaud, Marc. "Quebec's New Middle Class in Search of Social Hegemony." In *Quebec: State and Society*, ed. Alain C. Gagnon, 150–185. Toronto: Methuen, 1984.

Rioux, Marcel. *Jeunesse et société contemporaine*. Montreal: Presses de l'Université de Montréal, 1971.

———. *Un peuple dans le siècle*. Montreal: Boréal, 1990.

Rioux, Marcel, and Yves Martin. *La société canadienne-française*. Montreal: HMH, 1971.

Robillard, Yves, ed. *Québec Underground*. Montreal: Médiart, 1973.

Robitaille, Georges. "Un grand saut en avant." *Relations*, no. 290 (February 1965): 61.

Rocher, Guy. *Le Québec en mutation*. Montreal: Hurtubise HMH, 1973.

———. "La sécularisation des institutions d'enseignement." In *Jean Lesage et l'éveil d'une nation: Les débuts de la Révolution tranquille*, ed. Robert Comeau, 168–177. Montreal: Presses de l'Université du Québec, 1989.

Savoie, Claude. *La véritable histoire du FLQ*. Montreal: Éditions du Jour, 1963.

Taylor, Charles. "Nationalism and the Political Intelligentsia: A Case Study." *Queen's Quarterly* 72, no. 1 (Spring 1965): 150–168.

———. "Le pluralisme et le dualisme." In *Québec: État et société*, ed. Alain G. Gagnon. Montreal: Québec/Amérique, 1994.

———. "La révolution futile." *Cité libre* 15, no. 69 (August–September 1964): 10–23.

Trudeau, Pierre Elliott. "Un manifeste démocratique." *Cité libre* 9, no. 22 (October 1958): 1–31.

Vachon, André. "Parti pris: De la révolte à la révolution." *Relations*, November 1963, 326.

Vaillancourt, Yves. *L'évolution des politiques sociales au Québec, 1940–1960*. Montreal: Presses de l'Université de Montréal, 1988.

Architecture and Urban Planning

"A Sense of Place." *Progressive Architecture*, February 1966, 186–189.

Aquin, Hubert. "Essai crucimorphe." *Liberté*, no. 28 [vol. 5, no. 4] (July–August 1963): 323–325.

Archigram. Paris: Centre Georges Pompidou, 1994.

Aubin, Henry. *City for Sale*. Montreal: Éditions l'Étincelle; Toronto: J. Lorimer, 1977.

Baker, Jeremy. "Expo and the Future City." *The Architectural Review*, no. 846 (August 1967): 151–154.

Banham, Reyner. "A Home Is Not a House." *Art in America* 53, no. 2 (April 1965): 70–79. Illustrations by François Dallegret.

———. *Age of the Masters: A Personal View of Modern Architecture*. New York: Harper and Row, 1975.

———. "L'uomo all'Expo." *Casabella*, no. 320 (November 1967): 48–50.

———. *Megastructure: Urban Futures of the Recent Past*. London: Thames and Hudson, 1976.

———. *The New Brutalism: Ethic or Aesthetic*. London: Architectural Press, 1966.

Barles, Sabine, and André Guillerme. *L'urbanisme souterrain*. Paris: Presses universitaires de France, 1995.

Beaulac, Claude, and Iskandar Gabbour. "L'incidence du développement sur la croissance spatiale de l'agglomération montréalaise 1950–1976." *Plan Canada* 21, no. 3 (September 1981): 90–98.

Beaulieu, Claude. "De la nécessité de bien organiser les villes." *Architecture, bâtiment, construction* 10 (April 1955): 38–41.

Beauregard, Ludger. "Les centres d'achats de Montréal." *Revue de géographie de Montréal* 27, no. 1 (1973): 17–28.

Bernier, Jacques. *La Petite Bourgogne*. Bulletin spécial no. 1. Montreal: City Planning Department, City of Montreal, March 1965.

Blake, Peter. "Downtown in 3-D." *The Architectural Forum* 125, no. 2 (September 1966): 31–48.

———. "Vincent Ponte: A New Kind of Urban Designer." *Art in America* 57, no. 5 (September–October 1969): 62–67.

———. "Quebec's Shimmering Vitrine." *The Architectural Forum* 126, no. 5 (June 1967): 29–39.

Blondin, Michel. *Le projet St-Henri: Description et analyse d'un projet centré sur la participation des citoyens*. Montreal: Conseil des oeuvres de Montréal, 1965.

Blouin, André. "De l'urbanisme, de l'Homme et de l'architecture." *Architecture, bâtiment, construction* 12 (April 1957): 58–61.

———. "Le coeur de Montréal." *Habitat* 4, no. 3 (May–June 1961): 10–15.

———. "L'exposition universelle." *Architecture, bâtiment, construction*, April 1963, 24.

———. "L'exposition universelle." *Architecture, bâtiment, construction*, April 1965, 30–31.

———. "Montréal au xxᵉ siècle." *Journal of the Royal Architectural Institute of Canada* 33 (November 1956): 420–423.

———. "Rénovation urbaine à Montréal." *Architecture, bâtiment, construction* 12, no. 144 (April 1958): 59–64.

Blumenfeld, Hans. *The Modern Metropolis: Its Origins, Growth, Characteristics, and Planning*. Selected essays edited by Paul D. Spreiregen. Cambridge, Mass.: MIT Press, 1967.

Boyarsky, Alvin. "Buildings." *Architectural Design*, no. 3 (March 1970): 156–157.

Bryant, R.W.G. "En quête d'une politique régionale en matière d'espace vital." *Cité libre* 13, no. 52 (December 1962): 22–28.

———. "On ne loge que les riches." *Cité libre* 15, no. 81 (November 1965): 12–16.

———. "Pensées d'un banlieusard." *Cité libre* 15, no. 70 (October 1964): 25–26.

"Building." *Forum* 125, no. 5 (December 1966): 19.

Durgel, Guy. *La ville aujourd'hui*. Paris: Hachette, 1993.

Bussière, Yves Daniel. "L'automobile et l'expansion des banlieues: Le cas de Montréal, 1901–2001." *Revue d'histoire urbaine* 18, no. 2 (October 1989): 159–165.

Bussière, Yves Daniel, and Y. Dallaire. "Tendances socio-démographiques et demande de transport dans quatre régions métropolitaines canadiennes: Eléments de prospective." *Plan Canada*, May 1994, 9–16.

Canty, Donald. "Philadelphia's Giant Shopping Machine." *The Architectural Forum* 125, no. 4 (November 1966): 38–43.

Castells, Manuel. *Luttes urbaines et pouvoir politique*. Paris: François Maspero, 1975.

Central Mortgage and Housing Corporation. *Housing and Urban Growth in Canada*. Ottawa, 1956.

———. *Principles of Small House Grouping*. Ottawa, 1954.

Chalk, Warren. "Hardware of a New World." *The Architectural Forum* 125, no. 3 (October 1966): 47–50.

Chapleau, Gaston. "Cité-Ondes, Cité-Familles." *Architecture, bâtiment, construction* 12, no. 138 (October 1957): 33.

———. "Le projet Dozois, progrès ou recul." *Architecture, bâtiment, construction* 12, no. 130 (January 1957): 15.

Charney, Melvin. *Montréal: Plus or Minus?* Montreal: Montreal Museum of Fine Arts, 1972.

———. *The Adequacy and Production of Low-Rental Housing*. Ottawa: Central Mortgage and Housing Corporation, 1971.

Choko, Marc H. "Dossier habitation." Typewritten report, University of Montreal, 1974.

———. *Les Habitations Jeanne-Mance: Un projet social au centre-ville*. Montreal: Éditions Saint-Martin, 1995.

Choko, Marc H., Jean-Pierre Collin, and Annick Germain. "Le logement et les enjeux de la transformation de l'espace urbain: Montréal, 1940–1960." *Revue d'histoire urbaine* 15,

no. 2 (October 1986): 127–136; 15, no. 3 (February 1987): 243–253.

Cimon, Jean. "L'exposition universelle de Montréal ou le fleuve retrouvé." *Cité libre* 14, no. 55 (March 1963): 27–29.

City of Montreal. *2,000,000 People in Your Own Basement*. Montreal, 1965.

City Planning Department. *An East-West Expressway*. Montreal: City of Montreal, 1948.

———. *Caractéristiques physiques de la région*. Bulletin technique no. 4. Montreal: City of Montreal, 1966.

———. *Centre-ville*. Bulletin d'information no. 8. Montreal: City of Montreal, October 1974.

———. *Études de circulation, été 1945*. Montreal: City of Montreal, 1946.

———. *Études de circulation, été 1946*. Montreal: City of Montreal, 1946.

———. *Études de circulation*. Montreal: City of Montreal, 1949.

———. *Étude de la forme: Région de Montréal*, no. 2. Montreal: City of Montreal, 1966.

———. *Familles et ménages, 1951–1961*. Bulletin technique no. 2. Montreal: City of Montreal, 1964.

———. *La vague d'expansion urbaine: Étude sur les variations de la densité dans la région de Montréal*. Bulletin technique no. 1. Montreal: City of Montreal, 1964.

———. *Le centre ville de Montréal*. Bulletin technique no. 3. Montreal: City of Montreal, 1964.

———. *Métropole: Les Cahiers d'urbanisme*, no. 1. Montreal: City of Montreal, January 1963.

———. *Métropole: Les Cahiers d'urbanisme*, no. 2. Montreal: City of Montreal, April 1964.

———. *Métropole: Les Cahiers d'urbanisme*, no. 3. Montreal: City of Montreal, October 1965.

———. *Montréal 2000: Esquisse du plan témoin régional présentée aux membres du conseil de la Ville de Montréal le 24 avril 1967*. Montreal: City of Montreal, 1967.

———. *Planning for Montreal: Master Plan Preliminary Report*. Montreal: City of Montreal, 1944.

———. *Population emplois 1964–1981*. Bulletin technique no. 7. Montreal: City of Montreal, 1971.

———. *Relevé visuel, région de Montréal*. Bulletin technique no. 6. Montreal: City of Montreal, 1969.

———. *Répertoire des noms des rues*. Bulletin d'information no. 3. Montreal: City of Montreal, September 1965.

———. *Répertoire des noms des rues*. Bulletin d'information no. 1. Montreal: City of Montreal, November 1963.

———. *Répertoire des noms des rues*. Bulletin d'information no. 5. Montreal: City of Montreal, June 1968.

———. *Superficies des municipalités*. Bulletin d'information no. 2. Montreal: City of Montreal, August 1964.

———. *Toponymie*. Bulletin d'information no. 4. Montreal: City of Montreal, June 1966.

———. *Urbanisation: A Study of Urban Expansion in the Montreal Region*. Bulletin technique no. 5. 2nd edition. Montreal: City of Montreal, 1968.

———. *Zonage du flanc sud du Mont Royal*. Montreal: City of Montreal, 1962.

———. *Zone A: Hochelaga/maison neuve*. Bulletin no. 3. Montreal: City of Montreal, May 1967.

———. *Zone E: Saint-Henri*. Bulletin no. 2. Montreal: City of Montreal, June 1967.

———. *Zone F: Les vieux ménages à Pointe-Saint-Charles*. Bulletin no. 4. Montreal: City of Montreal, May 1967.

———. *Zone F: Pointe-Saint-Charles*. Bulletin no. 1. Montreal: City of Montreal, May 1967.

City Planning Department, General Studies Division. "Rôle potentiel des villes satellites." Typewritten report, 1966.

City Planning Department, Urban Development Division. *Remembrement du territoire: Aménagement de Rivière-des-Prairies*, vol. 1. Montreal: City of Montreal, c. 1968.

Clairoux, Benoît. *Le métro de Montréal, 35 ans déjà*. Montreal: Hurtubise HMH, 2001.

Cohen, Jean-Louis, and André Lortie. *Des fortifs au périf*. Paris: Picard / Pavillon de l'Arsenal, 1992.

Collin, Jean-Pierre, and Gérard Divay. *La Communauté urbaine de Montréal: De la ville centrale à l'île centrale*. Montreal: INRS-Urbanisation, 1977.

"Commenti: Montreal troppo geniale." *Casabella*, no. 316 (May 1967): 61.

"Computer Community." *The Architectural Forum* 125, no. 5 (December 1966): 19.

Conseil de développement social du Montréal métropolitain (Montreal Council of Social Agencies). *Rapport de la Commission d'audiences publiques populaires sur l'autoroute est-ouest à Montréal*. Montreal, 1971.

Cormier, Anne. "L'Île-des-Soeurs, le plus merveilleux domaine résidentiel en Amérique du Nord." ARQ: *Architecture/Québec*, February 1993, 18–19.

De Lorimier, Jean-Louis, ed. *Expo 67*. Toronto: Thomas Nelson and Sons, 1968.

Déclics: Art et société, le Québec des années 1960 et 1970. Quebec City: Musée de la civilisation; Montreal: Musée d'art contemporain / Fides, 1999.

Demchinsky, Bryan, and Elaine Kalman Naves. *Storied Streets: Montreal in the Literary Imagination*. Toronto: Macfarlane Walter and Ross, 2000.

Denis, Pierre-Yves. "Conditions géographiques et postulats démographiques d'une rénovation urbaine à Montréal." *Revue de géographie de Montréal* 21 (1967): 150–164.

Drapeau, Jean. *Cité-Famille: Un projet d'habitation et de relogement conçu d'après les besoins et les habitudes des familles de Montréal*. Montreal, 1957.

Drouin, Martin. "Les campagnes de sauvegarde de la maison Van Horne et du couvent des Soeurs grises ou les questionnements d'une identité urbaine (Montréal, 1973–1976)." *Journal of the Society for the Study of Architecture in Canada* 26, no. 3–4 (2001): 25–36.

Ellis, Cliff. "Professional Conflict over Urban Form: The Case of Urban Freeways, 1930 to 1970." In *Planning the Twentieth-Century American City*, ed. Mary Sies and Christopher Silver, 262–279. Baltimore: Johns Hopkins University Press, 1996.

Elte, Hans. "Cultural Centres." *Journal of the Royal Architectural Institute of Canada* 42 (May 1965): 51–54.

"Études de circulation pour le centre de Montréal." *L'Architecture d'aujourd'hui*, no. 118 (January 1965): 94–95.

"Expo 67." *The Canadian Architect*, February 1963, 116–118.

"Expo '67." *The Architectural Review*, no. 846 (August 1967): 86–166.

Fiset, Édouard. "Introduction d'un concept urbain dans la planification de l'exposition." *Journal of the Royal Architectural Institute of Canada* 42 (May 1965): 55–58.

———. "Projects." *Journal of the Royal Architectural Institute of Canada* 41 (January 1964): 53–56.

"Focus." *The Architectural Forum* 125, no. 1 (July–August 1966): 81.

———. *The Architectural Forum* 125, no. 3 (October 1966): 65.

———. *The Architectural Forum* 125, no. 5 (December 1966): 40–41.

Folch-Ribas, Jacques. "Urbanisme et architecture à l'exposition internationale." *Vie des Arts*, no. 48 (Fall 1967): 16–17.

Gareau, Jean. "Provincial News." *Journal of the Royal Architectural Institute of Canada* 41 (February 1964): 15–21.

Germain, Annick, ed. *L'aménagement urbain: Promesses et défis*. Quebec City: Institut québécois de recherche sur la culture, 1991.

Germain, Annick, and Damaris Rose. *Montréal: The Quest for a Metropolis*. Toronto: Wiley, 2000.

Giurgola, Romaldo, and Jaimini Mehta. *Louis I. Kahn*. Boulder: Westview Press, 1975.

Goldberg, Michael A., and John Mercer. *The Myth of the North American City: Continentalism Challenged*. Vancouver: University of British Columbia Press, 1986.

Gourney, Isabelle, and France Vanlaethem, ed. *Montréal Metropolis, 1880–1930*. Montreal: Canadian Centre for Architecture, 1998.

Goyer, Jean-Pierre. "Montréal et sa banlieue." *Cité libre* 13, no. 43 (January 1962): 25–28.

Graham, Gerald G. *Canadian Film Technology, 1896–1986*. Toronto: Associated University Presses, 1989.

Hamilton, Mina. "Designing a Cultural Center." *Industrial Design*, September 1964, 56–61.

"Habitat '67, Montreal." *Arkitektur: The Danish Architectural Press*, no. 4 (August 1967): A145–A164.

"Habitat '67, Montréal." *L'Architecture d'aujourd'hui*, no. 130 (February–March 1967): 28–29.

Hanna, David B. "Les réseaux de transport (chemins de fer, tramways, rues) et le développement urbain à Montréal." From the conference *El desarrollo urbano de Montréal y Barcelona en la época contemporanea: Estudio comparativo*, University of Barcelona, 5–7 May 1997.

Hayes, Bob. "Rebirth of Huge Downtown Area Proposed in Morgan's Plan." *The Gazette* (Montreal), Friday, July 1960, second section, 19–34.

———. "Victoria Square – Park-Pine Boulevard Urged." *The Gazette* (Montreal), Friday, July 1960, second section, 19–34.

Hecker, Zvi. "Proposition pour un nouveau centre à Montréal." *L'Architecture d'aujourd'hui*, no. 158 (October–November 1971): 27–30.

Henket, Hubert-Jan, and Hilde Heynen, ed. *Back from Utopia: The Challenge of the Modern Movement*. Rotterdam: 010 Publishers, 2002.

"High to Come to the Fair/Exhibition." *The Canadian Architect*, March 1963, 104.

"Horizon 2000, Montréal." *Architecture, bâtiment, construction* 23 (April 1968): 32–38.

"Il centro di Ville Marie a Montreale, città nella città." *l'a*, no. 56 (June 1960): 119.

"Il padiglione italiano all'Expo '67 di Montréal." *l'a*, no. 141 (July 1967): 146–176.

"Île-des-Soeurs." *Architecture, bâtiment, construction* 22 (January 1967): 20–23.

"Immeubles de bureaux, Place Ville-Marie, Montréal." *L'Architecture d'aujourd'hui*, no. 111 (January 1964): 2–7.

"Institute News." *Journal of the Royal Architectural Institute of Canada* 40 (November 1963): 9.

J.P. "On veut des cafés terrasses, rêverie d'un promeneur solitaire." *Cité libre* 15, no. 70 (October 1964): 27.

Kahn, Louis. "Form and Design." *Architectural Design*, April 1961, 151–152.

———. "Toward a Plan for Midtown Philadelphia." *Perspecta*, no. 2 (1953): 26.

Kolehmainen, Aila, and Esa Laaksonen, ed. *Drawn in Sand: Unrealised Visions by Alvar Aalto*. Helsinki: Museum of Finnish Architecture, 2002.

Kultermann, Udo, ed. *Kenzo Tange: 1946–1969, Architecture and Urban Design*. New York: Praeger, 1970.

"La bolla più grossa." *l'a*, no. 135 (January 1967): 608.

"La casa dello studente." *l'a*, no. 147 (June 1968): 598.

Lalonde, Girouard, and Letendre, Engineers. *Plan directeur: Routes à caractère métropolitain*. Montreal: Montreal Metropolitan Corporation, 1961.

Larue, Monique, and Jean-François Chassay. *Promenades littéraires dans Montréal*. Montreal: Québec/Amérique, 1989.

"Le nouveau centre d'affaires de Montréal." *L'Architecture d'aujourd'hui*, no. 84 (June–July 1959): 82–83.

Legault, Guy R. *La ville qu'on a bâtie*. Montreal: Liber, 2002.

"L'exposition universelle de 1967." *Journal of the Royal Architectural Institute of Canada* 40 (March 1963): 89–90.

Lincourt, Michel, and Harry Parnass. "Métro éducation Montréal." *L'Architecture d'aujourd'hui*, no. 153 (January 1971): 54–59.

Linteau, Paul-André. *Histoire de Montréal depuis la Confédération*. Montreal: Boréal, 1992.

Longpré, Claude. "Pitié pour les architectes." *Cité libre* 12, no. 34 (February 1961): 28–30.

Lortie, André. "Grandes voiries: Permanence des tracés et fluctuation des écritures." In *Infrastructures, villes et territoire*, ed. Claude Prélorenzo, 155–160. Paris: L'Harmattan, 2000.

———. "Jacques Gréber et l'urbanisme: Le temps et l'espace de la ville." Ph.D. diss., Université de Paris XII, 1997.

———. "Paris–CDG, l'aeroporto e la città." *Casabella*, no. 604 (September 1993): 22–31.

M'Bala, José. "Prévenir l'exurbanisation: Le plan Gréber de 1950 pour Montréal." *Revue d'histoire urbaine* 29, no. 2 (March 2001): 62–70.

Marsan, Jean-Claude. *Montréal en évolution: Historique du développement de l'architecture et de l'environnement urbain montréalais*. Montreal: Fides, 1974.

McGrath, T.M. *History of Canadian Airports*. Toronto: Lugus, 1992.

McKenna, Brian, and Susan Purcell. *Drapeau*. Toronto: Clarke Irwin, 1980.

McNally, Larry. "Roads, Streets, and Highways." In *Building Canada: A History of Public Works*, ed. Norman R. Ball, 51. Toronto: University of Toronto Press, 1988.

Meyerson, Martin, and Edward C. Banfield. *Boston: The Job Ahead*. Cambridge, Mass.: Harvard University Press, 1966.

Moholy-Nagy, Sibyl. "Expo 67, Montréal." *L'Architecture d'aujourd'hui*, no. 133 (September 1967): ix–xi.

Mumford, Eric. *The CIAM Discourse on Urbanism, 1928–1960*. Cambridge, Mass.: MIT Press, 2000.

N.D. Lea and Associates, for the Transportation Planning Committee of the Canadian Good Roads Association. *Urban Transportation Developments in Eleven Canadian Metropolitan Areas*. Ottawa, 1966.

Nepveu, Pierre, and Gilles Marcotte, ed. *Montréal imaginaire: Ville et literature*. Montreal: Fides, 1992.

"Nuns' Island, Montreal." *The Canadian Architect* 15, no. 6 (June 1970): 32–39.

Parenteau, Roland. "Régions riches et pauvres du Québec." *Cité libre* 15, no. 70 (October 1964): 6–12.

Pawley, Martin. "The Shape of Trade." *Architectural Design*, no. 2 (February 1970): 55.

Persitz, Alexandre. "Propos sur Montréal '67." *L'Architecture d'aujourd'hui*, no. 135 (December 1967–January 1968): 90–99.

Ponte, Vincent. "Montreal's Metro." *Subways*, 8 December 1977.

———. "The Multi-Leveled City Center." *Institute on Planning and Zoning* (Dallas), 1–23.

Prideaux, Tom. "Architecture's Leap into the Future." *Life* 62, no. 17 (28 April 1967): 32–41.

"Progetto canadese per Osaka '70." *l'a*, no. 146 (December 1967): 526–527.

Projet de rénovation d'une zone d'habitat défectueux et de construction d'habitations à loyer modique. Montreal: City of Montreal, 1954.

Proulx, Daniel. *Le Red Light de Montréal*. Montreal: VLB, 1997.

R. "Den canadiske regerings pavillon på Expo 67." *Arkitektur: The Danish Architectural Press*, August 1967, A157–A192.

"Rassegna." *Casabella*, no. 306 (December 1965): 48–49.

Richards, J.M. "Multi-Level City." *The Architectural Review*, no. 846 (August 1967): 86–96.

Roncayolo, Marcel. *La ville et ses territoires*. Paris: Gallimard, 1990.

Ronner, Heinz, and Sharad Jhaveri. *Louis I. Kahn: Complete Work, 1935–1974*. 2nd ed. Basel and Boston: Birkhäuser, 1987.

Rumilly, Robert. *Histoire de Montréal*, vol. 5. Montreal: Fides, 1974.

"Safdie, David, Barott et Boulva, 'Habitat 67,' Montréal, Canada." *L'Architecture d'aujourd'hui*, no. 119 (February–March 1965): 96–99.

Safdie, Moshe. *Beyond Habitat*. Edited by John Kettle. Montreal: Tundra, 1970.

Sartogo, Piero. "Habitat 67, analisi di una esperienza." *Casabella*, no. 320 (October 1967): 52–53.

Schoenauer, Norbert. *Architecture Montréal*. Montreal: Southam Business Publications, 1967.

Sévigny, Marcel. *Trente ans de politique municipale*. Montreal: Écosociété, 2001.

Sies, Mary, and Christopher Silver, ed. *Planning the Twentieth-Century American City*. Baltimore: Johns Hopkins University Press, 1996.

Sky, Alison, and Michelle Stone. *Unbuilt America: Forgotten Architecture in the United States from Thomas Jefferson to the Space Age*. New York: McGraw-Hill, 1976.

Surveyer, Nenniger, and Chênevert, Engineers. *Cité de Montréal: Projet autostrade nord-sud à proximité du boulevard Saint-Laurent*. Montreal, May 1959.

Svenson, Göte. "Bostadt spolitiken nål och medel." *Arkitektur: The Swedish Review of Architecture*, no. 9 (September 1967): 521–530.

"The 1967 International Exposition at Montréal." *Journal of the Royal Architectural Institute of Canada* 40 (April 1963): 70–71.

Therrien, Marie-Josée, and France Vanlaethem. "Modern Architecture in Canada, 1940–1967." In *Back from Utopia: The Challenge of the Modern Movement*, ed. Hubert-Jan Henket and Hilde Heynen. Rotterdam: 010 Publishers, 2002.

Vachon, Bernard. "La création de Candiac en banlieue de Montréal: Essai d'analyse spatiale et financière d'une trame d'appropriation du sol en milieu péri-urbain." *Revue de géographie de Montréal* 27, no. 1 (1973): 29–39.

"Y67, projet pour l'exposition de Montréal." *L'Architecture d'aujourd'hui*, no. 120 (April–May 1965): 102.

Zeckendorf, William, with Edward McCreary. *The Autobiography of William Zeckendorf*. New York: Holt, Rinehart and Winston, 1970.

Zevi, Bruno. "L'Italia all'expo 1967 di Montreal." *l'a*, no. 141 (July 1967): 142–144.

Fiction

Bessette, Gérard. *La bagarre*. Montreal: Cercle du livre de France, 1958. *The Brawl*. Translated by Marc Lebel and Ronald Sutherland. Montreal: Harvest House, 1976.

Carrier, Roch. *Le deux millième étage*. Montreal: Éditions du Jour, 1973. *They Won't Demolish Me!* Translated by Sheila Fischman. Toronto: Anansi, 1973.

Cohen, Leonard. *Beautiful Losers*. Toronto: McClelland and Stewart, 1966.

Cloutier, Eugène. *Les inutiles*. Montreal: Cercle du livre de France, 1956.

Ferron, Jacques. *La nuit*. Montreal: Parti pris, 1965.

Godbout, Jacques. *Le Couteau sur la table*. Paris: Seuil, 1965. *Knife on the Table*. Translated by Penny Williams. Toronto: McClelland and Stewart, 1968.

———. *Salut Galarneau!* Paris: Seuil, 1967. *Hail Galarneau!* Translated by Alan Brown. Don Mills: Longman Canada, 1970.

Gravel, Pierre. *À perte de temps*. Montreal: Parti pris; Toronto: Anansi, 1969.

Hood, Hugh. *Around the Mountain: Scenes from Montreal Life*. Toronto: Peter Martin Associates, 1967.

———. *Flying a Red Kite*. Toronto: Ryerson, 1962.

———. *The Fruit Man, the Meat Man & the Manager*. Ottawa: Oberon Press, 1970.

———. *White Figure, White Ground*. Toronto: Ryerson, 1964.

Layton, Irving. *A Red Carpet for the Sun*. Toronto: McClelland and Stewart, 1959.

———. *Collected Poems*. Toronto: McClelland and Stewart, 1965.

Moore, Brian. *The Revolution Script*. Toronto: McClelland and Stewart, 1971.

Naubert, Yvette. *Les Pierrefendre*. Montreal: Cercle du livre de France, 1972.

Renaud, Jacques. *Le Cassé*. Montreal: Parti pris, 1964. *Broke City*. Translated by David Homel. Montreal: Guernica Editions, 1983.

Richler, Mordecai. *The Street*. Toronto: McClelland and Stewart, 1969.

Index

Complexe La Cité (*Cité Concordia*)
Private collection, Milan

Head Office of Hydro-Québec
Private collection, Milan

L'Acadie Interchange
Private collection, Milan

Place Victoria (Montreal Stock Exchange Tower)
Private collection, Milan

Champlain Bridge
Private collection, Milan

Palais de justice

Place Bonaventure
Private collection, Milan

Marriott Château Champlain
Private collection, Milan

Port Royal Apartments
Private collection, Milan

*La Ronde and
Jacques-Cartier Bridge*

Printed in Canada

Published simultaneously in French under the title *Les années 60: Montréal voit grand*

Library and Archives Canada Cataloguing in Publication

The 60s : Montréal thinks big / edited by André Lortie; contributors, Marcel Fournier ... [et al.].

Exhibition held at the Canadian Centre for Architecture, Montréal, Québec, Oct. 20, 2004–Sept. 11, 2005.
Issued also in French under title: Les années 60 : Montréal voit grand.
Includes bibliographical references.
ISBN 1-55365-075-1

1. City planning–Québec (Province)–Montréal–Exhibitions.
2. Architecture–Québec (Province)–Montréal–Exhibitions. 3. Montréal (Québec)–History–Exhibitions. I. Fournier, Marcel, 1945– II. Lortie, André, 1958– III. Canadian Centre
for Architecture. IV. Title: Sixties. V. Title: Montréal thinks big.

NA9016.C3M65 2004   711'.4'07471428   C2004-905423-6

Canadian Centre for Architecture
1920 Baile
Montreal, Quebec
Canada H3H 2S6
www.cca.qc.ca

Douglas & McIntyre Ltd
2323 Quebec Street, Suite 201
Vancouver, British Columbia
Canada V5T 4S7
www.douglas-mcintyre.com

Credits

Unless otherwise indicated, photographs were made by Michel Boulet, Senior Photographer, and Michel Legendre, Technician/Photographer, from CCA Photographic Services.

Fig. 4, 71, 72 © ABC, material reprinted with the express permission of CanWest Interactive Inc., a CanWest Partnership
Fig. 90 Drawing © The Estate of Normand Hudon / ABC, material reprinted with the express permission of CanWest Interactive Inc., a CanWest Partnership
Fig. 6, 8, 30, 67, 84, 88, 132, 133, 163, 164, 174, 188, 205, 206, 213, 214, 218, 219 © CCA
Fig. 7, 220 © Archives Hydro-Québec
Fig. 9, 10, 11, 105 © *The Gazette*
Fig. 14, 194 © Archives Radio-Canada
Fig. 15 © The Estate of Alexander Calder / SODRAC, Montreal, 2004
Fig. 21 © Daniel van Ginkel and Blanche Lemco van Ginkel
Fig. 22, 145, 147, 200, 211 © Bernard Lamarre
Fig. 23, 27, 29 © Luc Durand, architect, O.A.Q., E.A.U. Geneva
Fig. 23, 29 © Deidi von Schaewen
Fig. 12 © *Liberté*
Fig. 13 © *Cité libre*
Fig. 31 © The Estate of Hugh Hood
Fig. 32, 33 © Courtesy of Groupe Ville-Marie Littérature
Fig. 35 © Michel Saint-Jean
Fig. 36, 46, 57, 61, 173 © Jeremy Taylor
Fig. 44 © Courtesy of the Montreal Museum of Fine Arts
Fig. 47 © Gilles Carle / The Estate of Guy L'Écuyer, with the permission of the producer, the National Film Board of Canada
Fig. 48, 49 © David Miller
Fig. 64 © A. Janin & Compagnie ltée (now Janin Atlas)
Fig. 65 © SNC-Lavalin
Fig. 77, 86 © Harold Ship
Fig. 82, 83 © Archives of Pei, Cobb, Freed, and Partners, Architects
Fig. 85, 100, 216 © The Estate of Jean Ouellet
Fig. 87, 139, 140, 141, 142, 196, 197 © Victor Prus
Fig. 89 © Lohan, Caprile, Goettsch, Architects
Fig. 92, 157, 208, 209, 221 © Van Ginkel Architects
Fig. 97 © Alvar Aalto Foundation
Fig. 101 © Brian Merrett
Fig. 106, 187, 189 © Mayerovitch and Bernstein, with the permission of Lionel Mincoff
Fig. 109, 111 © Yukari Ochiai
Fig. 115 © Gouvernement du Québec, ministère des Transports. Reproduction authorized by Les Publications du Québec
Fig. 116, 117 © 2004, Central Mortgage and Housing Corporation (CMHC). All rights reserved. Reproduced with the consent of CMHC. All other uses and reproductions of this material are expressly prohibited.
Fig. 122 to 125 © Développements Urbains Candiac Inc.
Fig. 126, 127 © William D'Onofrio
Fig. 128, 130 © Bobrow Architects
Fig. 129 © Metropolitan Structures of Canada / Bobrow Architects
Fig. 131, 134 © Metropolitan Structures of Canada
Fig. 137 © The Cadillac Fairview Corporation Limited
Fig. 138 © Hyman M. Tolchinsky, architect, with permission of Edward Reichmann (Three-Star Construction)
Fig. 155 © The Estate of Eugène Beaudoin / SODRAC, Montreal, 2004
Fig. 156 © Bruno Bédard
Fig. 160, 161, 225 to 238 © University of Nebraska-Lincoln, Photo Joseph Messana Architectural Image Collection

Fig. 162 © Reproduced with the permission of Benjamin News Inc., Montreal
Fig. 165 © Time Life Pictures, Getty Images
Fig. 166 © Paris Match
Fig. 167, 168 © André Blouin
Fig. 171 © Peter Desbarats
Fig. 176 © 1977, Louis I. Kahn Collection, University of Pennsylvania and Pennsylvania Historical and Museum Commission
Fig. 177 © Smithson Family Collection, with the permission of Emap, London
Fig. 178 © Yona Friedman, with permission of Éditions Denoël
Fig. 179 © Peter Cook
Fig. 180 © Courtesy, The Estate of R. Buckminster Fuller
Fig. 182 Drawing © Peter Cook, with the permission of the Walker Art Centre for *Design Quarterly*
Fig. 183 © Permission to reproduce, courtesy Moshe Safdie and Associates
Fig. 184 © Zvi Hecker, with the permission of Éditions Jean-Michel Place, Paris
Fig. 185 © François Dallegret / SODRAC, Montreal, 2004
Fig. 186 © Michel Lincourt and Harry Parnass, with the permission of Éditions Jean-Michel Place, Paris
Fig. 193, 195 © Harold Ship
Fig. 204 © Le Groupe Arcop, fonds Affleck, Desbarats, Dimakopoulos, Lebensold & Sise
Fig. 215 © Société de la Place des Arts de Montréal
Fig. 223 © Reproduced with the permission of Éditions Jean-Michel Place, Paris
Fig. 224 © *The Architectural Review*

Every reasonable attempt has been made to identify the owners of copyrights. Errors or omissions will be corrected in subsequent reprints.